PHILIPPINE HISTORY
AND GOVERNMENT
Through the Years

PHILIPPINE HISTORY
AND GOVERNMENT
Through the Years

- FRANCISCO M. ZULUETA
- ABRIEL M. NEBRES

National
Book Store

Philippine History and Government Through the Years

Published by

National
Book Store

Quad Alpha Centrum Bldg.
125 Pioneer Street
Mandaluyong City 1550
Tel. 631-80-61 to 66 • Fax 634-03-76
www.nationalbookstore.com

PHILIPPINE COPYRIGHT, 2003 by
Francisco M. Zulueta &
Abriel M. Nebres

2006 Reprint

ISBN 971-08-6344-4

Cover Design by
Francisco M. Zulueta

Printed by
Navotas Press
Navotas, Metro Manila

Pambansang Awit ng Pilipinas

Bayang magiliw,
Perlas ng silanganan,
Alab ng puso
sa dibdib mo'y buhay.
Lupang hinirang,
duyan ka ng magiting
Sa manlulupig, di ka pasisiil.
Sa dagat at bundok, sa simoy
at sa langit mong bughaw,
May dilag ang tula at awit sa
paglayang minamahal.
Ang kislap ng watawat mo'y
tagumpay na nagniningning,
Ang bituin at araw niya kailan
pa may di magdidilim.
Lupa ng araw, ng luwalhati't
pagsinta,
Buhay ay langit sa piling mo.
Aming ligaya na pag may
mag-aapi
ang mamatay nang dahil sa iyo.

Bayan Ko

Ang bayan kong Pilipinas
Lupain ng ginto't bulaklak,
Pag-ibig ang sa kanyang palad
Nag-alay ng ganda't dilag.

At sa kanyang yumi at ganda
Dayuhan ay nahalina;
Bayan ko, binihag ka,
Nasadlak sa dusa.

Ibon mang may layang lumipad,
Kulungin mo at umiiyak;
Bayan pa kayang sakdal dilag
Ang di magnasang makaalpas.

Pilipinas kong minumutya,
Pugad ng luha ko't dalita,
Aking adhika
Makita kang sakdal laya.

To the Filipino People,

Upright and resilient, who dramatized their courage, bravery, fortitude, heroism and tenacity of purpose, with greater vigor and determination which exemplified the Filipino character at its highest and loftiest measure, their rejection of foreign and home-grown tyranny and misrule in the Battle of Mactan, Bataan Peninsula, Corregidor Island, EDSA 1 and EDSA 2.

Even as we remain paupers among the people of the world, we are rich with the imperishable memories of our history. We are strong and resolute to build on for a better tomorrow. We are indeed full of hope with faith in GOD and in ourselves.

Preface

This book was conceived and written to meet the need for a more comprehensive, well-balanced, documented, easy to understand and up-to-date literature in Philippine History and Government for colleges and universities. It has developed out of the authors' experiences in teaching the subject and other related fields of study for many years, both in the undergraduate and graduate levels. It is their beliefs that students, teachers, researchers, professionals and lovers of history will undoubtedly benefit from this literature.

According to Dr. Jose Rizal, "In order to understand the destiny of a people, it is necessary to open the book of its past."

The primary purpose of this book is to present Philippine History and Government within a manageable time frame. Feedback from students and teachers was carefully considered because, for them, since Philippine history, as a subject, is a part of the curriculum in the secondary level, its approach and style of presentation must be portrayed in a fascinating manner that will motivate and induce students to read, appreciate and understand the subject better by way of focusing on significant events and facts, without giving much emphasis on trivial issues.

It begins with the land and people, and discusses the various changes of its political, social, economic and cultural dimensions. It touches on the dramatic epic of the Filipino people's quest for justice, economic, security, peace and order, equality and freedom from foreign colonizers and the dictatorship.

The history of our nation is the story of the Filipino people who, long abused by people in power, suddenly woke up and collectively demonstrated their rare courage, fortitude and tenacity of purpose, which exemplifies their character at its

highest and loftiest measure to gain freedom. The history of
the Filipino people was written in the blood of our heroes and
martyrs and the tears and sweat of a people who had risen
against oppressive regimes.

Since the Filipinos have faith in God, the goodness of man
will always triumph over evil. They consider society as a body
in a state of improvement and humanity as a changing scene,
in which nothing is permanent. They admit that what
happened to them over the years was painful, but this will be
superseded by something better tomorrow – this is Philippine
History and Government through the years.

For any inaccuracy and misinterpretation of events and
facts, the authors are responsible and they hope for the
indulgence and understanding of the readers. Indeed, they
would gratefully acknowledge the help they would extend to
rectify the error. William Shakespeare once said, "To err is
human, to forgive, divine." For enrichment, terms and
concepts to understand and questions to answer are provided
at the end of each chapter to test the comprehension of
students.

The significant events, persons, places and concepts are
provided to serve as easy reference for students and
researchers.

It is hoped that, through this book, the reader's awareness
and interest in our history and government and other issues
affecting our lives will be enhanced.

The authors would like to express their profound
gratitude and appreciation to: Dr. Celia A. Zulueta, beloved
wife of Dr. Zulueta, former Chairman of the Department of
English, College of Arts and Sciences, University of the East,
Claro M. Recto Avenue, Manila, and at present, Professorial
Lecturer of English and Literature, College of Arts and
Sciences, Pamantasan ng Lungsod ng Maynila, Intramuros,
Manila, for editing the manuscript, and Dr. Carmelita Zulueta-
Kasuya, Assistant Professor, Institute of Industrial Science,
University of Tokyo, Tokyo, Japan, for her continuous support;

The faculty and students of the College of Arts and
Sciences, Pamantasan ng Lungsod ng Maynila and the
Philippine Christian University, who graciously shared some
of their insights and experiences in teaching and studying
history, respectively, as a discipline;

The late Teodoro A. Agoncillo, Filipino historian and
professor, Milagros C. Guerrero, author and professor of
history, respectively. Department of History, University of the
Philippines, the authors' most admired professors of history
for providing impetus to write this book.

Many of our academic associates who have provided
valuable inputs and collegial asupport.

Mrs. Letty G. Custodio, Reprint Coordinator, National
Bookstore, Inc., for her valuable support.

Mrs. Emelita M. Nebres, beloved wife of Prof. Nebres,
for computerizing the manuscript.

The Philippine Daily Inquirer for the photos used in this
book;

The various scholars, authors, writers and critics whose
works have been a rich mine of information needed in the
preparation of this book; and

Finally, the students and teachers of Philippine History
and Government in the Pamantasan ng Lungsod ng Maynila,
Philippine Christian University and other colleges and
universities, whose interest in the subject has been a source of
inspiration.

Francisco M. Zulueta
Abriel M. Nebres

Manila
July 24, 2002

Contents

On Agrarian Grievances. The Muslim
Opposition to Spanish Misrule. The
Development of Philippine Nationalism. The
Influx of Liberal Ideas. The Opening of
Philippine Ports to International Trade and
Community. The Emergence of the Middle
Class. The Effects of European Liberalism. The
Influence of the French Revolution. Racial
Prejudice. The Secularization Issue. Study
Guides.

The Objectives of the Propaganda Movement.
The Great Reformists. Jose Rizal – A Nationalist
Martyr. Graciano Lopez-Jaena. Marcelo H. Del
Pilar – Exponent of Justice. The La Solidaridad.
The Hispano-Filipino Association. The End of
the Reform Movement. Katipunan Initiation
Rites. Membership in the Katipunan. The Flags
of the Katipunan. Andres Bonifacio. The Great
Plebian. Emilio Jacinto – The Brains of the
Revolution. Discovery of the Katipunan. Study
Guides.

The Cry of Balintawak. The First Encounter of
the Katipuneros. The San Juan Hostile
Encounter. The Reign of Terror. The Katipunan
in Cavite. The Tejeros Convention. The Naik
Military Compact. The Trial and Execution of
Bonifacio. The Revolution Continues. The Biak-
na-Bato Republic. The Pact of Biak-na-Bato.
Failure of the Pact of Biak-na-Bato. Study
Guides.

Filipinization of the Catholic Church. Monsieur
Chapelle and Filipinization. The Religious
Schism. Significance of Religious Schism. Study
Guides.

The American Policy on Filipinization. The Taft
Commission and Filipinization. Training for
Self-government. Filipinization of the National
Government. The Jones Law. The Philippine
Legislature under the Jones Law. The National
Civil Service. The Harrison Administration. The
System of Government under Harrison. The
Wood Administration. The Wood-Forbes
Mission. Murphy, the Last American Governor-
General. The Independence Mission. The OS-
ROX Mission. The Hare-Hawes Cutting Act. The
Tydings-McDuffie Law. The Framing of the
Constitution. Preparation for Independence. The
Problem of National Security. The National
Language. On Economic Problems. On Social
Justice. On Social Problems. Results of the
American Occupation. On Development of
Education. On Public Health and Welfare. On
Trade, Commerce and Industry. On
Transportation and Communication. On
Individual Freedoms. On Political
Consciousness. On Negative Results. Study
Guides.

The Japanese Offensive Attack. The Japanese
Invasion Begins. Bleak Christmas. The Retreat

Chapter 1

The Land And The People

The Philippines is a varied land – rugged mountains, valleys, high flat mountains, forest, irregular lands even and long coast lines, fertile plains, bays and lakes, rivers and volcanoes. It is an archipelago consisting of more than 7,000 islands and islets. The largest island is Luzon followed by Mindanao.

There are big ranges comprising the mountain systems throughout the archipelago. The virgin forests cover some 40,000 square miles, which produce various kinds of timber for domestic and export consumption. The Philippine hardwood; e.g., narra, apitong, guijo, lauan, tangili, tindalo and yakal abound in the Philippine forests. Aside from the timbers, the Philippine forests had medicinal plants and herbs, nipa, palms, resins, rubber, abaca and rattan gums.

Forest Resources. The narra tree (pterocarpus indicus) is the national tree of our country. It symbolizes the Filipino character and ideals at their highest and loftiest measure. The narra is the best wood for furniture-making; e.g., cabinets, tables, chairs and beds. It is also used for flooring, ceiling, staircase, balusters and walls for aristocratic homes and luxurious offices. Its durability and beauty commands a high price and are highly in demand.

Fish and Marine Resources. The Philippine bays, lakes, rivers and seas abound with various types of fish, shells, crustaceans, seaweeds, corals and pearls and other forms and classes of marine and aquatic resources. The various common fish are milkfish, lapu-lapu, talakitok, kanduli, tamban, tanguingui, dalagang bukid and tilapia.

1

The smallest fish in the world is said to have been found in Lake Buhi Camarines Sur. This is locally known as *tabyas*. Turtle Islands in the Sulu Sea is a breeding ground for big turtles whose meat and eggs are the gourmet's favorite. Beneath the deep serene blue waters of Palawan and Sulu are found the pearl beds. It may be worth mentioning that the world's largest natural pearl called "Pearl of Allah" was found in Palawan by a muslim diver.

Mineral Deposits. The Philippines is very rich in mineral deposit; e.g., gold, silver, iron, copper, lead, manganese and zinc. Non-metallic minerals; e.g., limestone, asbestos, asphalt, clay and oil are abundant in our country.

Typhoons. The Philippines is always visited by typhoon starting in the month of May up to the latter part of December. This is the reason while the archipelago is lashed by strong and gusty winds every year, submerging low areas with water and consequently, taking a heavy toll of human lives and destruction of property.

Earthquakes. This natural phenomenon resulting from the movement of a part of the earth's surface due to the faulting rocks to volcanic forces is frequently experienced by the Filipino people. The most tragic and frightful earthquake to rock Manila and its suburbs happened on June 3, 1863. it destroyed Manila Cathedral, many churches, bridges, buildings and houses. It was estimated that more than 400 people perished and many were injured. The most destructive earthquake that occurred in the Philippines was on August 17, 1976 with a tremendous forces of 8.2 magnitude on the Richter scale with epicenter in Mindanao Gulf, it was accompanied by tidal waves. Hundreds of people died and rendered many families homeless and destroyed property running to millions of pesos.

Volcanoes. Volcanoes are vents in the earth's crust through which lava steam and ashes are expelled either continuously or at irregular intervals. There are around fifty volcanoes in the archipelago, majority of which are inactive. The most famous of these volcanoes is Mayon Volcano in the

Bicol region, "the perfect cone." A joy to behold because of its majestic and serene beauty, but it has a grim, horrible and tragic history. It has recorded eruptions of 38 times from 1616 to 2001 causing terrible losses to human lives and destruction to property.

The most frightful cataclysmic eruption of Mount Mayon was on February 1, 1814. The avalanche of its flaming rocks and molten lava and billowing smoke utterly destroyed the town of Cagsawa and buried hundreds of people. Only the belfry of the buried town remains above the ground, a mute witness to the frightful tragedy.

The famous volcano, which is a delight to many tourists and artists are the tiny volcano in Taal Lake in Batangas Province. It has erupted a number of times and destroyed the nearby towns and villages, causing the death of hundreds of people and destruction to property.

Mount Pinatubo sits in the center of the Zambales Range in Central Luzon. When it erupted in 1991, after more than 400 years of dormancy, it produced some 5 billion cubic meters of pyroclastic flow materials.

The Philippine Institute of Volcanology and Seismology (Philvolcs.) said it would take approximately 10 to 15 years for the rains to wash such a large volume of debris down the volcano slopes.

On top of the economic damage and social problems – thievery, prostitution, mendicancy and dislocation, the residents are exposed to a potentially fatal health hazard each day. The debris spawned by Mt. Pinatubo contains silica particles that cause silicosis, a lung disease that, like AIDS, has no known cure as yet, and which becomes apparent only 20 years or more after the first exposure to silica.

Lahar comes from volcanic eruption and the Philippines has had active volcanoes long before the coming of man, yet only known now has lahar become an immediate, urgent reality. The onset of the rainy season continues to show fears among many Central Luzon residents. Farmers who used to pray for rains that their fields might be irrigated, today implore the gods to spare them from continuous rains.

Other volcanoes in the Philippines are Mount Apo, Mount Banahaw, Bulusan Volcano in Sorsogon, Kanlaon Volcano in Negros Occidental, Hibok-Hibok Volcano in Camiguin Island and Calayo Volcano in Mindanao.

Fauna. Fauna are the animals of certain regions. The Philippines abounds in different kinds of animal life. Almost all kinds of specie exist in our country except the kangaroo of Australia, the polar bear of the arctic region, the camel of the Middle East countries and the moose of Canada.

There are unique animals found in the Philippines. These are the tamaraw (Bubalus mindorensis) in Mindoro, a small wild buffalo, having thick brown hair and short massive, horns; the tarsier (semus tarsius) a small, aboreal, nocturnal primate, having a long thin tail and very big eyes and the smallest monkey in the world; the mouse-deer (tragulidae) a very small deer-like of Balabac Island which is the world's smallest deer; and zebronkey, half zebra and half donkey which was bred at the Manila Zoo in 1962.

There are almost 26,000 species of insects in the archipelago and the largest insect is the giant moth (attacus atlas) with big wings and having nocturnal habits.

There are various kinds of birds in the Philippines, e.g. the kalaw, which makes a loud call from the mountain. The peacock (pavo cristatus) the male of the peafowl, distinguished by its long, erectile greenish iridescent tail coverts that are brilliantly marked eyelike spots, the hawk (accipitridae) which screams as it soars into the sky and king – fisher (megaceryle, alcyon), insect – eating with a large head and long stout bill and usually crested and brilliantly colored.

Flora. The various plants of particular region that exist in great quantities all year round of a certain country. In the Philippines, millions of flowers of various sizes, colors, petals and scents bloom especially in the month of May.

Among the beautiful flowers of our country are the lovely

sampaguita, the Philippine National flower, a very popular
flower with white petals and pleasing smell; usually made into
leis and placed around the neck of visiting heads of state,
dignitaries and prominent personalities. The *dama de noche,*
that blooms at night captivate lovers, because of its distinctive
odor, the bougainvilla, when in bloom, delights the eye with
such exotic brilliance, the Doña Aurora, is a small shrub with
multiple leafy calyx holes of yellow-cream and small yellow
flowers, blooms throughout the year and is very floriferous,
the *cadena de amor,* a fast-growing climber with masses of
pink or white flowers develop on sprays which end in
numerous tendrils, and the Banaba, which will remind you of
the lilacs and springtime when admiring the lovely blossoms
which display a color of deep purple when opening, fading
light blue when a few days old.

There are hundreds of varieties of orchids that bloom in
the archipelago. The waling-waling is considered to be the
queen of the orchids world. Its native habitat is in the forest of
Mindanao, and it is not found anywhere else in the world.

Fruits of different sizes, shapes and tastes grow in
abundant in quantity. These are the sweet mangoes, bananas,
lanzones, star apples and papayas. The durian, having a hard
prickly rind with highly flavored, pulpy flesh and an offensive
odor are found in Mindanao "Tastes like heaven, but smells
like hell." There are numerous kinds of medicinal plants like
sambong, lagundi, oregano, pito-pito and ampalaya to name
a few.

Climate. Nature was generous in giving the Philippines
plenty of fertile soil, along with a climate that is healthful and
moderately warm. There are two distinct climatic seasons –
wet and dry. The wet season is from the early part of June to
October, and dry season starts from the first week of November
to April.

Rainfall is frequent in our country, so that flowers of all
kinds bloom everyday.

Agriculture. The science of cultivating land in the raising
of crops such as rice, corn, coconuts, sugarcane, coffee, tobacco

are abundant. Other agriculture products are bananas, pineapples, cabbages, onions and sweet potatoes. Our main exports are coconut and sugar.

The People. The Filipino people are a mixture of races even though they are basically Malay. They are a blending of the East and West undoubtedly, the Filipinos at the coming of the Spanish colonizers were brown-skinned like their Malay ancestors. The intermarriage between the Filipinos and the foreigner particularly light-skinned and high-bridged nose consequently led to the class known as the *mestizos.* In Philippine society, the type of *mestizos* implies that the individuals referred to are Spanish-Filipino. All other half-breeds are classified by the origin and nationality of their parents, thus a Filipino with a Spanish father or mother is called Spanish *mestizo.* The feeling and attitude of perceived inferiority and hostility between a *mestizo* and the "native" is felt because of this social and economic status. This resulted with disagreeable connotation, e.g., arrogant, boastful or pretentious. Today, the uneasy feeling between the Filipino and the mestizo still exists, though gradually fading out.

Majority of the Filipinos are the Tagalogs, Visayans, Ilocanos, Bicolanos, Pampageños, Pangasianares, Ibanag and Zambals, other indigenous groups include the Igorots, the Apayaos, Bontoks, Ifugaos, Mangyans of Mindoro, Tagbanuas of Palawan, Badjaos and the Samals of Tawi-Tawi, the Maranao of Lake Lanao, the Agta of Palanan, the Atis of Negros, the Ilongots of Nueva Viscaya, the Tinguians of Abra and the Negritos of Pinatubo.

Filipino Traits. As a people the Filipinos over the years have come to value certain traits like hospitality, pakikisama, close family ties, respect for the elders, loyalty and fatalistic attitude.

Hospitality. This is a unique trait that commends itself to a friend or foreigner. If you happen to drop in at an unholy hour of the day and sensing that you are hungry, the Filipino readily prepares the best food, even if there would not be enough food for the next meal.

Pakikisama. This Filipino trait has not been fully understood from its connotations, which may be translated unrestrictedly and loosely as a manifestation of camaraderie and good faith. The person is labeled "mabuting makisama" if he is not selfish, and participates cheerfully in community work, and masamang makisama "if he is incapable of empathy."

Today, because of politics and the age of materialism, the term pakikisama has been debased into an attitude that makes a crook well-liked or admired if he can help people even if he subverts justice.

Close Family Ties. The family is the oldest social institution. It is the primary social group and the first agency of socialization. It is the smallest unit of society and everything revolves around. The Filipinos posses a genuine and deep love for the family. The father is the head of the family and normally, the breadwinner and the one who rules. The mother is the housekeeper, the educator, the laundry woman and the cook. The Filipino family is composed of the grandparents, the parents, the children, aunts, uncles and other relatives. The grandparents are always consulted on matters affecting the family.

Respect for the Elders. This is one Filipino trait that has an enduring force that has remained in the book of unwritten laws. The Filipino parent exercises almost absolute power over their children and what even decisions they made are respected. It is quite unthinkable and surprising for a son or a daughter to do an important decision without consulting the parents. Respect to show regard or consideration for others is always observed. Children are not condoned talking back to those who are older than they are. The elders believe that they can demand obedience among the young members of the family – right or wrong. For the elders, academic degrees required in college does not impress them and cannot compare favorably with their long experience. For them, the young have the knowledge; theirs the wisdom, collective responsibility is evidently felt in the Filipino family. The members who are lucky to be better off have to look after the welfare not only of their immediate family but also of other relatives. The custom, right or wrong, in the family as a social institution, comes first.

Loyalty. This is one trait of the Filipino, to be faithful to commitments on matters relating to personal relationships. For them, this is very strong and enduring. Friendship is such a sacred association and implies mutual help under any kind of condition. A friend is considered a member of the family and is expected to share its hardships and sufferings as well as its fortunes and happiness. This concept of loyalty to a friend as a dimension of concern, explicitly explains why many Filipinos remain aloof from the United States because of the thought of not receiving enough aid due to them, during the World War II, the American and Filipino soldiers fought valiantly against the enemies in the name of democracy and freedom. For the Filipinos, it is unthinkable that the United States showed not value such friendship, knowing that they stood by her side during the darkest hour.

For the Americans, this attitude is beyond comprehension for their understanding of friendship is different from that of the Filipinos. The relationship with the Americans is business-like and impersonal and will not allow sentimentalism and sympathetic feeling to be an obstacle to the fulfillment of their objective. This attitude the Americans have demonstrated cannot be understood by the Filipinos, hence the misunderstanding between the Americans and the Filipinos with respect to material aid continues to exist.

Superstition. Superstition is an irrational set of beliefs of the ominous significance of a particular thing or circumstance and phenomenon. The Filipinos believe that faith can move mountains. The events surrounding the EDSA phenomenon, which has a moral dimension, a fight to finish between the forces of good and evil, is an eloquent manifestation among Filipinos for whom faith has been a durable peg for historical upheavals.

It is interesting to remember that, from the time of the Spanish conquistadors who prevailed with cross and sword, to the katipuneros who treated their tribulations as highlights in a stylized play, the Filipinos have looked to religion as a rallying point. The peaceful uprising in EDSA will always be remembered as the Filipino people's shining moment in history because they stood up to answer the call for love of country. Their only weapons against a formidable force were songs, prayers, religious icons, and yellow daisies to oust a dictator through a dramatic end. This EDSA event, which the whole world watch with awe as it unfolds was considered a miracle for the Filipinos.

, *Fatalism.* Fatalism is doctrine that all events are predetermined or subject to a fate. The Filipinos are by nature fatalistic and submit to fate. It seems that no amount of logic and scientific explanation can remove him from this fatalistic attitude. He believes that every fate or misfortune that comes along his way is attributed to fate. This fatalism is exemplified in the common expression "Bahala na, may awa ang Panginoong Diyos." It is dangerous to travel by sea because of the bad weather, "Bahala na." The equivalent of Spanish expression, "Que sera, sera" (what ever will be, will be). This fatalistic attitude has been ingrained in the Filipino sense of resignation.

Filipinos have the propensity and passion for gambling. It is not surprising to see people, young and old make a bet in jueteng, cara y cruz, bingo, lottery sweepstakes, black jack, horse-racing, cock fighting and even basketball ending. This passion for gambling can make a family miserable, since the hard-earned money may be lost because betting involves risks.

Gambling, as a game of chance for stakes, make the Filipino, especially the youth, enticed to this kind of game. Gambling cheats and corrupts our poor and demeans our Christian values. A poor and impoverished society lured to gambling when people should be working, struggling for a better life, and educating their children now, one sees gambling everywhere. Some ill effects of gambling are neglect of duties and responsibilities, broken marriage, home and family relations, loss of self-respect and moral integrity, prostitution, poverty, high crime rate and even sale of precious personal and real property.

Extreme Personalism

Filipinos are extremely personalistic. A typical Filipino views the social environment in terms of personal relationships. The extent to which one is able to relate personally to things and people determines the recognition of their existence and the value attached to them. Filipinos have a difficulty dealing with all forms of impersonal stimuli because of this personalistic view about his environment. This is one of the reasons why one is uncomfortable with bureaucracy, with rules and regulations and with other standard operating procedures to be observed. Personal relationships, which are always involved in any transaction make this, most often, are difficult to turn down. Preference is usually given to family and friends in matters of hiring personnel, delivery of services and even voting for candidates during elections. Consequently, this extreme personalism often leads to graft and corruption and other malpractices in our government institutions.

Extreme Family-Centeredness

While concern for the family is considered an important trait of the Filipinos, its extreme excessiveness becomes detrimental to the welfare of a larger community. The use of one's office and power to promote the interest of one's family results in the utter lack of concern for the common good.

Lack of Discipline

The Filipinos have an aversion for following strictly a set of procedures to observe order and discipline. They are impatient to get what they want fast. This results in the use of short-cuts or the "palusot" syndrome, "nakaisa," "nakalamang," and "nakadaya," in the Filipino vocabulary words loaded with implied values. In several instances, they are guilty of the "ningas – cogon" tendency. They start out projects with full enthusiasm and interest, which abruptly die down, leaving things unfinished. What a waste!

Lack of National Consciousness

A proper understanding of one's history is a very important factor in the development of national consciousness because it will serve to demonstrate how the present is influenced by the past. Why is there a weak state of national consciousness among Filipinos? How did it happen?

A state where national consciousness is absent or fragile can only succumb to the Western power that is more skillful, subtle, and wear the facade of benevolence (goodwill) aided by the deliberate and systematic miseducation of the exploited.

Westernization has virtually dulled the minds of the Filipinos so that, as a result, a crisis of identity was created. It is so pervasive that Filipinos were unaware of their own lack of national consciousness.

Colonial Mentality

The Filipinos suffer from "National Amnesia" and "Colonial Mentality." This condition may be attributed to two dimensions – lack of patriotism and national integration and the strong preference for imported goods, foreign ideas and ways.

The Filipinos have a penchant for adapting and incorporating the foreign elements into their image. This is manifested in their preference for foreign fashion, entertainment, life styles, technology, language and consumer items.

Passivity and Lack of Initiative

While it is true that Filipinos can adjust to circumstances

in a given environment and is possessed by some creative talents, they are generally passive and lacking in initiative at times. One has to be told what has to be done. The strong reliance on the government and people in authority tend to make Filipinos complacent. They can tolerate inefficiency, poor service and even violation of human rights. In many ways, it can be said that Filipinos are too patient for along suffering ("matiisin"), easily resigned to one's fate, even if they are oppressed and exploited.

"Kanya-kanya" Syndrome

Most Filipinos have a selfish and self-serving attitude that generates a feeling of envy towards others; particularly, when one's peer has gained honor or prestige because of hard work. They demonstrate some hostile attitudes and feelings by recoursing to unfounded and malicious criticism – "tsismis" and "intriga" to bring others down. This "crab mentality" that characterizes many Filipinos is counter productive.

One evident manifestation of the "kanya-kanya" syndrome is one's personal ambition and the drive for power and status that is completely insensitive to the common good. Purely personal and in-group interests reign supreme in this kind of attitude.

The "kanya-kanya" syndrome often results in the non-cooperation of members of the community.

Lack of Exhaustive Study and Self-Analysis

The Filipinos have a tendency to be superficial and sometimes even somewhat flighty. Confronted with serious problems, both personal and social, there seems to be no deliberate and intelligent alternative plan to solve the problem. In most cases, they joke and laugh about serious problems affecting them. Anyway, these problems are "not mine alone." If there are strategies to solve these problems, they are only panacea. They easily accept and are even satisfied with the superficial explanations and hasty solutions to the problems.

Another factor related to this issue is that Filipinos give too much emphasis on form ("maporma") rather than on substance. In most cases, they have a tendency to be satisfied with rhetoric and substitute this for reality. Empty rhetoric and endless beautiful words uttered by many politicians, that come into print and broadcast media are very much a part of their daily lives. There seems to be a tendency that, as long as the right things are said, as long as the proper documents and reports are presented, as long as the proper committees and task force are constituted, as long as government officials are recognized, Filipinos are deluded into believing that the government really means business.

There have been a lot of investigations in Congress about alleged irregularities committed by high-ranking officials in the government in aid of legislation. After this legislative inquiry, what's next?

The Filipinos really lack self-analysis on problems that confront them. They easily accept form rather than substance. This emphasis on form is reinforced by an educational system that is often more on form than substance, and a legal system that tends to substitute law for reality.

Other Filipino Character Traits that Distinguish them from Other People of the World

The Filipinos are by nature extravagant. They are fun-loving and this can be seen in various fiestas held every year in honor of a Patron Saint throughout the country with pompous and pretentious extravagance. The baptism of a child, the wedding of a member of the family, the birthday of a loved one, the school graduation of a son or daughter, the passing the board or bar examination, winning a beauty contest is celebrated with a party.

The Filipinos have the tendency to be indolent, a character trait brought about perhaps by warm tropical climate and the abundance of natural resources that nature has provided the archipelago.

The tendency to procrastinate, otherwise known as the "mañana habit" and the virtual lack of punctuality, deridingly dubbed "Filipino time" is a part of the Filipino character.

The parochial practice of "tayo-tayo," otherwise known as the "compadre system."

The propensity to be over critical of the actions and thoughts of others that do not conform with one's beliefs.

The exaggerated "amor propio," too much self-esteem and extreme sensitiveness, which often times indicate a feeling of insecurity.

The weak character traits of the Filipinos are, however, offset by their strong and resilient character. Most admirable of these character traits are readily recognized.

Hard Work and Industry

Filipinos have the capacity for hard work, if given the opportunity and better working conditions. The desire to raise one's standard of living and to acquire the basic essentials of a better life for one's family, with appropriate incentives, undoubtedly makes the Filipino work very hard. This is clearly shown by one's willingness to risk taking jobs in a foreign land with a different culture, not to mention the social cost.

Flexibility, Adaptability and Creativity

Filipinos have the capacity to adjust and to adapt to conditions and circumstances in a given environment, both physical and social. Filipino migrant workers are unfazed by uncertainty or lack of information about a foreign land in pursuit of job opportunities. Filipinos are also creative, resourceful and fast learners. They have the ability to improvise and make use of whatever is on hand in order to create and produce new things out of discarded scraps, for survival.

"Pakikipagkapwa-tao"

Filipinos have a deep sense of concern for one's dignity and respect. This "pakikipagkapwa-tao" is manifested in a basic regard for justice and fairness to others. The Filipino's gesture to emphathize with others as a way of extending support in times of need; for instance, "pakikiramay," the sensitivity to other people's feelings – "pakikiramdam" and "pagtitiwala" are bonds that promote feelings of closeness to one another and become foundation of unity.

Joy and Humor

Filipinos have a propensity to cheer and laugh and have a fun loving approach to the ups and downs of life. Laughing at themselves and the mess they are in is an important coping mechanism. In many instances, they are playful, sometimes cynical, and laugh at those they love and at those they hate and make jokes about their misfortune. This sense of humor, certainly, provides emotional balance and optimism.

Faith and Religiosity

Filipinos have a deep faith in God. Their innate religiosity enables them to comprehend and genuinely accept reality in the context of God's will and plan. To a Filipino, success is a blessing from above. Likewise, tragedy and misfortune are accepted with an open heart. Filipinos live very intimately with the religion and prayers have been important parts of their lives.

The spirit of cooperation and neighborliness is exemplified in the bayanihan system. This is the applied synthesis of their Malayan spirit and culture.

The tenacity in the pursuit and defense of national ideals,

the strength of will and flexibility of character and capacity
for self-adjustment and improvement shows the Filipino
character trait.

"Palabra de Honor" (Word of Honor) is the virtue that
defines the sanctity of commitments and obligations is
contractual and personal relations. Today, it is one of the many
virtues we must revive in order to establish the moral code
and expectation of the public from the government; and
inversely, of the government from its citizens.

"Delicadeza" is the virtue that determines the person's
sensitivity to what is right or wrong. A sense of prudence and
propriety is implicit in a person with delicadeza. "Delicadeza"
in a person of authority also serves as an early warning device
in recognizing the traps of graft and corruption; whether in
the guise of "pagtanaw ng utang na loob" or the innocent gift.

"Kaayusan" is a Filipino character trait of orderliness. It
begins in the home as an early mental discipline, instilled in
the children by the parents.

"Kagalingan" is the Filipino trait, which relates to the
spirit and compulsion for competence in whatever job or
profession a person is working at, whether manual or mental.
"Kagalingan" results in the worker with a strong personal
drive to improve his skills and level of excellence and a habit
for initiative.

The Filipino's character traits can be compared to the
molave tree – sturdy and resilient and the bamboo, pliant,
which bend with the strong winds, but never breaks.

Regional Traits. The Filipinos in different regions have
their peculiar and distinguishing character traits. From the
north, the Ilocos Region stands along mountain ranges and
seas that are occasionally restive and violent. The land
especially during the dry season, is extremely arid and when
cultivated yield insufficient products for the family for the
whole year.

The Ilocanos are perceived to be industrious, hardworking, patient and thrifty. Because of the pressure of economic opportunities and alternatives they are forced to migrate to other places. In Hawaii and in other parts of the United States one finds an Ilocano. Of all the Filipinos, the Ilocanos are known to be regionalistic. The Central Plain comprisisng the provinces of Bataan, Bulacan, Nueva Ecija, Pampanga, a small part of Tarlac, Rizal, Cavite, Laguna, Batangas, Quezon, Marinduque and Mindoro, including Manila, the capital of the Philippines, and the center of political, economic and cultural activities and is at the heart of the region and the Tagalog zone. The Tagalogs feel "superior" to the rest of their Filipino brothers. Their lifestyle is neither frugal nor extravagant. Generally, they prefer to stay in their places of origin rather than migrate to greener pastures to seek their fortune. A number of Tagalog personalities excel in literary, music and art. Among the best literary greats in the Tagalog region are Jose dela Cruz, popularly known as Husing Sisiw, Francisco Balagtas and Jose Corazon de Jesus, in Tagalog; Fernando Ma. Guerrero and Claro M. Recto, in Spanish, Jose Garcia Villa and Nick Joaquin, and in English.

From the Bicol Region, the Bicolanos are known for their religiosity. They are perceived to be peace-loving people. They are fond of spicy foods. It is observed that the region is abundant with natural resources; hence, it may be inferred that the Bicolanos tend to have bigger families.

From the Visayan Region, the Visayans are said to be happy-go-lucky people. They are interested in the meaning of the good life. They are ready to spend their hard-earned money just to enjoy life to the fullest. Whether this assumption is correct or not, only the Visayans can attest to this. Generally, the Visayans are perceived to be spendthrifts; they are also adventurous. The Visayan girls can leave their homes and go to Manila and other cities without hesitation or anxiety about their decision to follow the glitter of their adventure. It is in this regard that it may be inferred the Visayan girls are more self-reliant than the Tagalogs.

The Visayans are said to be hedonists and crave for pleasure as a way of life. They have passion and love for music.

From the Mindanao Region, the Muslims, considered the staunch advocate and lover of freedom, are also adventurous. They are perceived to be men of honor and would stick to their word to fulfill an obligation. They are proud of their culture and way of life. While a big portion of the Philippines had been subjugated and Christianized by the Spanish colonizers, the Muslims fought valiantly to protect their territory, religion and freedom.

The various traits of the Filipinos, representing the major geographic regions in the Philippines, is reflective of the cross-section of its people.

Other Important Information About the Philippines

The Philippines is the first Asian nation to achieve independence through revolution and establish a Republic led by General Emilio Aguinaldo in 1898-1901. It is also the first Southeast Asian nation to gain independence from a colonial power on July 4, 1946. The Philippines is the only Christian nation in Asia. The Philippines is a nation of many languages and dialects. The Filipinos are said to speak English fluently compared with other Asians. The National Language of the Philippines is "Filipino." The Filipinos are considered the most literate people in Southeast Asia with a literacy rate of 89.27%. This is because the Filipinos put a high premium on the value of education.

On Beautiful Scenes and Wealth of Natural Wonders

The Banawe Ifugao Rice Terraces, in Northern Luzon, built more than 2,000 years ago by the Ifugao on the slopes of the mountains is an attractive place for the tourists. Many writers acclaimed the Banawe Rice Terraces as the "Eighth Wonder of the World."

The Mayon Volcano in Albay Province, "the perfect cone" and its majestic beauty is indeed a scenic spot to behold. The small Taal Volcano in Lake Taal, in Batangas, fascinates local and foreign tourists. Other scenic beauty and wonders in the Philippines that delight tourists, excursionists and travelers are the world-famous Pagsanjan Falls, the legendary Mount Banahaw in Laguna, the awesome chocolate hills in Bohol, the historical Montalban Caves of Rizal, the Tiwi Hot Springs of Albay, the fascinating Beach of Boracay, the serene Lake of Sorsogon and the magnificient Maria Cristina Falls in Mindanao.

The beautiful sunset of Manila Bay is a delight to the poets and artists and promenaders at the Luneta and the long stretch of Roxas Boulevard, Manila.

Indeed, nature has blessed the Philippines with beautiful scenes and places where one can go and relax after a hard day's work, and experience its beauty and wonders.

Before the Discovery of the Philippines

Long before Ferdinand Magellan arrived in the archipelago in 1521, which was later called the Philippines, it was practically unknown to historians. It was only through archeological records and extensive researchers in ancient narratives, factual or imagined and other stories written by Chinese chronicles and Muslim scholars bear witness that the Philippines had early relations already with her neighbors. In effect, these records are eloquent manifestations of the existence of civilization, which are indications of our Oriental character.

The first man in the Philippines, inferentially, in spite of the extensive researches about the physical history of the archipelago in recent years by historians and archeologist to describe exactly its origin, it seems that no adequate pieces of evidence and concrete information are available. What the geologists perhaps did was to resort to a theory that during the Pleistocene Period characterized by widespread glacial ice, the waters around what is now the Philippines fell several feet below the present elevation. Consequently, a boundless area of land lay open and formed some kind of land bridges connecting the archipelago with Asia.

The discovery of skullcap of a man in Tabon Cave in Lipuan Point Palawan in 1962 is a proof that man existed in the Philippines several centuries ago. By inference, the primitive man came to the archipelago by way of land bridges with his prehistoric culture. With him were animals, e.g., the elephants, rhinoceros, boars and deer. This man was described to be stocky and had sturdy muscles and have thick hair, lived in caves with bark or leaves of trees joined together as their clothing, and survive on fruits and other raw food. In as much as no fossil remains regarding the activities of the ancient men of great age, inferentially, this leads to the conclusion that he vanished without leaving any trace.

The Inhabitants of the archipelago, after the disappearance of the ancient man, about 30,000 years ago, the negritos from Borneo as the land of origins came to the Philippines using Palawan and Mindoro as point of entry by way of walking on land bridges. Several centuries after their arrival, the huge glaciers of ice of the world melted and raised the sea levels and submerged the land bridges, cutting off the archipelago from the Asian mainland.

The negritos are small people below five feet tall in height, with dark skin, black kinky hair, black eyes and flat noses, they used bow and arrow when hunting and fishing. They wandered in the forests gathering wild fruits and root crops and lived in houses made of branches of trees. Their clothing were made of bark of trees and leaves tied together. These primitive people have a culture that belonged to the Paleolithic Period. They made fire by rubbing two dry bamboo sticks together to give them warmth and light at night. The Negritos were the first inhabitants in the archipelago.

The Malaysians.   After the submersion of land bridges another group of people came to the archipelago by ships who were culturally advanced. They were tall in height, light-skinned and have long faces and originated from Indo-China and landed in Luzon. Their houses were built with wood and covered with grass. They practiced dry agriculture and produced upland rice, gabi, yams and other root crops. Their clothing were made of beaten tree barks and decorated with various printed decorative designs. They cooked their food in bamboo tubes. They survived by way of hunting and gathering fruits. Their implements were of polished stone axes.

In the course of time, another migratory wave came to the archipelago. They practice a primitive form of agriculture known as "kaingin." They are stocky and dark-complexioned with thick lips and big noses and are classified by the anthropologists to belong to the Neolithic Period.

By deduction, the Apayaos, Bontoks, Gadangs, Kalingas, Igorots, Ilongots and the Tinguians of Luzon, the Tagbanuas and Bataks of Palawan, the Bagobos, the Bilaans, the Manobos and the Tirurays of Mindanao are of Indonesian descent.

The continuous wave of immigrants brought with them particular culture describing their way of life. Because of their advanced culture, improved implements and methods of agriculture were introduced.

It may be inferred that the last of the prehistoric immigrants where the Malays who came by way of sail boats moved by wind through the direction of Palawan and Mindoro, and another group into Visayas and Mindoro through the Celebes Sea. The culture and the way of life of this group includes irrigated agriculture, the smelting and manufacture of tools, utensils, weapons and various ornaments of iron and metals, the manufacture of clay pottery, art of weaving and the manufacture of jewelry and other adornments made of shells, flowers, leaves and plumage, metal soon became part of the materials used and it became possible to work with more challenging materials such as gold and semi-precious stones. Their houses were made of wood and bamboo and palm leaves for the roof and raised above the ground. The carabaos were used in farm activities. They raised various crops and other agricultural products and planted fruit-bearing trees.

Another group of Malay migration arrived at the early part of the 13th century. These people were quite advanced from other migrants because they had already an alphabet and syllabary found in a clay pot discovered in Calatagan grave. These were the Christian Filipinos from whom the Tagalogs, Ilokanos, Bicolanos, Kapangpangans descended. The last group of Malay migrants who settled in the archipelago from the 14th century to the 16th century constituted the Muslim Malays who introduced the Islamic religion in Mindanao.

Data about these waves, of migrants are hypothetically considered, however, more accurate. Information to establish their authenticity as concrete facts are still necessary, though.

The Bornean Datu. The Malay settlement at Panay is told in the Maragtas, an epic about the ten datus, headed by Datu Puti. At about the 13th century, Borneo was at a state of agitation because Sultan Makatunaw was arbitrarily treating his subjects; so, these ten chieftains decided to leave for an unknown destination in search for freedom.

With them were the families who sailed without any definite destination. After a few days of sailing, these Bornean chieftains reached Panay, which was at that time ruled by a datu, Marikudo and his wife. Datu Puti assured Marikudo that their intentions were peaceful and all they wanted was to purchase land where he and his men and their families could settle. After consulting with his elders, Marikudo sold his land to the new settlers. It may be interesting to note that the purchase price was ridiculously low – a gold salakot and a gold necklace for Maniwantiwan, Marikudo's wife. The sale was sealed by a part of friendship and followed by a customary feast after which Marikudo and his people bade farewell to Datu Puti and his guests.

With the chieftains and their families settled in Panay, these datus sailed in different regions. The three datus Puti, Balensusa and Dumangsil reached the coast of Batangas and were delighted by the scenic beauty of the region around Lake Taal and the fertility of the soil that holds promise; so they decided to settle there. While Datu Puti and his men were satisfied with the peaceful environment, they returned to Borneo. The families of Dumangsil and Balensusa sailed to Laguna and the Bicol region. The seven datus in Panay found the place peaceful so they decided to divide the island into three districts namely: Hantik (now Antique) under Datu Sumakwel; Irong-Irong (now Iloilo) under Datu Paliburong; and Aklan (now Aklan and Capiz); under Datu Bangkaya. It may be worth mentioning that the Bornean colonies in the Philippines apparently prospered. It was perceived that Datu Sumakwel ruled well because of his age and wisdom. The datus formed a sort of political organization known as "Confederation of Madyaas" led by Datu Sumakwel for purposes of protection and for maintaining harmonious relations among the families.

The Filipino People. From the interracial mixture of the prehistoric Negritos, Indonesians and the Malays, the Filipino people was born. The succeeding course of events, prior to the arrival of the Spanish colonizers the Filipinos intermarried with Chinese, Indians, Arabs, Japanese and other Asians. At present, Filipinos who migrate in other countries to look for greener pastures, intermarry with foreigners-Canadians, Australians, French, Irish, Italians, Mexicans and other nationalities.

The Cultural Influences of India. India's civilization has a dramatic influence in Philippine culture. The ancient Filipino system of beliefs, their rituals and sacrifices were of Indian origin. The term bathala (supreme god of the ancient Tagalogs) came from the Sanskrit Bhattara Guru, which means "the highest of the supernatural beings" and other religious and philosophical ideas originated from India. The ancient alphabet where Tagalog language are Sanskrit terms such as asawa (spouse), diwa (thought), lakambini (princess), and puri (honor), ina (mother), mana (inheritance), guro (teacher), dala (fish net) to mention a few are India's influences. The Sarong (skirt) worn by women and the potong (turban) a man's headdress worn chiefly by Muslims consisting of a long cloth of silk or linen, and the rich and intricate embroidered shawls of the present-day Muslim Filipino women show Indian character. The Filipino literature and folklore, e.g., Darangan, a Maranao epic, the Ramayana and Mahabharata are Hindu epics and other tales and fables with which ancient Filipinos entertained their children found their way to Filipino culture.

Many Indian influences are shown in decorative art and metal work. The boat-lute, a stringed musical instrument, which is still used in Muslim communities is of Hindu origin.

The veil and cord placed on the bride and groom during the wedding ceremony in the Philippines apparently are Hindu influences.

Inferentially, about five percent of the Filipino blood is Indian. This is the reason why the Filipinos are capable of enduring pain and possess fatalistic outlook in life.

The Cultural Influences of China. The Chinese influence on Filipino life is reflected on Philippine languages; particularly in Tagalog mode of dressing, certain customs on marriages, respect for elders and adoption of Chinese surnames of many Filipino families.

An examination of some Philippine languages, particularly in Tagalog, shows that they have their Chinese origin:

Chinese	*Tagalog*
am-pau	ampa'u
bi-hun	bihon
bi-koe	biko
he-bi	hibi
in-kong	ingkong
ma-ni	mani
mi-ki	miki
pan-sit	pansit

From the Chinese, the Filipino learned the use of polo shirts with Chinese collar, sleeved jackets, loose trousers and the cheongsam style for women. The marriage arrangement of children, the practice of employing a go-between in marital negotiations, the wearing of white shirt and dress during the wake and funeral processions, a custom of Chinese character.

The Filipinos also learned the use of umbrellas, porcelain, gongs, the manufacture of firecrackers, gun powder, mining methods and metallurgy. Food preparation like pansit, siopao and mami were Chinese influences.

A few records on account of the Philippine relations with China, reveal that trade relations started as early in the early part of the 9th century. During the Sung Dynasty (960-1127), Chinese goods began to flow into the Philippines.

The Introduction of Islam. Islam is a religious faith of the Muslims, as set forth in the Koran, which teaches that Allah is the only God and that Muhammad is his prophet. The spread of Islam in the archipelago was brought about by the Arab traders, missionaries and teachers who introduced their religious beliefs among the natives. Mukdum, a noted Arabian scholar and missionary, was primarily responsible in introducing Islam. This was followed by Rajah Baginda, Muslim Malay prince, from Sumatra. Other Muslim missionaries to propagate Islam in Sulu was Abu Bakr. Upon his arrival in Sulu, he married Baginda's daughter, Princess Paramisuli. When Rajah Baginda died, Abu Bakr exercised his powers as sultan and founded the Sultanate of Sulu. The spread of Islam in all parts of Sulu was rapid and, as a result, the natives were converted.

Study Guides

A. Terms/Concepts to Understand

aboreal   irrational
pretentious   passion
fatalistic attitude   personalism
socialization   bureaucracy
explicit   aversion

B. Questions to Answer

1. Describe the land of the Philippines.

2. What earthquake that rocked Manila and its suburbs was the most frightful and caused a lot of damage to human lives and property?

3. What can you say about the Philippine climate?

4. Is "pakikisama" as a Filipino trait developmental? Explain your answer.

5. Why do Filipinos have a passion for gambling?

6. What is meant by extreme personalism? Explain your answer by giving some instances.

7. How can we inculcate among the Filipinos the value of discipline?

8. How can we free ourselves from the parochial practice of "tayo-tayo" or the compadre system?

9. What are the regional traits of the Ilocanos?

10. Do you believe that the Negritos are the first inhabitants in the Philippine archipelago? Explain your answer.

Chapter 2

The Pre-Spanish Civilization

Long before the Spaniards and other foreigners landed on Philippine shores, our forefathers already had their own civilization and were living in well-organized independent villages called *barangays*. The name barangay originated from *balangay,* a Malay word which means "sailboat." It may be inferred that the sea-faring Filipinos, to give meaning to their nostalgic memories as they sailed in the high seas towards the Philippine archipelago, named their villages after boats which brought them safely across the seas until they reached the Philippine Islands.

System of Government

During the pre-Spanish period, there were many barangays. Some barangays were big in land area and in population. It may be of interest to note that among them, were Maynilad (Manila), Sugbu (Cebu), and Maktan (Mactan). The barangay was the unit of government and consisted of from thirty to one hundred families and was ruled by a chieftain called *datu* who was the Chief executive, legislator, judge, and supreme commander of the barangay in time of war. The position of the *datu* is obtained through succession. In the event that the datu had no son to bequeath his power to in case of death or being incapacitated, the position was usually handed to a member of the barangay who commanded respect, wealth, intelligence and strength.

The federations of the barangays during the pre-Spanish period was evident and one of the oldest confederations was the "Confederation of Madya-as" which was established by Bornean datus. It was composed of the settlements of *Hantik* (Antique) Aklan and Irong-Irong (Iloilo) and was under the overall rule of *datu* Sumakwel, considered the wisest and the oldest datu of ancient Panay. The rulers of bigger barangays assumed the title of *rajah* or *lakan*.

Perhaps the primary reason why early barangays were formed was because of mutual protection against enemies and the subsequent marriage of the *lakambini* (princess) and the *lakan* (prince) of different barangays which eventually led to the unification of some barangays. Barangay relations were established because of intermarriage of persons in one barangay to other barangays. Friendship with each other was usually sealed by the traditional ceremony, the blood compact, called sandugo (one blood) and anchored on mutual respect and alliance. The participating parties in the compact drew blood from their arms and mixed the blood with wine and drank from the same cup.

The primary duty of the datu was to rule and govern his people and ultimately to promote their welfare and interests. The subjects were loyal to their chieftain during wars and voyages. They also helped him in cultivating the land, harvesting the crops and the construction of his house. They paid their taxes and other obligations to the chieftain in the form of crops or form of services.

Laws. Laws are for the common good and for the welfare of the whole barangay. The early Filipinos had laws that were both oral and written. The oral laws were the customary laws that constituted the bulk of laws in the barangay and were handed down orally from one generation to generation. The written laws were written and promulgated by the chieftain and the elders from time to time when necessity arose and announced publicly throughout the barangay by one known as *umalahokan*. These ancient written laws were embodied in the Code of Kalantiyaw (1433) and was written by Datu

Kalantiyaw. It contained various crimes committed and these were dealt with the corresponding penalties.

The Code of Kalantiyaw consisted of eighteen orders as follows:

First Order. Ye shall not kill; neither shall ye do harm to the aged; lest ye incur the danger of death. All those who disobey order shall be condemned to death by being drowned in the river or placed in boiling water.

Second Order. Ye shall obey; let all your debts with the chief be met punctually. He who does not obey shall receive for the first time one hundred lashes. If the debt is large, he shall be condemned to thrust his hand thrice into boiling water. For the second time, he shall be condemned to be beaten to death.

Third Order. Obey ye; let no one have women that are very young nor more than he can support; nor be given to excessive lust. He who does not observe this order shall be condemned to swim for three hours for the first time, and for the second time, he shall be lacerated with thorns.

Fourth Order. Observe and obey ye; let no one disturb the quiet of the graves; when passing by the caves and trees where they are, give respect to them. He who does not observe this order shall be killed by ants, or beaten with thorns until he dies.

Fifth Order. Ye shall obey; he who makes exchanges for food, let it be always done in accordance with his word. He who does not comply, shall be beaten for one 'hour; he who repeats the offense shall be exposed for one day among the ants.

Sixth Order. Ye shall be obliged to revere sites that are held in respect, such as those of trees of recognized worth, and other sites. He who fails to comply shall pay with one month's work in gold or in money.

Seventh Order. They shall be put to death; he who kills trees of venerable appearance; he who enters the house of the chief without permission; he who shoots arrows at night at old men and women; and he who kills sharks or crocodiles.

Eight Order. Slavery for one year shall be suffered by those who steal away the women of the chiefs, keep ill-tempered dogs that bite the chiefs, and burn the fields of others.

Ninth Order. All these shall be beaten for two days; who sings while traveling by night; who kill birds known as *manual;* who tear the documents belonging to the chiefs; who tell malicious lies; and who mock the dead.

Tenth Order. It is an obligation of every mother to teach matters pertaining to lust secretly to her daughters and prepare them for motherhood. Let not men be cruel or harm their wives when they catch them in the act of adultery. He who shall disobey this order will be killed by being cut to pieces or thrown to the crocodiles.

Eleventh Order. They shall be burned; those who by their strength or cunning have mocked at and escape punishment; or who have killed young boys; or try to steal away the wives of old men (*agorang*).

Twelfth Order. They shall be drowned; all those slaves who interfere with their superiors, or their owners and masters; all those who abuse themselves through their lust; those who destroy their anitos by breaking them or throwing them down.

Thirteenth Order. They shall be exposed to the ants for half a day; those who kill black cats during a new moon, or steal anything from the chiefs and old men, however small it be.

Fourteenth Order. They shall be made slaves for life; those who have beautiful daughters and refuse to marry them off to the sons of the chiefs, or hide them in bad faith.

Fifteenth Order. Concerning beliefs and superstitions. They shall be beaten; those who injure or kill the young of manual (sacred bird) or white monkeys.

Sixteenth Order. The fingers of the following will be cut off; those who break the idols of wood and clay in their *olongas* (altars) and temples; those who destroy the daggers of the priestesses used for sacrificing pigs, or break their drinking jars.

Seventeenth Order. Those shall be put to death; who prefane sites where idols are kept and where the sacred things pertaining to their gods and chiefs are found. He who performs his necessities in these places shall be burnt.

Eighteenth Order. Those who disobey the above orders, if they are chiefs, they shall be put to death by being stoned and crushed; and if they are old man, they shall be placed in rivers to be eaten by sharks and crocodiles.

1433

KALANTIYAW
Third Chief of Panay

The laws, which were prescribed during the pre-Spanish period were formally recognized as binding and were enforced by a sanction. A number of laws covered many subjects that are found in modern legal codes; e.g., persons and family relations; legal separation and divorce, obligations and contracts, property rights, inheritance, loans and crimes. Under the Code of Kalantiyaw, insult, murder, arson, rape, incest, trespassing, witchcraft and sacrilegious acts were punishable by death or by slavery or heavy fine. On the other hand, minor crimes, e.g., cheating in business transactions, adultery, perjury, theft and disturbing peace of the night by singing were punished by exposure to the ants, by flogging, by cutting the fingers of one hand or by swimming continuously for several hours.

The various punishments meted out to guilty persons may appear harsh and barbarous to contemporary man, but the laws have to be applied. A law was a process with a purpose and participated in man's actions and aspirations for a better society.

Anybody caught violating the law was arrested and brought before the chieftain to be judged according to merits of the case, and if found guilty, the corresponding penalty was promptly imposed. This effect is in consonance that "justice delayed is justice denied." The enactment of a law is usually done when the chieftain of a certain barangay wanted to make a law. He called in the elders of the community and presented his plan to promote and protect the welfare of his constituents, and if approved, this became a part of the barangay laws.

Judicial Process. The quest for justice is a basic human need. Conflicts and misunderstandings occurred in any society. All trials involving criminal and civil cases were usually decided peacefully before a court, although not always in some cases, disputes between parties were resolved by arbitration in a body composed of elders from other barangays acting as arbiters.

Trials were held in public where the plaintiffs and defendants pleaded their own case. It may be inferred that, since there were no lawyers at that time, trials were conducted expeditiously without delay as the litigants presented their respective witnesses. Before testifying to the veracity of their testimonies, and to show their honesty and integrity, the witnesses took an oath to this effect and take the consequence: "May the crocodile eat me if I tell a lie!" "May the lightning strike me, if I tell any falsehood!" "May the moon frown upon me if I tell a lie!" For them, their oath was sacred and inviolable. Perjury, which is the willful utterance of a false statement under oath before a court, upon a point of legal injury was inferentially rare in early trials. The barangay courts decided cases in favor of the litigants who presented sufficient proofs and evidence and more witnesses to prove their cases. The chieftain who acted as the judge and executive, enforced his judgment by openly declaring the winner of the case and compelling the defeated party to respect the judgment of the barangay court.

Trial by Ordeal. In all criminal cases, when there was doubt to establish the guilt of the accused, trial by ordeal to show that God with His infinite wisdom, protected the innocent and punished the guilty.

To determine the guilt of the accused, various modes were adopted; e.g., the river ordeal where the suspects plunged into the river or lake with lances, long, shafted weapons with metal heads, and he who came to the surface first was adjudged as the culprit; the boiling water ordeal where the suspect was ordered to place a stone in a hollow utensil or vessel and compelled him to dip his hands into the vessel to take out the stone. The suspect who refused vehemently to obey the order was regarded as the guilty party; in the candle ordeal, the suspects were given lighted candles of the same size. The suspect whose lighted candle died first was regarded the guilty person. These methods of trial by ordeal may appear crude and absurd because it appears contrary to all reasons and seemed ridiculous but this kind of ordeal is still practiced in other parts of the Philippines. In Northern Luzon. The Ifugao's in some parts of the Cordillera, the ordeal by wrestling was still existing and this is called *bultong.* The defeated wrestler in the contest was considered the culprit and consequently, may lose his life as a just punishment.

Religious Beliefs. The freedom to choose one's religious belief and faith and to worship according to individual conscience is the right of every Filipino. The ancient Filipinos believed in their supreme god, the *Bathala* and other deities. The Bathala was the creator of earth, heaven and man. Below the Bathala were deities with their divine character and the purpose for which they existed. The god of agriculture was

Idiyanale; the god of death, *Sidapa;* the rainbow god, *Balangaw;* the war god, *Mandarangaw; Lalahon,* the goddess of harvest; and *Agri,* the fire god.

The early Filipinos were pagans and worshipped ancestral spirits called anitos (Tagalog) or diwatas (Bisayan). They offered prayers and food to their anitos. To these anitos, the sacrifices were performed by priest or priestesses called *Katalona* or *babaylan,* and consisted of food, wine, pigs and gold. They also believed that the anitos were not all good; that is why, they offered prayers and sacrifices to win their good will and favor, and for the bad, to appease their anger.

They also worshipped and venerated almost any object that had influence and close to their daily lives an indication of the importance of the relationship between man and the object of Nature.

Ancient Filipinos kept alive the memory of their dead members of the family by carving and fashioning idols of stones, ivory or gold, which they called *likha* and adored them with respect and honor as if they were alive.

They also believed in the immortality of the soul and life after death. The good soul would travel to heaven and the bad soul would go to hell and suffered the wrath of their god.

Burial. The early Filipinos respect for the dead was eloquently manifested in taking good care in burying their dead loved ones. The corpse was placed in a coffin made out tree barks and fibers woven into mats and were accompanied with receptacles of food and other belongings to accompany the dead on his journey to another world and buried near the house on top of the hills overlooking the seas and the valleys. It may be interesting to note that there were burial jars excavated in Tabon Caves where Jar burial practice in the Philippine was considered one of the most intriguing subjects in Philippine culture.

Usually, during the mourning period, members of the family and relatives of the dead wore rattan bands around their arms, legs and necks; used white garlands, and abstained from eating meat and drinking wine. There was much weeping among the members of the family and friends. For the mourning attire of the member of the family, man wore white shirts and for woman, white skirts. The relatives of the dead even hired professional mourners to sing a chant to contemplate the good deeds and achievements of the dead.

A distinction of mourning for a dead man was called *maglahi;* for dead woman, *morotal;* and for a datu, *larao.* Mourning for a datu was observed with a better ceremony than the ordinary mortal. When a datu died, the whole barangay was immediately informed and prohibitions were relayed; e.g. all wars and petty quarrels were ordered stopped; singing in the boats coming from the sea or from the river was prohibited; all warriors carried their spears with points downward and their daggers with hilts reversed, and wearing of loud colored clothes was not allowed.

The expression of grief ceased after the dead was laid to rest; however, eating and drinking continued until the ninth day after the death of a person, *"pasiyam,"* where relatives and members of the barangay pray for the soul of the departed.

Prophecy and Superstitions. The early Filipinos, like other people elsewhere in many lands had their own prophecy and superstitions. They interpreted various phenomena, e.g., the continuous *howling* of dogs at night the flight of flock of birds and the singing of lizards were signs of good or bad omens depending upon the conditions. As regards the future, the ancient Filipinos had the tendency to believe with fortune tellers who were endowed with extraordinary powers to predict the future and fortune of any person that was in store for him.

They believed in black magic and sorcerers and the *mangkukulam* made people sick by pricking a toy with a pin; *tikbalang,* who appeared in the form of horse, the *aswang,* who with bat-like wings and half-bodied and suck blood of victims, the *tiyanak,* who sucked the blood of babies of pregnant women.

They also believed in various magical powers of amulets

to ward off evil or to bring good fortune such as *anting-anting* or *agimat* insured a man against dangers and charms to attract a prospective lover such as the *gayuma* which made a man lovable to all women; the *odom,* a Bicol magic herb which makes the possessor invisible to human eye, a charm known to the Tagalog *tagabulag*; the *wiga,* a Visayan charm and *sagabe,* charm for the Tagalog that could make the possessor walk or swim in a river without getting wet.

These superstitious beliefs were not eradicated with the coming and influence of Western civilization. The enduring force never dies and some of then are still practiced in some parts of the Philippines. Some of them are worth mentioning; e.g., the appearance of a comet is associated to ill omen like pesticide, war, drought, earthquake and other calamities; a woman who is conceiving should not eat twin bananas; otherwise, she is likely to give birth to twins; a wedding gown should not be fitted by the bride before the wedding day; otherwise, the wedding ceremony will not be pushed through. If a black cat crosses one's path, it means bad luck. Before placing the coffin in the tomb, children are carried across it; and back again to the other side. One should not sweep the floor while somebody is lying in state (wake). Do not let the coffin bump against the wall. Say "tabi-tabi po, baka kayo matapakan" to a mound. If a woman is in the family way, she should not stand a sponsor in a baptism or wedding ceremony.

Economic Life and Living Standards

During the pre-colonial days, economic life and living standards of the Filipinos, especially in many remote barangays had no significant change. Farming was the main source of livelihood. There were two methods of cultivation – the ordinary method of tilling the soil using wooden plows and harrows drawn by carabaos in plain and irrigated land and the *kaingin* method in which trees were cut down and cleared by setting fire together with shrubs and bushes; and then, the land was planted with rice using pointed and stardy sticks to bore holes on the land and seeds were planted in every hole. Land cultivation yielded rice and a variety of crops. Productivity was increased through the use of indigenous irrigation systems; like the world-famous and breathtaking Ifugao rice terraces, in Cordillera mountain.

The acquisition of public and private land ownership was also recognized. The arable land along the slopes of the mountains was considered public property and can be cultivated by anybody. On the other hand, the rich and cultivated lands were considered private property for the datus.

The chief staple food was rice. There was an abundance of sugar cane, corn, coconuts, hemp, cotton, bananas, cacao, oranges and various tropical fruits and vegetables. Fishing thrived in most settlements along the rivers, lakes and seas. Various industries, e.g., mining, lumbering, metal craft, wood working, ship building, tool making, poultry raising and weaving were the main source of income.

Lumbering and ship-building flourished because of the abundance of thick virgin forests with various kinds of hardwoods for ship and boat-building.

Weaving to form a fabric was common home industry where women used crude wooden looms, to weave textiles, such as sinamay from hemp.

The pre-Spanish Filipinos had domestic trade and commerce among the villages in different barangays. Barter was the most common mode to trade by exchange of commodities.

There was foreign trade with China, Japan, Borneo, Sumatra, Java, Siam (Thailand), India and other neighboring Asian countries. The early Filipinos knew about coin, a piece of gold or metal stamped and issued by the authority for use as money in exchange in their various business transactions among themselves and with foreign traders. It is interesting to note that the pre-colonial Filipinos adhered to honesty as a moral dimension as two Chinese traders Chao Jukua (1225) and Wang Tayuan (1349) testified that the Filipinos were honest in their commercial transactions as evidenced when they paid their debts to the Chinese upon their return the following years or so.

Education. Education during the early Philippines was both academic and vocational. Archival documents showed that in ancient Panay, a school house called *bothoan* was under the charge of an old man in the barangay. The subjects taught to the children were reading, writing and arithmetic. The art of using weapons and *lubus* (acquiring amulets) to ward off evil or to bring good fortune were prevalent. The father assumed the role of the teacher to train his sons to be hunters, farmers, fishermen, miners, lumber man, shipbuilders and warriors. On the other hand, the mother trained her daughters in household chores; e.g., cooking, sewing, gardening and weaving. It was also the duty of the mother to teach her daughter sex hygiene and prepare them for motherhood.

Languages. Language as a part of culture, in the early Philippines, there were more or less a hundred languages and dialects that were spoken; however, learning one Filipino language was relatively easy, perhaps because all of then originated from a common linguistic source, the Malayo-Polynesian language.

Among the native languages, the Tagalog was regarded by the Spanish historians and writers to have been the best. According to Father Chirino, there were four qualities of the four best languages of the world and these are Hebrew, Greek, Latin and Spanish.

The differentiation among the Philippine languages inferentially as been the result of forming new words and phrases to fit the environment and the prevailing conditions.

A comparative study of some Philippine languages and Malayo-Polynesian shows that the former were derived from the latter.

Malayo-Polynesian	Tagalog	English
ama	ama	father
anaj	anay	termite
babaji	babae	female

Malayo-Polynesian (cont'd.)	Tagalog	English
bangkaj	bankay	cadaver
manuk	manok	chicken
pitu	pito	seven

On Philippine languages, Tagalog and Kapampangan show the close affinity to Malay language, whether Bahasa, Indonesia, or that of Malaya. Some Malay and Tagalog words show close affinity and some examples are:

Malay	Tagalog	English
abu	abo	ash
alun	alon	waves
amok	hamok	attack
babi	baboy	pig
bangon	bangon	rise up
bongsu	bunso	youngest

Writing. The early Filipinos had their own system and style of writing from Father Chirino's account, almost all of the natives knew how to read and write. The alphabet was called *baybayin*, which originated from Asokan alphabet of India. The alphabet has 17 letters: 14 consonants and 3 vowels. "A" is represented by one symbol, but "e" and "I" are indicated by one character alone, and so are "o" and "u." The early writers used a knifepoint to incise their script on bamboo tubes and back of trees. They must have written from top to bottom, left to right per vertical column, as was practiced by the Tagbanuas of Palawan and Manyans of Mindoro.

Literature. The ancient Filipinos already had their own literature stamped in the history of our race and eloquently show our customs, beliefs and traditions in everyday as evidenced in folk stories, ancient plays and short stories. Our ancestors also had their own alphabet which was different from that brought by the Spaniards. The first alphabet used by our forefathers was similar to that of the Malayo-Polynesian alphabet. It may be of interest to note that whatever records our ancestors left were either burned and destroyed by the Spanish friars in the belief that they were works of the devil or written on materials that easily perished like dried leaves, the bark of trees and bamboo cylinders.

Other records that remained showed folk songs that proved the existence of our own literature. It may be assumed that some of these were passed on by word of mouth until they reached the hands of some publishers and printers who took interest in printing the manuscript of the ancient Filipinos.

The literature of the early Filipinos were either oral or written. The literature is characterized by legends, folk tales, folk songs, epigrams, riddles, chant, epics, and proverbs. The ancient literature was made up of stories about life, adventure, love, horror and humor where one can derive lessons about life. These were useful because they helped them improve their lives and appreciated the beauty of the environment.

Epics were long narrative poems depicting the series of heroic achievements or events and these were the following: Bidasari-Moro epic, Biag ni Lam-ang-Ilocano epic, Maragtas, Visayan epic,Kumintang epic, "Dagoy" at "Sudsod" – Tagbanwa epic, Tatuang, Bagobo epic, Hudhud and Alim, Ifugao epic, Indarapatra and Sulayman were famous Muslim epic and have been handed down orally from generation to generation. The Ilocano Biag ni Lam-ang was written by Pedro Bukaneg who was said to have been thrown by his parents down the Abra River while still a baby because he was blind. Fortunately, a woman who found him gave him to an Agustinian priest and was christened Pedro Bukaneg. He was cared for and sent to school and became proficient in Spanish and Samtoy (Ilocano dialect), and consequently, known as the Father of Ilocano literature.

"Biag ni Lam-ang" was a long poem of adventure among Ilocanos. It was first recorded in the 17th century and was believed to be as old as other existing Philippine epics. "Hudhud," an Ifugao folk epic that centered in the story of the feast and their hero Aliguyon. "Alim" dealt with the lives of gods and goddesses Alisuna and Panbari, a mortal, and the origin of Panay and Negros. "Ibalon" – this as a Bicol epic which told the story of Ibalon, a fertile and beautiful land and how in a time of disaster, it was protected by Baltog (its founders), Handiong and Bantong, all three superhuman heroes.

The early Philippines was rich in myths and legends not only because of ancient Filipino ritualistic nature but also because each regional group had its own particular folklore and its own way of explaining the beginning of life in its own dialect.

Music. The ritualistic rhythm accompanying any chore performed in the daily lives of the people resulted into song. The Negritos of Bataan, Zambales, Mindoro and Tayabas (Quezon) and other areas, the ethnic groups of Mountain Province and the Muslims in the South had a number of musical instruments, which are still played even today.

Among the various musical stringed instruments were the Kudyapi, a boat-like shape stringed instrument with metal strings, Jews harp made of bamboo, the bamboo violin with abacca strings and the gangsa, the bamboo guitar. The gitgit resembles a violin and has a body and pegs made of wood with strings made of abacca or human hair and played with a bow of human hair. The kubling of the Dumagats is a bamboo version of the ancient Jew,s harp, the Ilokano kutibeng, a guitar with five strings.

On wind instruments, Bangsi of Hanumuo is a three-stopped bamboo flute blown at the end and Keleleng or Balingbaling (nose flute) where the sound is produced by wind blown through the nose, Palendag, a lip valley flute, sanuhay, a pipe with reed and suling, a ring flute were used by Muslims in Mindanao. Percussion sounds are produced by the metal and these are the gangsa, bangibang, gongs, agund, Kulintang, and gabbang of Sulu produce tones of different pitches. For the early Filipinos, music performed a personal function for it was a way of expressing their emotions.

The Bamboo Organ of Las Pinas. This bamboo organ

can be found in the old Catholic church of Las Pinas and the
only organ of its kind in the world and built in 1818 by Father
Diego Cerra, a recollect priest. This musical instrument is a
historic relic of the living glories of our musical art. Over the
years, it has survived the ravages of wars, typhoons,
earthquakes and fires which have swept over our land. Today,
it is one of the greatest tourist attractions. This Philippine
heritage truly reflects the Filipino ingenuity and love for music.

Dance. The early Filipinos were known to be good
dancers and they loved to dance whenever they hear music.
Famous dances included balitaw and dandansoy which won
recognition and honors among the various folk dances in the
Philippines. One of the favorite dances in the Ilocos Region
was the *kinotan* or ants' dance where a group of dancers
demonstrated gestures in an excited manner toward a person
being attacked by ants. Another Ilokano dance was the
kinnallogong, wherein a man and woman danced facing each
other, with the man remaining stationary, while the woman
danced toward him with a hat on her hand and tried to put it
on the man's head, the panjalay, the Muslim wedding dance
and the tadek, the Tinggian love dance. Their dances reflect
their exotic culture.

Art. The early Filipinos, during the Pre-colonial period,
had pieces of evidence of crude tools and weapons with artistic
designs. Later, the improvements were seen in the form of
beads, bracelets and other body ornaments and these began
to flourish. With the introduction of the hand loom, woven
textiles with various decorative designs and different shades
and colors were printed and came to be worn. The weapons
such as daggers, bolos, knives, spears, swords and other
bladed weapons were manufactured with artistic decorative
designs. Drawings in local pottery such as flowers, leaves and
different forms of animals adored the pots and jars. Different
methods of decorative design such as simple dots, straight
and curved lines were applied in objects. Different designs
and colors were applied on the body and face of primitive
Filipinos as a form of art. The Lanao Muslims pride themselves
with wood curving and wood painting, while the Igorots in

the Mountain Province curved various marvelous folk art in wood, e.g., wooden bowls, spoons, forks and smoking pipes.

They tattooed their bodies with different decorative designs representing animals, birds, flowers and geometric figures to enhance their bodily beauty and show their war exploits. The more enemies a warrior had killed in battle, the heavier he tattooed bore his body. This way very common among men although women were less tattooed. It was observed that the Visayans were the most tattooed people. The early Spanish writers called them Pintados or Painted people.

Clothing and Accessories. Before the coming of the Spaniards, the Filipino people were already wearing clothes. The men wore a colorless, short-sleeved jacket called *Kanggan* and strip of cloth, known as *bahag*, wrapped around the waist and passing down between the thighs. The color of the jacket was blue or black which indicated the rank of the wearer, but the chief was red. The men had a head gear consisting of a piece of cloth, called *putong* wrapped around the head that showed the wearer's "manliness." They wore necklace, gold bracelets, called *Kalambigas*, and gold anklets and they were barefooted.

The women's dress consisted of the upper and lower parts where the upper was the *baro* which was the jacket with sleeves, while the lower part, called *saya* for the Tagalogs and *patadyong* for the Visayans was a loose skirt about their waist and let fall to their feet. A piece of colored cloth, called *tapis,* was usually wrapped around the waist. They wore heavy jewelry consisted of gold necklace, gold bracelets, large gold earrings and gold rings. The women tied their long hair with a knot at the back of their heads. Since gold was a common commodity, both men and women made good use of it to adorn their teeth.

Houses. Our forefathers lived in houses made of wood, bamboo and palm leaves or cogon grass. Each house has a bamboo ladder which could be drawn up at night or when the family was out. The lower part of the house called *silong* was enclosed by stakes and bamboos where their fowls and cattles were taken care of for safekeeping. There was also a gallery called *batalan*, where jars of water were stored for washing dishes and other kitchen utensils. It is interesting to note that our ancestors lived in tree-houses built on top of the trees presumably to prevent them from enemies and other intruders. The Ilongots and Kalingas of Northern Luzon and the Mandayas and the Bagobos of Mindanao lived in such houses. On the other hand, the *Bajaos* of Sulu constructed their houses in their boats and *paraos*.

Social Stratification. Philippine society was a layered structure showing three classes – the nobles, the freemen and the slaves. The nobles consisted of the datus, their families and relatives. They wielded tremendous power and political privileges in the barangay. In the Tagalog region they carried the title of Gat or Lakan and occupied the highest position in society and called *Maharlika*. The freemen were called *timawas* who were born free and former slaves who were set free by their masters, and composed of the middle class in the barangay. Occupying the lowest stratum were the dependents or slaves called *alipin* among the Tagalogs. Slavery in society is acquired by birth, by captivity in war, failure to pay debts and punishment of a crime committed for which he was sentenced. These inequalities range from the distribution of exercise of power and status in society.

Among the Tagalogs, the slaves were two kinds – the *aliping namamahay* and *aliping sagigilid*. The *aliping namamahay* has his own family and house and served his masters during planting and harvesting seasons, rowed the boat for him and served his visitors. He can marry without the consent from his master and could not be sold. On the other hand, the *aliping sagigilid* had no property of his own, lived with his master, and could not even marry without the latter's consent and could be sold anytime.

Woman's Position. Women before the Spaniards came to Philippine shores, enjoyed a unique position in society. Laws according to their customs gave them the right to be equal to men. They could own and inherit property, engage in trade and industry, and succeeded to datu of a barangay in the absence of a male heir and had the exclusive right to give names to their children. As a sign of respect to show esteem and consideration for, when accompanying women, men walked behind them.

The Family. As the basic unit of society, it was closely knitted and strong. The children were given the needed attention, affection, and discipline by their parents to preserve its solidarity. The children were brought up to obey and respect their parents, elders, and datu and the barangay laws. The father, as the head of the family, worked hard to provide the basic essentials, food, shelter and clothing. His word was law to the children. The mother, on the other hand, looked after the physical, social, emotional and educational needs of the children. She was the housekeeper and enjoyed the privilege of naming their children. If she gave birth to a baby girl who was beautiful she named her *maganda*. If the baby happened to a boy who was robust and manifested signs of physical strenght, the name could be *malakas*.

Inborn Courtesy and Politeness. The early Filipinos were courteous and polite and this was eloquently demonstrated when two persons of equal rank met on the road, usually they removed their putong (turban) as a sign of courtesy and politeness. Whenever a person addressed his superior, he promptly removed his putong, and bowed low. The word "po" which is equivalent to "sir" as he addressed his superior had been a part of a polite language. The women were always shown courtesy everywhere.

Marriage Traditions. The handling down of beliefs and customs handed down from generation to generation, especially even for months had been a part of life of ancient Filipinos. Some practices were not followed strictly, were a man belonging to one class married a woman of the same class. It was observed that, as a matter of customs, it was possible for a noble to marry a slave or a woman to marry somebody outside her social rank. A man's legal wife was called *asawa*.

Children born out of wedlock were not entitled to property inheritance. The patience and spirit of dedication on the part of a man to win the hand of the woman he was offering love to was evident. This custom had persisted and its enduring force can still be seen in some remote villages. The man had to fetch water and chopped wood for the girl's family. Usually the young girl was tightly guarded by the parents. When the parents thought the suitor would be a good son-in-law and husband to their daughter, consent to marry their daughter was given. As a matter of condition imposed by the parents of the prospective bride, a dowry, called *bigay-kaya* in the form of land or gold was given the parents of the prospective groom. In addition to the dowry, the man must also give a certain amount of money as payment for the mother's care and effort in rearing the girl to womanhood. When all the arrangements had been threshed out for the forthcoming marriage ceremony, *pamamalae* took place.

The announcement of the betrothal differed according to the social status of the contracting parties. For the nobles, a go-between was hired by the groom to bring the bride to his house. The groom's father usually gave the bride a gift. The priestess took the hand of the man and the woman and announced before the guests that the two were to be united in matrimony where, over a bowl of uncooked rice, pronounced them man and wife. With a loud shout, the bride threw rice to all the guest and responded with also a loud shout and the ceremony was over.

Marriage among the freemen was different. The rice ceremony was omitted. For the slaves, marriage was consummated and was simple without an officiating priestess. When the man said to a woman, "Will you marry me?" and the woman responded "Yes" they were considered man and wife.

For mixed marriages, if the couple belonged to different social classes, for instance, a freeman and a slave, their children were equally divided among the parents. In cases, where the father was a freemen and the mother was a slave, all children belonging to the father became freemen and those belonging to the mother became slaves.

Succession and Inheritance. On the law of succession, the first son of the datu of the barangay succeeded his father. In the event that the first son died without leaving an heir, the second son succeeded as datu. If there was no male heir, the eldest daughter became the head of the barangay.

On inheritance of property, the legitimate children automatically inherited the property of the parents. The property was divided equally among the children although in some cases, either the mother or the father might show a little partiality to her favorite daughter or son as the case may be, a few pieces of jewelry and the son, a few pieces of gold. If the couples have no legitimate sons or daughters, the property of the couple went to the nearest relatives.

Study Guides

A. Terms/Concepts to Understand

civilization   babaylan
code   prophecy
flogging   extraordinary power
veracity   epic
perjury   social stratification

B. Questions to Answer.

1. What was the political unit of government during the pre-Spanish Philippines?

2. What were the reasons why our forefathers formed the confederation of barangays?

3. Enumerate the various duties and responsibilities of the datu.

4. What are some of the provisions of the Code of Kalantiyaw that you think are still relevant in our present times?

5. How do you evaluate the provisions of the Code of Kalantiyaw in terms of the content and penalty?

6. What is religion?

7. Enumerate some functions of religion that you find meaningful in your life.

8. What can you say about some superstitious beliefs of our ancestors that are still existing in some places, especially in the rural areas?

9. Describe the economic life and living standards of the Filipinos during the pre-colonial days.

10. What is social stratification? Describe the social stratification that existed during the pre-Spanish era.

Chapter 3

Assimilation of the Philippines into the Spanish Rule

The beginning of the 16th century marked the political and scientific advancements in Europe and brought tremendous changes in many parts of the world. As a matter of fact, the continuous political stability and the growth and development of trade and industry, improvements in military technology and navigation, the awakening in Europe of the interest in the Orient, consequently led to the territorial expansion. The Philippines fell because of the powerful Spanish military skill superiority, and experience. Gradually, the independence of barangays could no longer maintain their freedom and slowly and unsteadily succumbed to the superior force of the Spanish power. This eventual loss of undue restrictions and the opportunity to exercise their rights and powers transformed every facet of the Filipino primitive way of life – political, social, economic and cultural.

Major Events before the "Discovery" of the Philippines

Long before Ferdinand Magellan, a Portuguese navigator, came to the Philippine shores in 1521, the archipelago had already been discovered by the Filipino ancestors. The issue on who discovered the Philippines has been a ticklish and intriguing question that stirred discussion among students in history classes. For the occidental people it was a "discovery," but for the Filipinos, it was more of a rediscovery. Evidently, the West came to know the island because of early Portuguese and Magellan's voyages. The Portuguese were ahead of the Spaniards in search for new trade routes. In 1487, the Portuguese navigators rounded the Cape of Good Hope, and a few years later, Vasco de Gama discovered a route to India by sailing eastward from the Cape. Christopher Columbus failed to convince the King of Portugal that he could reach the East by sailing westward. He sailed into the Atlantic Ocean with three ships in October 12, 1492, and he "discovered" America or the New World.

This "discovery" began the rivalry between the Portuguese and Spain because of their interest in colonizing new lands. On May 3, 1493, Pope Alexander VI issued a papal bull, a formal document, which divided the world into Portuguese and Spanish spheres to reconcile their conflicting interests. The decree contained that all non-Christian lands lying west of the Azores and Cape Verde Islands should belong to Spain. On the other hand, all lands lying east of the demarcation line should belong to Portugal. A year later, Portugal and Spain agreed in the Treaty of Tordessillas on June 7, 1494 to move the demarcation line 370 leagues west of Cape Verde Islands for the maintenance and promotion of their interests.

Magellan's Expedition. Ferdinand Magellan, a Portuguese navigator and widely known for his achievement during the age of geographical exploration and discoveries, had curved a name in history. He was rewarded for his service to the crown as an officer and soldier. He persuaded Charles I of Spain that the Moluccas (Spice Islands) could be reached by sailing west through the Atlantic Ocean. Magellan received the approval of the King to head the expedition. On September 20, 1519, with five ships and with a fleet of 237 men, began their voyage. Sailing the eastern coast of South America, they headed on a passage and discovered a place, which now bears his name, the Straight of Magellan in 1520. After four months of hardships that seemed insurmountable, the three ships finally crossed the Pacific Ocean. On March 17, 1521, the Spaniards sighted a group of islands. The first meeting between the natives and the Spaniards took place in a very small island of Homonhon.

The Spaniards left Homonhon and sailed to Limasawa, an islet south of Leyte. This small island was ruled by a native king. Rajah Kolomba. Magellan and his men were welcomed warmly by Kolombo and eventually, made a blood compact on March 29, 1521 as a testimony of their friendship and brotherhood.

On March 31, 1521, on Easter Sunday, the first Catholic mass in the Philippines was celebrated on Limasawa's shore. After the mass on the same day, Magellan planted a big wooden cross on top of a hill overlooking the sea. Taking possession of the land in the name of Spain, he named the island the *Archipelago of Saint Lazarus.*

On April 1, 1521, Magellan sailed for Cebu and on the same day, he made a blood compact with Rajah Humabon to establish friendly relations and converted about 800 natives, with Humabon, his wife and a daughter to Christianity. A mass was celebrated. After the mass, Magellan had a wooden cross erected on the very spot where the first Filipinos, Rajah Humabon, Queen Juana, and about four hundred of their followers were baptized. The natives venerated the cross believing it has miraculous power. This Magellan's cross still exist and can be found on the corner of Magallanes and Burgos Streets, Cebu's most famous landmarks. Magellan gave Queen Juana a statue of the child Jesus as a gift and preserved up to now and is venerated as the patron of Cebu.

The Battle of Mactan. Lapu-lapu, chief of Mactan and enemy of Rajah Humabon was hostile to the Spaniards. Magellan went to Mactan to force Lapu-lapu to submit to Spanish sovereignty and to pay tribute. This fearless chieftain vehemently refused and Magellan was irked and the ensuing hostility consequently resulted in a fierce battle. Magellan was wounded with a poisonous arrow in his right leg; his iron helmet knocked off and bamboo spear struck him fatally. Lying prostate with face down on the ground that caused him embarrassment and humiliation, Lapu-lapu's valiant fighters pounced and killed him. His men, demoralized, finally left the place. Magellan died, and Antonio Pigafetta, official chronicle of the expedition, recorded the event and wrote: "our mirror, our light, our comfort, our true guide." By vanquishing Magellan, Lapu-lapu has been considered the first Filipino to have successfully defended his territory against Spanish aggression.

Significant Results of Magellan's Expedition. Magellan's expedition could be considered as one of the greatest maritime exploits of mankind, because it proved that the East could be reached by sailing westward from Europe. His expedition completed the first circumnavigation of the world. His "discovery" of the Philippines, virtually brought the archipelago and the people the awareness of Europe. It also paved the way to Spanish colonization, and as a result, Christianization of the Philippines.

It may be interesting to note that, the triumph and glory of the journey, which should be bestowed on Magellan, was reaped by Sebastian del Cano who commanded the ship Victoria that reached the Port of Seville.

The Treaty of Zaragoza (1529). The Treaty of Zaragoza was purportedly held to define the respective territorial jurisdictions of Portugal and Spain in the Pacific and to solve the problems of ownership of the island of Moluccas. The treaty stipulated that the King of Spain will sell the rights over Moluccas to the Portugal for 350,000 gold ducats ($ 630,000.00), and a new demarcation line was fixed at 297 ½ leagues east of the Moluccas. Portugal gained the rights of ownership over all lands of the west of the line. On the other hand, Spain gained the right of ownership over all the lands found east of the line. Because of the scant knowledge of the exact position of the demarcation line which determined the marking of the boundaries, Spain sold the Moluccas which lay within the Portuguese sphere of influence and claimed ownership over the Philippines.

The Villalobos' Expedition. The primary purpose of the Villalobos' expedition headed by Ruy Lopez de Villalobos was to establish permanent settlements in the Philippines. After sailing across the Pacific, he reached the island of Saranggani, South of Mindanao and was tempted to establish a settlement. With the acute scarcity of the provisions, and hostility of the natives, in addition to the impending mutiny of his men, Villalobos sailed to the Moluccas where he was forced, unconditionally, to surrender to the Portugees.

Before his death on April 4, 1546, he was able to land in the islet of Leyte. Bernardo dela Torre, a member of the expedition, gave to the Samar-Leyte region the name *Felipinas,* in honor of Philip, the Spanish crown prince and latter Philip II.

The Legaspi Expedition (1564). The primary objective of the Legaspi Expedition was to establish Spanish sovereignty over the archipelago. Philip II, who succeeded to the throne, upon renunciation of Charles I, decided to for go all claims to the Moluccas. He wrote to the Mexican Viceroy to prepare an expedition to the Philippine Islands and establish a permanent settlement that could be used for spice trade.

Miguel Lopez de Legazpi, a Spanish-born soldier and lawyer with chief adviser and navigator was Fray Andres de Urdaneta, a noted scholar, and a priest of high moral character and integrity, sailed from Mexico in November 1564. The expedition sailed westward across the Pacific and stopped at Guam to obtain supplies and other provisions. The voyage arrived in Cebu on April 27, 1565. Because the Spaniards found the natives hostile, they decided to sail to the neighboring islands and landed in Limasawa on March 9, 1566, and a few days later, they landed at Bohol where the chieftain and Legaspi made a blood compact. While in Cebu, Legaspi had also a treaty with the chieftain, Rajah Tupas to seal friendship and goodwill. The traty heralded the conquest of the archipelago.

The provision of the treaty was one-sided on the ground that the prosecution of the Filipinos who committed crimes against the Spaniards with no corresponding reciprocity, a similar penalty imposed to the Spaniards committing crimes against the natives. This treaty, in effect, signified the virtual loss of freedom of the Filipinos.

The first permanent settlement in the Philippines was established by Legaspi in 1565 and called the settlement in Cebu, San Miguel, but later renamed it *Santisimo Nombre de Jesus* in honor of the sacred statue, the Holy Child Jesus, Cebu, which Legaspi founded, is the oldest city in the Philippines.

Legaspi and his men moved to Panay because of the continuous attacks and hostility of the natives and the shortage of supplies. In 1570, Legaspi instructed Martin de Goite to explore the region and consequently, found a fortified place, Maynilad. Thereafter, a blood compact with Rajah Sulayman, a Muslim chieftain was concluded. The pact of friendship did not ward off the suspicion of the Muslims that the Spaniards had come to impose their rule among the natives and exact tribute. Sulayman refused to submit to the Spanish condition, owing homage to them as a subject or subordinate. Tension, as a result of the hostilities ensued, and de Goite and his soldiers burned the town to the ground.

The Conquest of Manila. De Goite left Maynilad after the victory and returned to Panay and informed Legaspi of the existence of the Muslim Kingdom along the shore. It was a rich kingdom because trade and commerce flourished with Chinese, Borneans, Siamese and other neighboring countries engaged in business transactions every day.

Legaspi's intense desire to colonize Maynilad, made him gather a strong expedition consisting of 27 ships, 280 Spaniards and some Visayan allies, which left Panay and reached Maynilad Bay in May, 1571.

The conquest of Maynilad by the powerful force of the Spaniards was a bloodless event. Lakan Dula, last king of Tondo, realized that it was virtually useless to repeal the superior power of the colonizers, so, instead of starting a fight which will be an exercise of futility, he welcomed Legaspi and his men. He also persuaded Rajah Sulayman, his nephew, and

Rajah Matanda to surrender peacefully to Legaspi. Thus, Legaspi and his men landed at Maynilad without resistance.

Even if Lakandula and Sulayman gave up their fight against the foreign invaders of Maynilad, Filipinos in Central Luzon defied Spain. A fearless Pampango by the name of Bambalito rallied the warriors of Macabebe, Betis and other neighboring barangays to carry on the resistance against the Spaniards. The show of high powered fire arms of the Spaniards and the death toll among the Filipinos, demoralized Bambalito's forces and they finally gave up their cause.

Manila – A Glimpse of History. Legaspi entered the city and proclaimed Manila as the capital of the Philippines on June 24, 1571, the Feast Day of St. John the Baptist, by virtue of the royal decree signed by King Philip II. He was the country's first civil and military governor. "Thus, with the permanent colonization by Legaspi, the Indios (natives) lost the freedom they earlier enjoyed."

It may be interesting to note that before Goite and Legaspi arrived in Manila, it was an "oversized barangay" a compact aggroupment around a recognized chieftain. One of the first major Spanish constructions was Fort Santiago from which developed the colonial capital and the walls that eventually enclosed it. Located at this historical place was the last incarceration cell of Dr. Jose Rizal.

The early development of Intramuros shows that the stone walls emerged from 1593 to 1650. The walls were surrounded by a moat, with waters coming from Pasig River.

Intramuros, the "Old Manila" was the stronghold of the Philippines for almost four hundred years until its destruction in 1945. When the Japanese forces entered the city, it was the center of activities – political, economic, religious and educational.

"Manila" was said to come from the words "may nilad," a place full of "nilads" – a small tree with white flowers. "Manila," the English name as we call today, was a lot different from Manila at the time of our ancestors.

Legaspi died of a heart attack in Manila on August 20, 1572. His untimely death was deeply mourned by both Spaniards and the Filipinos while serving his God, his king and the people of good will.

The last Spanish conquistador, Juan de Salcedo, grandson of Legaspi, youthful and valiant soldier, was the last Spanish conqueror who subdued to superior force Lim-Ah-Hong, the first threat to Spanish rule in the Philippines who was finally captured in 1575.

Political Structure of the Colonial Government. For more than 250 years, the Philippines was a crown colony of Spain. Spain administered the political affairs through the council of the Indias (Consejo de Indias). This was a very powerful body vested with all government powers – legislative, executive and judicial. The royal edicts called the Laws of the Indies and the medieval Spanish legal code, Las Siete Partidas were the legal bases of Spain's colonial policy in the Philippines. The laws contained in these documents were found not applicable to prevailing conditions in the Philippines.

The government, which Spain established in the Philippines, was centralized in structure. The whole country was under the control of a highly centralized government, headed by a governor-general. He was appointed by the viceroy of Mexico and later by the Spanish King. He was the sole representative of the Spanish crown in the archipelago. As captain-general, vice-royal patron and president of the Royal Audencia, he wielded tremendous military, ecclesiastical and legislative powers. The governor-general has the power to suspend the implementation of any royal decree order, if he thinks that the conditions in the colony did not warrant its implementation. Because of these awesome powers, the governor's paternalistic centralized government became the primary source of graft and corruption in the Philippines.

The Royal Audencia. The Royal Audencia was established on May 15, 1585 by virtue of the Royal Decree of the Spanish Crown. The primary function was to act as the supreme court of the Philippines and served as an advisory body of the governor. It was also empowered to check the abuses of the governor-general in the exercise of the administrative functions and prerogatives.

The residencia was a judicial system introduced by Spain to investigate outgoing governor-generals and other Spanish officials during their term of office for the purpose of punishing corrupt and dishonest officials found guilty after the investigation. It may be of interest to note that, the investigation was conducted by the in-coming governor-general and other high officials or a special judge assigned for this purpose.

Another institutional body was the *visita,* a secret investigation conducted by an official sent by the Council of the Indies in Spain to look into the conduct and behavior of high ranking officials in the colony.

The *visitador-general* was an investigating officer sent by the king of Spain to check Philippine conditions and to look into administrative complaints against erring governor – general, and other Spanish officials.

The *residencia* and the *visita,* virtually did not serve their intended purposes as a check to the corrupt administration for it was quite easy for errant Spanish officials to influence and to bribe the officials investigating the case, or to get a reversal of the decisions as the case may be, rendered by the investigating body through political connections in the Philippines or in Spain.

The Encomienda System. During the first decades of the Spanish regime, the Philippines was divided into political jurisdiction called encomiendas. Theoretically, the encomienda was a right vested by the king upon a Spaniard who had helped in the settlement of a country as a reward for his services. The encomiendero has the duty to collect taxes in his jurisdiction. In return, he has the obligation to promote the welfare of the inhabitants and to assist the missionaries to convert the natives to the Catholic faith.

In the later years of the eighteenth century, the encomienda became the basis for the development and establishment of the provinces.

The Provincial Government. The structure of the colonial provincial government was divided into types – the alcaldia – mayor, or province where peace and order had already been established and maintained and under a civil official, the alcalde-mayor. The *corregimientos* are the territories that were not completely pacified and placed under a politico-general called *corregidor.*

The alcalde mayor of the alcaldia (regular province) exercised awesome executive, military and judicial powers. This office was exclusively for Spaniards. The alcalde mayor enjoyed a unique privilege, the right to engage in trade called the *indulto de comercio,* which virtually gave him a monopoly of trade in the province. This privilege was abused by many alcaldes mayor who enriched themselves through various activities involving graft and corruption; e.g., dictating prices of goods in the provinces and coercing the natives to sell their produce at very low price. The provincial governor was also a big money lender who loaned money at usurious interests, which were obtained from the Obras Pias and other government lending institutions. No one could question him because he was also the highest judicial official in the province and the only person authorized to interpret the law. What was ironic was that the administrator of justice did not even have decent background in law that oftentimes there was gross miscarriage of justice.

Such power the governor wields of the province made him "the most corrupt official in the bureaucracy in the Philippines." The penisular government, cognizant of the scandalous administration of the province, passed and approved the reform decree of 1844, abolishing the *indulto de comercio* and prohibiting the provincial governor from engaging in any kind of trade. Another reform decree separating the executive from the judicial functions of the provincial governor was passed in 1886. The executive functions were vested in the provincial governor, while the judicial functions were vested in a judge of the court of first instance who was a full-fledged member of the bar.

In spite of the two reform decrees purportedly designed to improve bureaucratic provincial administration to mitigate the long agony of the people, the same incompetent and corrupt officials continued to dominate the administrative operations of provincial governments.

Municipal Government. Every province was divided into pueblos (towns). The pueblo was the local government and was headed and administered by a petty governor or gobernadorcillo, which is equivalent to our town's mayor today. Each pueblo consisted of several villages or barangays depending on the land area and population and was placed directly under the village – the *cabeza de barangay.* This position in the municipal government was open to Filipinos. During the early years of the Spanish rule, this position was occupied by a pre-colonial chieftain. However, in the later years, the office of the gobernadorcillo became elective, while that of the office of the cabeza de barangay remained an appointive position by the governadorcillo.

The administrative functions of the governadorcillo included administration of justice and public works, maintaining the municipal jail, and to supervise the collection of taxes.

The privileges he enjoyed included the exemption from the payment of taxes and forced labor. The power he wielded from his position gave him a lot of opportunities to enrich himself through corrupt practices.

Graft and corruption committed by municipal officials were very common notwithstanding their gross incompetence. The people normally did not file any complaints against erring and abusive officials, because it will be an exercise of futility. The unfortunate victims of injustice had to contend with hopelessness and resignation and distrust toward the government.

The Union of Church and State. One basic principle of

Spanish government on governance was the Union of Church and State. This disgusting political set up was aggravated by the virtual enchroachment of the Church upon the civil jurisdiction of the government. This condition of being united between the Church and the State enabled the archbishop and heads of the clergy to occupy significant positions in the government. The friars controlled the press and the entry of books and other printed materials in the Philippines.

Although the laws of the Indies offered some help for the natives, the friars' interference in the colonial administration of civil affairs caused much oppression and untold suffering among the people.

Study Guides

A. Terms/Concepts to Understand

assimilation	insurmountable
succumb	sovereignty
territorial expansion	expedition
prostrate	circumnavigate
navigation	reciprocity

B. Questions to Answer

1. What were the various factors that led to the territorial expansion of the Spanish colonization?

2. What were the different expeditions sent to the East by Spain and what were the results?

3. Who gave the name "Philippines" to our country?

4. What significant role was played by the missionaries in the conquest of the Philippines?

5. Identify the various reasons why the Philippine archipelago was easily conquered by the Spanish colonizers.

6. What was the primary purpose of the Villalobos expedition?

7. Why was Miguel Lopez de Legaspi hailed by some historians as a great colonizer?

8. Enumerate the significant results of Magellan's expedition?

9. Describe the fatal death of Magellan in the hands of Lapu-Lapu and his men.

10. Why is Intramuros called the Walled City?

Chapter 4

The Philippines Under Spanish Colonial Regime

The Spanish colonial policy was virtually designed not only to keep the Philippines under complete control but also to exploit her rich natural resources. The onerous system of taxation, the arbitrary and unjust forced labor, the monopolistic galleon trade and stringent trade and agricultural policies, consequently brought about a distorted and unbalanced economy.

On Taxation. This is the power of the state to impose and collect revenue for public purpose to promote the welfare of the people of a particular society. One of the laws of the Indies promulgated by the Spanish Crown was to require conquered inhabitants to pay tribute in recognition of Spanish sovereignty. For so many years, the Filipinos paid tribute to Spanish authorities amounting to eight *reales* or one peso, payable in cash or in kind. In 1589, the tribute was increased to ten *reales* and to twelve in 1851, but finally, abolished by virtue of a reform decree in 1884, but replaced by a personal *cedula* tax. A graduated poll tax based on the yearly income of the taxpayer. All residents about eighteen years of age, regardless of nationality or sex were required to pay the new tax. This burdensome tribute paid to Spanish sovereign covers taxes for support of the church, and the coastal areas for the protection of the natives from looters, burglars and marauders.

The natives were coerced to sell their harvest to the government at very low price. Under this unfair system, called *bandala*. The government required every province to satisfy the prescribed quota of goods assigned to it.

There were a lot of direct form of taxes the natives had to bear that were not sanctioned by the Spanish government policy on taxation. These arbitrary impositions, which were collected by the friars and civil officials of their personal greed and satisfaction included various forms of confiscation of agricultural harvest, poultry and livestock and compulsory payment of fees for masses, novenas and other religious rituals and activities of the Church.

While the rational of taxation was premised on the support of public welfare, e.g., health and sanitation, public works and safety of the natives, only a small amount was used for such purposes. A big amount of taxes extracted from the inhabitants went to the pockets of corrupt, arrogant and indolent Spanish civil officials.

To make the mode of taxation worse was that a big portion of taxes collected were spent for Spanish expeditions outside the Philippines. The amount that should have been spent for the colony's development was used to maintain government offices in Madrid such as Archives of the Indies. Consejo de Filipinas and the maintenance of diplomatic relations with Hongkong, Peking, Singapore and Japan.

On Forced Labor. The dehumanizing labor where the Spanish government required all male, healthy and physically able between the ages sixteen and sixty to render service for forty days virtually exploited the colony's human resources. This is called *polo*, where Filipinos were hauled out of their homes and were assigned to various projects, e.g., construction of churches, building and repairing bridges, cutting timber in the forest, working in shipyards and served as rowers for the galleon trade that plied the Manila-Acapulco route. The laborers were called *polistas*, the natives who rendered forces labor. In spite of the laws on the abolition of slavery, the Filipinos were treated like slaves. The polistas who where engaged in backbreaking hard labor under the scorching heat of the sun were not paid daily wages and food ration during their working days.

There were some Filipinos exempted from rendering forced labor upon payment of a certain fee called *falla*. The only few Filipinos who could afford to pay the arbitrary exemption fee were the *governadorcillos, cabesa de barangay* and the *principalia.*

While the Spanisrds were enjoyed a life of luxury and comfort the Filipinos had a miserable life. They developed a poor attitude and a strong distaste for manual labor and as a result, re-enforced the apparent tendency to be indolent. This negative effect on the Filipino psychology about manual labor could be attributed of the Filipinos preference to "white collar job." The Filipinos were not indolent, if given the proper working conditions.

The Tobacco Monopoly of Basco.   Jose Basco y Vargas established the tobacco monopoly in 1781. The increase in revenues of the government through the cultivation of tobacco and its export became a profitable venture that provided additional income to be financially viable and independent of Mexico. The cultivation of tobacco under government control was confined to Nueva Ecija, Cagayan Valley, Marinduque and Ilocos provinces. Each family in the tobacco districts under government monopoly was given a quota of tobacco plants to raise annually. The crops were purchased by the government through promissory notes instead of cash for their labors. In most cases, the government paid the poor farmers unredeemable treasury notes.

While the tobacco monopoly brought considerable profit to the government in terms of revenues and placed undeveloped lands to cultivation, the Filipino economic difficulties remained the same. In some designated areas, food production miserably declined because the government compelled the natives to produce tobacco only.

The tobacco monopoly led to the rampant abuses by government officials by certifying the native's produce to be of inferior grade while reporting to the government the same tobacco to be higher grade. The tobacco planters were forced to sell all their produce to the government. They could not even reserve a few leaves for their own personal consumption.

The government has the exclusive right to operate and to manufacture cigars and cigarettes, which were sold at prohibitive prices. Because of this unjust condition, the tobacco farmers were forced to engage in widespread bribery and smuggling to evade the strict regulations of the monopoly and to secure a better price for their tobacco.

The Galleon Trade. Long before the Spaniards came to the Philippine shores, the Filipinos had been trading with China and other Asian countries, by virtue of the doctrine of Merchantilism, the Spanish authority closed trade relations with other countries and allowed only two countries, China and Mexico to continue trade activities with the Philippines. For more than two centuries, foreign trade relations were maintained by the galleon trade or the Manila-Acapulco trade. Spain imposed stringent restrictions upon the galleon trade because of pressure exerted by the Servile merchants who were afraid that Chinese goods would flood the American markets, putting Spanish export products to a disadvantage. As a result, the galleon merchants were allowed only one part of entry in Mexico-Acapulco and only two ships each year to ply. Exports to Acapulco consisted mainly on Chinese and other Oriental goods brought by Chinese merchants. Manila became the distribution center of Chinese and Oriental goods.

The galleon trade virtually disrupted the growth and development of Philippine economy because Spain barred other European ships to embark their products to Manila and to other ports of the Philippines. Spain put different modes of barriers to block the influx of Chinese traders in the economy flourished consequently controlled the retail business. The Chinese also became known for the colony's money-lending business between foreign merchants and the Filipinos, especially the peasants. It may be interesting to note that the clergy was one of the primary investors in the Galleon trade. The *Obras Pias* or commonly called pious works was a foundation where money from trade was invested and appropriated, the profit accruing to charitable institutions like orphanages and charitable institutions were controlled by the friars. The Obras Pias virtually became a partner of commercial banks and other lending institutions that gained tremendous benefits from the traders.

The friars were so powerful that they could borrow money from Obras Pias and the government without any collateral and, in most cases, did not pay back their debts resulting in their bankruptcy.

Governor Fernando Manuel de Bustamante conducted an investigation to find out the causes of their bankruptcy and tried to institute administrative reforms by telling the friars to return the money loaned by the government in the Obras Pias, but in his attempt to rehabilitate and to stabilize the government finances, he met his untimely death allegedly in the hands of the friars in 1719.

Although the government dependence on the galleon trade to enhance revenue that resulted in utter neglect of the Philippines' agricultural and industrial development. The galleon served as the means of communication between the Philippines, Mexico and Spain, and consequently, helped the colony from undue exploitation of its rich natural resources, because the Spanish authorities were preoccupied with the galleon trade. The ships also brought in the colony new instruments and devices that, in effect helped in the development of technological and scientific awareness among the Filipino people.

On the Encomiendas. The encomienda was a right extended by the king upon a Spaniard who had helped to facilitate the settlement of a territory. By implication, it was a public office and the person was referred to as encomiendero, a holder of the encomienda and empowered to collect taxes from the people under his jurisdiction. In return, under the laws of the Indies, he was obliged to protect and defend the people under him against aggression and danger and helped to convert the natives to Catholicism.

The encomienderos abused their rights by way of forcing the natives to pay tribute beyond what the law prescribed.

The Filipinos had an option to pay the tribute in cash or in kind, but shrewd encomienderos coerced the natives to pay in cash by arbitrarily lowering the prices of their harvests. What made the situation worse was that the natives who could not come to terms in the manner dictated by the encomiendero, were brutally tortured or thrown to prison. Such as a despicable ordeal that many peasants were forced to leave their homes and found refuge in the mountains and upon their return, their houses were looted or razed to the grounds.

This thunderous and public outcry against the behavior of the encomienderos causing too much pain and distress among the natives led some humane ecclesiastic officials to inform the King about these unlawful practices. The clergy were Domingo Salazar, first bishop of Manila and Martin de Rada, superior of the Augustinians in the Philippines. They condemned these encomienderos and held them responsible for the various violence and atrocities committed against the natives.

Economic Retrogression. On the economic retrogression of the colony, the Spaniards blamed the indolence, which was inherent of the Filipino character, their inability for learning, and their perceived congenital inferiority of the *Indios*. Nevertheless, this was promptly debunked by Fathers Pedro Chirino and Antonio de Morga, about the allegation of the Spaniards by attesting to the marked growth and development of agriculture, trade and industry, skill and ingenuity of the natives. The economic retrogression was the government's imposition of numerous taxes and its utter insensitiveness to render service upon which taxes were extracted.

The Abolition of Slavery. The abolition of slavery could be considered one of the administrative accomplishments, which Spain had done for the people in the colony. This was certainly premised on the basic human right of every individual with human dignity. This move was affected through the efforts of Bishop Domingo Salazar and various heads of religious orders to ask the king to abolish slavery. The Bishop and the different religious orders signed a document accusing the Spaniards in the Philippines about the maltreatment of the Filipinos as slaves in the hands of the colonizers which was directly contrary to the law of God and the laws of the Indies.

King Philip II, after hearing and evaluating the complaint in the document of the Bishop and other religious clergy, issued the Royal Decree of August 09, 1589, emancipating all slaves in the colony.

On Cultural Development. Culture embraced language, art and religion. The colonial masters introduced the Spanish language – the lingua franca to the colony, but did not have a deliberate effort to propagate the language "for fear that the country may become Hispanized and ceased to be a monastic colony"; thereby the natives would understand better and might question arbitrary and questionable aspects of Spanish rule. Only the wealthy and educated middle class Filipinos learned to write and speak in Spanish.

Philippine literature was predominantly religious in tone, character and moral quality. The first printing press was introduced by Dominican friars in Manila in 1593, and in the same year, printed the first book in the Philippines. *The Doctrina Christiana.* The early Filipino printers were engravers at the same time who were trained by Spanish missionaries. Foremost among them was Tomas Pinpin of Mabatang, Abucay, Bataan. Siete Infantes de Lara and Bernardo Carpio.

Among the Filipinos who distinguished themselves in the fields of Philippine literature were Jose dela Cruz (Husing Sisiw 1746-1829) and Francisco Baltazar (1789-1862). The Florante at Laura of Baltazar's "awit" allegorically exposed the Spanish wrong doings in the archipelago.

On visual arts like painting and architecture interests also focused on religion. Chinese artisan curved various sizes of religious images made of wood or ivory for churches all over the Philippines. "Our Lady of the Rosary" known all over the Philippines as "La Naval," by the Catholic devotees was curved by a pagan Chinese craftsman.

The two Filipino painters won the attention of Spanish art establishment for their own entries in the Madrigal Exposition of Fine Arts. Felix Resurreccion Hidalgo, won a silver medal for his Christian Virgins Exposed and Juan Luna received his first gold medal for his Spoliarium.

On Religion. One of the important objectives of the Spanish colonizers was to spread Christianity. Undoubtedly, the establishment of *pax hispanica* in the Philippines was hastened through the concerted efforts of the Spanish missionaries. With the help of the soldiers, the missionaries easily conquered territories of the colony and converted the natives to Christianity.

The various missionaries who used their religious influence to facilitate the teaching of the Gospel and propagation of Catholic Christian faith were the Augustinians (1565), the Franciscans (1577), the Jesuits (1581), the Dominicans (1587) and the Recollects (1606). The entire colony was apportioned among the different religious orders with their corresponding missions, which were highly church oriented.

On Social Results. The Filipino conversion to Christianity inevitably meant the adoption of the Fiesta as a socio-religious event celebrating the feast day of a patron saint of a Catholic Town as an occasion of Thanksgiving for a bountiful harvest and other blessings. The fiesta that revolved on religion involves devotions and rituals that shape an individual's own belief system that never dies. These are exemplified by the colorful Ati-atihan Moriones festival and Obando, Bulacan fertility dance.

The fiesta was a costly social affair for it provided a horde of friends and strangers to temptation to avail some attractions of the celebration like gambling and cockfighting. The Filipinos look forward every year for the fiesta as a popular and enduring social celebration for it provided the natives a brief respite from the hard work of the year and afforded them the opportunity to renew their social affinity with relatives and friends.

On Architecture. The Spaniards introduced Western architecture with some modifications to suit the prevailing conditions. Many Philippine churches show influence of the baroque style, having massive walls and thick buttress and spiral motifs, ornate sculpture façade, and graceful, curving balustrades. San Agustin Church is the oldest church in the Philippines.

In Manila and in other cities and affluent towns, the stone houses of the well-to-do people were constructed in Spanish architectural style with the *azotea* and Andalucian courtyard. The house of Dr. Jose Rizal in Calamba, Laguna typified the character of Spanish architecture. Other ancestral houses of old rich people found in provincial capitol and the poblacion had the style of Spanish baroque.

On Education. Education in the Philippines during the Spanish era was not open to all Filipinos. The Spanish government had absolutely no intention of training the natives for eventual independence and self-government. During this period, some schools were exclusively established for education of some Spanish nationals in the archipelago. They were open only for the people who belonged to the upper social and economic class of society.

The educational system was controlled by the friars through different religious orders. The preparation, planning, control and supervision of curricular programs the chief feature of which was religion to secularize the colony's educational system were within the power and authority of the friars.

The University of Sto. Tomas, the oldest pontifical university of the Philippines was founded by the Dominicans in 1611. In 1630, the Colegio de San Juan de Letran was founded and in 1601, the Colegio de San Jose. Other religious educational institutions that were established were Colegio de Sta. Potenciana (1589), Colegio de Sta. Isabel (1632), College of La Concordia (1869) and Assumption Convent (1892).

In 1863, the Spanish government enacted and implemented an educational reform primarily designed to improve the state of education throughout the archipelago. The decree provided for the establishment of at least one primary school for boys and one for girls in every town. The decree also provided for the establishment of a normal school for male teachers under the supervision of the Jesuits and created a commission of eight members headed by the governor general. Instruction in the primary level for both boys and girls was free and the teaching of Spanish was compulsory.

While the government opened a higher level of education to the Filipinos, resulting in the emergence of the intelligentsia, a few years later, the Spaniards developed the fear that the natives will understand the value of education in relation to truth and fairness and they may in turn foment rebellion. This move from the Spanish authority literally negated the philosophy of education.

On the Economy. The abolition of the galleon trade in 1815 and the separation of Mexico from Spain made it necessary for the Spanish government to engage in trading relations with other countries. The government also allowed foreign investors to establish residence in the Philippines. Spain opened its ports in Manila and other parts of the country. Foreign banking institutions and other lending and credit facilities were open. The introduction of scientific farming through the use of new technology and other farm inputs accelerated agricultural production. The removal of stringent restrictions on foreign trade became a big boost for the economy and enjoyed a favorable balance of trade with Europe and neighboring Asian countries. Roads and bridges were built, shipping lines, inter-island and overseas were improved and communication systems were upgraded.

The opening of the Philippines to world trade and with the emergence of multifarious forces, e.g., scientific and technological, industrial, economic, social and political, resulted in economic changes and prosperity that improved the quality of life of the Filipinos.

Study Guides

A. Terms/Concepts to Understand

colonial empire   marauder
burdensome   scorching
influx   bankruptcy
exclusive   lingua franca
merchantilism   pontifical

B. Questions to Answer

1. What is taxation? Is this necessary for the welfare of the people?

2. What can you say about the forced labor imposed by the Spaniards in the colony?

3. Who are the polistas?

4. Under the forced labor imposed by the colonizers, who were exempted?

5. Explain the tobacco monopoly by Jose Basco.

6. Identify the disadvantages brought about by the galleon trade.

7. What is an encomienda? Explain your answer.

8. What is the significance of the abolition of the slavery?

9. Describe the nature, tone and character of Philippine literature during the colonial era.

10. Describe the cultural development and its contribution to contemporary society.

Chapter 5

Opposition Against Oppressive Spanish Sovereignty

It was evidently felt that in almost every part of the archipelago, the Filipinos vehemently resisted the imposition of Spanish sovereignty. At the outset, the Spaniards manipulated design through the use of religion. This was invariably successful because they were able to foster docility and resignation of the Filipinos to the political and social order established by the colonizers.

The miserable conditions affecting every facet of Filipino life brought about by the Spanish arbitrary and unjust economic and administrative policies resulted in and provided an intense motive among the inhabitants to resist and rebel against the ruling conquerors. The agitation grew and developed into a national awareness because the abuses perpetrated by the Spaniards throughout the colony became unbearable. The intense aversion toward the deceptive, administrative style of running the government by Spanish abusive officials and the various grievances led the people to revolt. These were:

1. Loss of power statue and influence of the native chieftains

2. Loss of power of the local priests who controlled the craft of magic and idolatry to Christian missionaries.

3. Intolerable conditions on agrarian and land tenure

4. Excessive and onerous system of taxation

5. Forced labor.

6. Malpractices of Spanish government officials in the bureaucracy, resulting to massive graft and corruption

7. Little participation of Filipinos in government affairs

8. Racial prejudice and discrimination against Filipinos

9. Misadministration of justice

10. Persecution of Filipino patriots

11. Abuses, viciousness and immorality of friars

12. Denial of human rights

13. Strict censorship of press freedom

These numerous and diversified complaints resulting in unjust acts causing too much pain and suffering can be seen and felt in the different incidents.

The various grievances of the Filipinos against Spanish misrule led to personal dissatisfaction; and consequently, the uprising by Rajah Lakan Dula and Rajah Sulayman (1574) Tamblot revolt (1621) and Bankan (1622). This stemmed from the unfulfilled promises of the Spanish authorities that their legitimate descendants be exempted from taxation.

Another cause of uprising was the denial of a Jesuit priest to give a decent Christian burial to Dagohoy's brother. Because of humiliation in the hands of the friars, he incited the natives of Bohol to revolt. Dagohoy and his men escaped to the mountains to be out of danger from Spanish harsh imposition of punishment. After several years of hiding in the mountains of Bohol province, the revolt initiated by Dagohoy was finally suppressed.

Other related personal dissatisfactions were the compulsory forced labor, unjust taxation, and mercenary Spanish soldiers committing violation of human rights in various places of the archipelago.

On Agrarian Grievances. Agrarian grievances became an expression of pockets of revolts, as mounting debts could not be paid by tenant farmers because of usurious practices imposed by the landowners in arbitrary increases in land rents and unjust eviction of farmers in the land. The absence of a proper land surveying system that caused fraudulent land measurements that often aggravated the problem of dissatisfaction. There were several cases of land rentals that were too high and the prohibition of the natives the privilege to gather firewood, forest products and fishing in rivers and lakes without paying taxes. These sporadic revolts spread like wild fire in many provinces, e.g., Batangas, Laguna, Cavite and Rizal. Government troops mobilized from Manila and the Provinces were peasants' restiveness became high to quell the rebellion.

The Muslim Opposition to Spanish Misrule. The Spanish demonstrative superior might in terms of arms and manpower capability and attempted to have the Muslim recognition of their power and authority by continuously engaging in war, but because the Muslim were best organized due to the enduring and cohesive force of Islam, the religious faith of the Muslims, as set forth in the Koran, not to mention their unity, they successfully opposed all efforts of the Spanish military and missionary strategies to integrate Sulu and other Muslim communities in Mindanao under Spanish control.

The acquisition of several gunboats reduced Muslim piracy and other multifarious activities and enable the Spanish government to establish and fortified military camps along the coast of Mindanao. In 1876, the Spaniards entered into a treaty with the Sultan of Sulu, affecting the recognition of Spanish sovereignty by way of returning the annual pension for the Sultan and his heirs.

The Filipinos are by nature peace-loving people. But because of economic exploitation, social degradation and massive graft and corruption committed by high government officials became the primary cause of revolts outburst violence in various parts of the country.

The Development of Philippine Nationalism. Nationalism or "devotion of national unity and independence" is the most important prerequisite to the formation of Philippine national consciousness and the desire for national advancement and ultimately independence. As a matter of fact, this is the *sine qua non* to the development of genuine national identity forged by a common history, culture and enduring traditions. This element of nationalism stemmed from the shared vision, racial, ethnic and nationalistic feeling among the Filipinos.

The Influx of Liberal Ideas. The influx of liberal Ideas from the West, the opening of the Suez Canal in 1869 and the opening of the Philippines to the world trade ignited and influenced the birth and development of Philippine Nationalism.

Influenced by various philosophical and political thinkers like Plato, Aristotle, Kant, Descartes, Rousseau, Locke, Voltaire, and Jefferson and other great minds contained in their books and treatise, liberal ideas leading to understand and mental consciousness started to gain grounds. Filipinos began to think about their deplorable condition and began to discuss about politics, justice, equality, freedom and human rights, and in the course of such a predicament, they became brave and assertive to redress their legitimate grievances and asked for government reforms which were long overdue.

The factors that contributed immensely to the emergence and development of Filipino nationalism were the liberal and revolutionary ideas they had learned from the intellectual thinkers of Europe and the West and the improved economic condition that eventually broke down the walls of isolation for so long and extended their contract and association with other nationalities of the world community.

The Opening of Philippine Ports to International-trade and Community. The opening of several ports throughout the archipelago exposed our country to international trade. The shortening of the sea travel between Manila and Spain, brought the Philippines closer to Europe. Transition and communication facilities brought more trades and other travelers to the country who, married Filipinos and eventually became residents in the Philippines and inevitably hastened the development of nationalism.

The abolition of strict censorship of the press that fostered the free discussion of social, economic and political problems brought meaningful reforms.

The Emergence of the Middle Class. The emergence of the middle class that constituted Filipinos who actively participated in agricultural production, commerce and industry improved their economic and social status and were able to send their children to better educational institutions that invariably and gradually changed the existing social order. The middle class became critical of the excesses of Spanish bureaucrats who occupied high positions in government.

From the new breed of Filipinos who belonged to the middle class sprang brave, articulate and idealistic young men of vision and educated in best schools in Manila and in Europe became the driving force were determined to institute reforms and changed the *status quo.* Planning together and graving a history of glory for the next generation, these young nationalists developed a feeling of pride to expose a corrupt regime and helped bring about national consciousness among the Filipino people.

The Effect of European Liberalism. The effect of European liberalism together with the opening of various ports in the Philippines which led to international trade, allowed intellectual developments and consequently and gradually undetermined Spanish colonial power. These can be seen from the appointments in the bureaucracy of liberal Spanish and some Filipino officials who came from the ranks of the middle class equipped by noble thoughts and orientations.

New progressive ideas flowed like water in the spring blended with intellectual ferment and humanism provided particularly strong to the educated Filipinos. John Locke *Two Treatise of Government* and the Jean Jacques Rousseau's *Social Contact* became the spring-board that influenced members of middle class to enable them to meet on common agenda for propaganda purposes. For Locke and Rousseau "no government is legitimate unless it represents and enforces the absolute and inalienable will of the people." It ceases to continue when it has lost the consent of the government.

The Influence of the French Revolution.   The French Revolution that began in 1789, that overthrew the Bourbon monarchy and ended with Napoleon's seizure of power in 1799, had provided some intellectual and political bases of the development of Filipino nationalism. The political and social condition in France was closely similar to the prevailing condition in the Philippines. A government ran by corrupt and incompetent officials reigned uncontested for quite a long time. The ruling classes had the monopoly of the political, economic and administrative powers and refused to give up such powers at all cost. The Church owned and administered vast tracts of land, controlled the educational system, trade, transportation and communication. The poor people who belonged to the lower social strata had to bear the economic difficulty brought about by the heavy burden of taxation and other impositions of Church and government, and to submit to abusive and immoral civil officials.

The illustrados, inspired by faith and devotion, who came from the middle class formed the corps and the vanguard of the Propaganda Movement, unveiled the magnitude of the political and economic issues affecting the country and persuaded the Spanish authorities that needed reforms were to be instituted to avert the impending outbreak of a revolution. Sensing that this strategy will be an exercise of futility and rendered their concerted efforts meaningless, these new breed of reformists, inspired by the lesson they learned from the French Revolution ignited their passion and launched the struggle for freedom and independence.

Racial Prejudice and Discrimination.   Ironically, the Spaniard introduced in the Philippines Christian religion that supports and upholds sound morals and promote solidarity; teaches brotherhood of all men and equality of all men regardless of race and color, but the Spaniards especially those who wielded power and who professed Catholicism as their religion, regarded the Filipinos as an inferior people and mockingly called them "Indios." This racial prejudice against the Filipinos existed in every place and evidently felt in government offices, schools and social gatherings. To aggravate the social perception and feeling of discrimination against Filipinos, the Spaniards regard them to have low mentality, incapable of acquiring education and only fitted for menial jobs. But Jose Rizal proved them wrong by surpassing Spanish writers in literary competitions, by distinguishing himself in the field of medicine and the physical and natural sciences, aside from being a man of letters, poet, painter and sculptor. The constant insinuation that the Filipinos were "impossible to expose to curiosity, analytical thinking and philosophical studies" and cultural inferiority compelled Jose Rizal to prepare the new edition of Antonio de Morga's *Sucesos de las Islas Filipinas*, with his annotations and incisive criticisms debunked the allegations of the Spaniards that the Filipinos were savages, ignorant and had no culture before the colonizers came to the Philippines. Racial prejudice apparently had wrought irreparable damage upon the Filipino mentality and began to see and regard Western culture as superior to their own. Perhaps this is the reason why many Filipinos have the Western mentality syndrome.

The Secularization Issue. The dispute on the secularization intensification involving the Spanish regular priests and the Filipino secular priests contributed to the development of nationalism. The issue between the Spanish clerics bent at all costs to protect and clinged to their position as the acknowledged people's religious custodian. On the other hand, the Filipinos priests were agitating for an equitable representation in parish religious administration, which were denied, because the Spanish clergy believed that the Filipino priests lack the necessary training. The secularization controversy centered on religious issues with racial prejudices and implications. The secularization controversy between the Spanish priests and Filipino priests focused on the control of curacies in the Philippines.

During the administration of Anda as governor (1770-1776) many parishes were secularized, but years later, the Filipinos were deprived in their parishes and the Spanish government gave them to the Spanish friars; hence, the Filipinos priests resented.

Among the Filipino religious leaders who arose and carried on this secularization controversy were Fathers Jose Burgos, Mariano Gomez and Jacinto Zamora. These three principled Filipino priests who will not compromise justice constituted the famous triumvirate – GOM-BUR-ZA. In the course of time, the secularization issue became a national issue and assumed a racial character that directly discriminate Filipino priests. Understandably, the Filipino people sympathized with the cause of the Filipino clergy.

One controversial issue where it became blown-up news was where the Spanish friars engaged the Filipino priests in a bitter fight over two of the riches benefices – a position granted to an ecclesiastic that guarantees a fixed amount of property or income. This was the shrine of Antipolo in Rizal and the curacy of San Rafael, Bulacan, which were being administered by Filipino clergy. The curacy of Antipolo was a very rich parish where collections of the month of May ran into thousands of pesos because of the influx of pilgrims who visited the shrine.

In the San Rafael curacy, it became vacant. As a matter of religious procedure, an examination had to be conducted to determine the most qualified, but the government for no justification, cancelled the examination for which seventeen Filipino priests had qualified, because the Recollects invoked the 1861 decree, for which the parish should be given to them.

These were similar cases of secularization involving various issues on administration of church activities in rich parishes in Bataan, Pampanga, Zambales, and Nueva Ecija where the native clergy protested in vain.

The struggle to secularize the parishes in the Phillippines increased the degree of racial conciousness, and eventually, helped bring about the emergence of nationalism.

The Liberal Spanish Governor Carlos Maria dela Torre (1869–1871) arrived in the Philippines in 1869. The Spanish liberals and the *illustrados* welcomed him. He was the most loved governor-general of the Philippines. He dismissed his bodyguards who wore colorful uniforms and medieval arms and walked about the city in civilian clothes and mingled with the Filipinos and treated them equally with the *mestizos*. He entertained the Filipinos in reception with high-ranking Spanish officials in his official residence. On one occasion, he was said to have encouraged the Filipino clergy led by Father Burgos, Gomez, and Zamora to go on with the secularization of the various parishes. The liberal governor also encouraged freedom of speech and expression and of the press. He abolished censorship of the press, put an end of flogging – a harsh punishment by beating and replaced imprisonment for erring Filipino soldiers.

Dela Torre antagonized the Spanish friars, particularly those who had been in the Philippines for a long time when he implemented the educational decrees of 1870, limiting secularization of education and government control of some educational institutions in the archipelago

The reactionary Spaniards and the friars denounced the administrative innovation of Dela Torre; for impliedly, the Filipinos were being encouraged to entertain revolutionary thoughts. The suspecting Spaniards were aware that the reforms of Dela Torre were sanctioned by the liberal government in the Philippines, was in effect, helping in the formation of national consciousness among Filipinos.

Governor Dela Torre's benevolence made him Spanish enemies, but he had acquired numerous Filipinos who love and respect him. His liberal regime ended when he was recalled to Spain.

The reactionaries in the Peninsula welcomed Rafael de Izquierdo, his successor. He ruled "with a crucifix in one hand and a sword in the other." His administrative style in running the affairs of government was the exact opposite of Dela Torre's for he ruled with an iron hand and employed coercive measures and policies to terrorize the Filipinos and asserted power and authority in the colony. He strengthened censorship and dismissed Spanish mestizos and Filipinos in the civil and military services in the government. He arbitrarily repealed the exemption from the taxes and forced labor that the Filipino workers had been enjoying in the arsenal and navy yard of Cavite and other parts of the archipelago.

Disgruntled Filipino workers at the arsenal and the navy yard revolted in strong protest against this unjust treatment from governor Izquierdo's despotic administration. The aftermath of this disastrous incident produced far-reaching effects that the Filipinos once again realized the basic idea that when righteous people govern, tranquility, justice and happiness would reign.

The Cavite Mutiny, on January 20, 1872, when nightfall began, a group of Filipino artillerymen, marines and workers in the Cavite arsenal, and a Filipino sergeant, led the mutiny. Immediately after the mutiny, many Filipino priests and patriots were arrested and incarcerated. They were charged of treason and sedition and tried by military courts and sentenced as those who revolted against constituted authority.

According to the friars, the mutiny was deliberate and part of well-planned and widespread conspiracy perpetuated by Filipino priests and actively supported by Filipino illustrados and prominent businessmen.

As soon as the news of the mutiny reached Manila and other neighboring provinces, a reign of terror followed and immediately governor Izquierdo ordered the arrest of Father Jose Burgos, Mariano Gomez, Jacinto Zamora and other prominent Filipino clergy, distinguished lawyers and well-known businessmen. The Spanish authorities accused the three Filipino priests as leaders of the conspiracy. They were tried in a mock trial and were sentenced to die publicly by the *garrote* (death by strangulation) on February 17, 1872.

The authorities made the execution of the three Filipino priests in public to sow fear and terror among the restive Filipinos from Manila and other neighboring provinces. The

Filipinos resented the execution of Fathers Gomez, Burgos and Zamora. They believed that the three priests were innocent and their death was a noble cause for Filipinos who had been victims of injustice in their own land. It may be inferred that the blood of these three martyrs of their fatherland, became the seed of Filipino nationalism.

Study Guides

A. Terms/Concepts to Understand

sovereignty	prejudice
docility	persecution
arbitrary	mercenary
unbearable	fraudulent
deceptive	reactionary

B. Questions to Answer

1. What were the various grievances of the Filipinos against the Spanish rule?

2. Give an example of the forced labor the natives experienced from the colonizers.

3. Enumerate the malpractices of Spanish government officials in the bureaucracy that resulted in massive graft and corruption.

4. Explain the meaning of misadministration of justice.

5. Why did Dagohoy revolt against Spanish rule?

6. Give some reasons why the Muslims opposed the Spanish rule.

7. How did the influx of liberal ideas from Europe and the other parts of the world influence Filipino nationalism?

8. Who constituted the middle class and what significant role did this group contribute to the development of Filipino nationalism?

9. How would you describe governor-general Carlos dela Torre?

10. Explain the secularization controversy. What can you say about the death of the three martyrs – Fathers Gomez, Burgos and Zamora and the development of Philippine nationalism?

Chapter 6

The Reform Movement and the Katipunan

The deliberate and unjust execution of the three Filipino martyrs Fathers Mariano Gomez, Jose Burgos and Jacinto Zamora, in effect, became as significant turning point in the history of the Filipino people, for it heralded the dawn of a new day — the reform movement. Some members of the wealthy Filipino families who belonged to the intellectual groups migrated to Europe and initiated a campaign for reforms by pen and by mouth to put an end to a corrupt regime. Meanwhile, the Filipino intellectuals in the Philippines were secretly communicating with Filipino patriots who defend their country and its interests in Europe and founded nationalist societies. This campaign for reforms was popularly known as the Propaganda Movement. Dr. Jose Rizal and other Filipino intellectuals that formed the corps of reformists brought to public notice through their speeches and writings that were full of passion and sentiment the flaws of the colonial government.

The Objectives of the Propaganda Movement. The Propaganda Movement was a peaceful campaign for reforms, which began in 1872. This was not a revolutionary movement that sought to change the whole political and social order as a means of creating a new one. The reformists behind this movement were just asking for reforms that directly affected the lives of the Filipinos and these were:

1. Equality of Filipinos and Spaniards before the law.

85

2. Assimilation of the Philippines as a regular province of Spain.

3. Restoration of Philippine representation in the Spanish Cortez.

4. Filipinization or secularization of the Philippine parishes.

5. Individual liberties for Filipinos, such as freedom of the press, freedom of speech, and freedom to redress grievances.

The nature of the movement was focused on the abuses of Spanish authorities – civil, military and ecclesiastical.

The Great Reformists. The wealthy and the middle class intellectuals comprised the Filipino reformists. They were principled and idealistic young men whose faith in their country and their fellowmen is boundless. This group of young Filipinos whose unwavering idealism for the welfare of their country cannot be compromised. These were Jose Rizal, Graciano Lopez Jaena, Marcelo H. del Pilar, Antonio Luna, Juan Luna, Mariano Ponce and other Filipinos who had contributed to the cause of the reform movement.

JOSE RIZAL – A NATIONALIST MARTYR, was born on June 19, 1861 was the most cultured of the Filipino reformists. At the age of eight, he wrote a Tagalog poem entitled, "Sa Aking mga Kabata" that teaches love of one's own language. He studied at the Ateneo Municipal, now the Ateneo University, operated by the Jesuits where he learned mathematics, poetry, rhetoric, painting and sculpture. Even as a young boy, he had already learned and felt the difficulties that attended the daily life of the Filipino people. His mother was a victim of a miscarriage of justice and was imprisoned. At the age of eighteen, he won first prize in a literary contest entitled *Juventud Filipina*. His allegorical play, *El Consejo de los Dioces* was adjudged the best in the competition, but he was denied the prize because he was a Filipino. He also studied medicine at the University of Sto. Tomas. He was considered a linguist, having learned and mastered different languages.

At the age of twenty-six, he had written the famous novel *Noli Me Tangere*, taken from the gospel of St. Luke which signifies "Do not touch me." Later, he wrote the *El Filibusterismo*. The Noli centered on the ills of society as a social cancer while the Fili delved on the reign of greed. The Noli unmasked the social, political and ecclesiastical conditions in the Philippines, the defects of public administration, the ignorance of the functionaries and their corruption, the immorality and vices of the friars and incompetence and corruption in the government. On the other hand, the Fili was in contrast with the Noli, a political novel in which Rizal predicted the coming of the Revolution. He was undoubtedly the inspiration of the revolution. He became a major exponent of reform and racial equality and infuriated with his trial on charges of treason, condemned and sentenced to die by musketry on the early morning of December 30, 1896, at Bagong Bayan, now the Luneta Park and was shot by the guardia civil surrounded by military cordon amidst the frantic and thunderous shouts of the Spaniards.

GRACIANO LOPEZ JAENA – The Fiery Orator, was born on December 17, 1836, in Jaro, Iloilo. He studied at the Seminary of Jaro operated by the Paulists – members of the Missionary Society of St. Paul, the Apostle. His study of religion and the atmosphere of the seminary and his associations with the seminarians did not influence his innate qualities as a person who usually resisted arbitrary authority and control. Endowed with superior intelligence and the power of keen observation, he was already aware of the sad condition of the country and the plight of the Filipinos. His prolific pen centered around the ignorance, abuses, vices and immorality of a certain friar named *Botod*. A tale entitled *Fray Botod* personified a big- bellied man who was callous, shrewd, ignorant and immoral. The friars saw in his Fray Botod their own picture, that often times had been object of public contempt and ridicule. Jaena had been the object of manhunt by Spanish authorities, so that he can escape from the menacing predicament, he left the Philippines and secretly enrolled in medicine at the University of Valencia in Spain.

Jaena, endowed with literary acumen, wrote speeches and delivered orations unveiling the deplorable social and political conditions of his country. On one occasion, a friar, Father Ramon Martinez Virgil wrote an article praising the friars for their "benevolent" role in the Philippines, when Jaena suddenly stoop up and debunked the friar's allegation and denounced the role of the friars in obstructing the progress of the Philippines through oppression, intolerance and fanaticism. He was obsessed with the idea that the Filipinos wanted a free press and the right to be represented in the Spanish Cortes so their vision and aspirations could be considered by the Spanish government.

In his desire to come out with a newspaper that will serve as a mouthpiece to articulate the grievances of the Filipinos, Jaena, together with the Filipino reformists founded *La Solidaridad* in 1889.

The objectives of La Solidaridad were explicitly expressed in its first editorial, to wit: Our aspirations are modest; our program is clear: to stop all retrogressive steps by the Spanish government, to adopt liberal ideas, to define progress, uphold democratic ideas in order to make these supreme in all nations.

The La Solidaridad collected libertarian ideas which were manifested daily in the field of politics, science, art, literature, commerce, agriculture and industry.

Discussion on all problems relating to the general interest of the nation sought solutions to those problems in a high-level and democratic manner.

With regard to the Philippines, since she needed help, not being represented in the Cortes, we should pay particular attention to the defense of her democratic rights, the accomplishment of which is our patriotic duty.

The newspaper was lovingly referred to by the reformists as the Sol and became the mouthpiece of the Filipinos in Spain and the archipelago. Jaena was the editor of the newspaper. His only compensation was free lodging, meals, clothing and little pocket money for his expenses. His articles and speeches reflected the power and the genius of a born writer and orator. Graciano Lopez Jaena died on January 20, 1896 in Barcelona, Spain, living a legacy of unwavering commitment for reforms.

MARCELO H. DEL PILAR – EXPONENT OF JUSTICE, was born on August 30, 1850 in Bulakan, Bulakan. He was a lawyer, journalist and political analyst involving political affairs of the Filipinos in Spain. He studied at the Collegio de San Jose; lately the, University Sto. Tomas and finished a law course in 1880. His sense of justice, freedom of the press and equality of men before the law led him to campaign against the abuses and interference of the friars in the government. He had the facility of the Tagalog language and used it to arouse the consciousness of his audience through his fiery and emotional speeches about the social and the political abuses by the friars. He founded the *Diariong Tagalog,* the nationalistic newspaper of the country. He wrote articles ridiculing the Spanish authority and exposed the injustices attendant to its administration.

Under del Pilar, the objectives of La Solidaridad were expanded to include a wider social and political freedom and removal of abusive friars in certain parishes. This political analyst and reformist died on July 14, 1896. He was the greatest journalist of purely Filipino blood.

The La Solidaridad. The newspaper of the reform movement as its mouthpiece brought to the attention of the various problems in the country. In one issue, the editorial carried the portrayal of the deplorable conditions in the Philippines and to carry on the legitimate aspirations of the Filipino people to attain democracy and freedom.

The Filipino reformists used pen names in the articles they wrote for the Sol for obvious reasons. Jose Rizal used Dimasalang and Laong Laan; Mariano Ponce used Tikbalang; Marcelo H. del Pilar, Plaridel and Antonio Luna, Taga-ilog. The Spaniards warned the Filipinos with severe punishment for reading the newspaper, but they did not succeed in intimidating them.

In the last issue of La Solidaridad, Marcelo H. del Pilar wrote his farewell editorial, full of endearing emotion and optimism by declaring: "We are persuaded that no sacrifice is too little to win the rights and the liberty of a nation that is oppressed by slavery."

The La Solidaridad contributed immensely to awaken the minds of every Filipino during the dark years of the Spanish administration to help bring about an atmosphere of freedom, equality and justice.

The Masonry and the Reform Movement. Masonry played a vital role in the Reform Movement. The Filipino reformists in Spain joined with Masonic lodges because of their utter disgust with the interference of the friars in Philippine social, economic and political life. Graciano Lopez Jaena brought together all Filipino Masons into one lodge. These Filipino patriots included Marcelo H. del Pilar, Jose Rizal and Mariano Ponce who were determined to carry on the fight for reforms. Lopez Jaena founded the first Filipino Masonic lodge called *Revolucion* in Barcelona on April 1, 1889. the lodge became the center of reform activities in Spain and became responsible for the maintenance of their unity. The leading Filipino Masons established lodges in the country. Serrano Laktaw founded *Lodge Nilad* on January 6, 1892 in Manila, the first Masonic lodge in the Philippines and recognized by the *Gran Oriente Español,* the Spanish mother lodge. The popularity of the Masonry attracted women to join it and the first woman to become a Mason was Rosario Villareal, who became a member of the lodge *Walana* on July 18, 1893. Other female members were Trinidad Rizal, Marina Dizon and Purificacion Leyva to name a few.

The Filipino Masonic lodges in Philippines and Spain were the centers of the Reform Movement. They became the sources of needed funds to support the campaign for reforms.

The Hispano-Filipino Association. At the outset, the reformists were working separately, later on, they pooled their resources and concerted efforts as a team so that their action and voices will be noticed by the government so they formed the association. This band of Filipinos was founded in July 1888, and its inauguration was on January 12, 1889 in Madrid.

It was interesting to note that its composition were Filipinos
and Spaniards who endorsed the granting of needed reforms
in the country. The society was called Hispano-Filipino
Association (Spanish-Filipino Association). Among the
prominent members of the association were Miguel Morayta,
a distinguished Spanish professor of history of the Universidad
Central de Madrid and Rizal's professor and Felipe de la Corte,
a prolific and respected author of several articles about the
Philippines. The principal objective of the society was for the
purpose of securing reforms for the Philippines. The president
was Miguel Morayta and the vice-president was Felipe dela
Corte. To facilitate the work of the society and to make the
movement work effectively, it was divided into three parts:
for the political, Marcelo H. del Pilar, literary, Mariano Ponce
and sports and recreation, Tomas Arejola.

Among the reforms the society envisioned were:

1. the compulsory teaching of Spanish in all schools;

2. the suppression of inhuman maltreatment and
    punishments in all penal jails;

3. establishment of the civil registry;

4. establishment of secondary schools;

5. reform in the University of Sto. Tomas to conform with
    the standards of the universities in Spain;

6. reforms in the bureaucracy;

7. construction of good roads and railways;

8. establishment of agricultural banks in the provinces.

It can be inferred that the Masonry, in effect, contributed
some changes in terms of reforms.

The La Liga Filipina. The La Liga Filipina was founded
on July 3, 1892 in a house in Ilaya, Tondo Manila. The members
of this civic association is open to all Filipinos who had the
interest for the welfare of the Philippines. The elected officers
were Ambrosio Salvador, President; Agustin dela Rosa, Fiscal;
Bonifacio Arevalo, Treasurer and Deodato Arellano, Secretary.

The members include prominent and civic-minded members of the middle class.

The aims of the La Liga as expressed in its constitution were:

1. Unite the whole archipelago into one compact, vigorous and homogenous body;

2. Mutual protection in every want and necessity;

3. Defense against all violence and injustice;

4. Encouragement of education, agriculture and commerce;

5. Study and application of reforms.

The aims of the La Liga were carried through the Supreme Council for the entire country, Provincial Council for every province and the Popular Council for every town.

Sensing that this league was dangerous, the Spanish authorities secretly arrested its founder, Rizal on the night of July 6, 1892 and ordered his deportation to Dapitan, Zamboanga, the following day by Governor-General Eulogio Despujol.

The La Liga could not sustain its avowed effort because some members became tired of paying their dues; hence, the society ceased.

The End of the Reform Movement. Jose Rizal's deportation to Dapitan and the poor radical members led by Andres Bonifacio believed that the envisioned reforms was an exercise in futility. Meanwhile, the conservative intellectual middle class organized themselves into a new group, the *Cuerpo de Compromisarios* where the members pledged to contribute financial aid to the Reform Movement in Spain. When they sensed that the association was no longer capable of maintaining and sustaining its goals, it finally ended.

Perhaps the failure of the reform movement to accomplish its avowed noble objectives could be the intervening factors such as:

1. The friars were so powerful that every good

impression the La Solidaridad had created and imprinted in the minds of Spanish officials in Spain were virtually counteracted by the influential and powerful newspaper of the friars, La Politica de España en Filipinas (The Spanish Politics in the Philippines).

2. The various societies established in the Philippines whose primary purpose was ultimately to campaign for the much-needed reforms did not have sufficient means to carry out and sustain their objectives.

3. The reformists were divided because of petty bickering and jealousies among the members, resulting in the weakening of the bond that tied them together.

While the intensive campaign and the deliberate effort of the La Solidaridad for needed reforms may not be evidently felt in the form of changes in the government, by implication, it also brought to the attention of the Spanish authorities the multifarious problems in the Philippines.

Bonifacio and the Founding of the Katipunan. Andrés Bonifacio, a man of little education but intelligent and a member of the La Liga, did not join the *Compromisarios* who were conservative intellectuals because he was poor. On the night when the news leaked out that Rizal was arrested and deported to Dapitan, Bonifacio with his plebian and patriotic associates Ladislao Diwa, Teodoro Plata, Deodata Arellano and a few others, met secretly in a house in Azcarraga Street (now Claro M. Recto Avenue) near the Railroad Station and founded the revolutionary society called Katipunan (Kataastaasan, Kagalanggalangan Katipunan ng mga Anak Bayan). The platform of the society was to liberate the country from the tyranny and abuses of the unwanted Spanish government and to secure its independence and freedom by armed conflict. He believed that the redemption of the Filipino people from the hands of the Spaniards could only be achieved through the use of radical and violent means.

Katipunan Initiation Rites. The Katipunan was conceived to unite the Filipino people and to fight at all cost for Philippine Independence. At the inception, a few brave men, determined with a noble purpose gathered around a flickering table lamp (lampara) signed the membership papers with their own blood and promised to eliminate Spanish imperialism. The agreement was to recruit new members by way of the triangle method in which the original member would enlist in two new recruits who did not know each other but only the original member who took them in. An agreement to pay an entrance membership fee was *one fuerte* (twenty-five centavos) and subsequently a monthly due of a *medio real* (about twelve centavos).

The Katipunan objectives under the leadership of Bonifacio centered around political, moral and civic. The political dimension in substance and strategy consisted and adhered in working for independence of the Philippines from Spain. The moral dimension delved on the teaching of good morals, integrity, honesty, self-worth, religious fanaticism and weakness of character. The civic objective revolved on the principle of self-help, self-reliance and the defense of the poor and the oppressed. All members were urged to observe the *"Kapatiran"* concept where all members had to help a sick comrade and in case of death, the society was to pay the funeral expenses.

The structure of the Katipunan was composed of three administrative governing bodies; e.g., the Kataastaasang Sangunian (Supreme Council), Sanguniang Bayan (Provincial Council) and Sanguniang Balangay (Popular Council). Administrative policies and implementation to their respective jurisdiction were duly observed.

The Judicial matters affecting the members of the society were referred to Sanguniang Hukuman (Judicial Council), which passed judgment on members who violated the laws and the secrets of the society.

Membership in the Katipunan. Membership in the secret society was divided into three grades – first, second and third. The first grade was called Katipon and wore a black hood with a triangle formed by white ribbons and letters – Anak ng Bayan (son of people), which was the password of the Katipon. The second grade was called Kawal (soldier) wore a green hood and a triangle consisting of white lines. Suspended around his neck was a green ribbon with a medal on which the Malayan letter K was inscribed. The password was GOM-BUR-ZA taken from the three martyred Filipino priests. The third grade was called Bayani (patriot) wore a red mask and sash with green borders and the password was RIZAL. The members adopted countersigns to recognize each other by placing the palm in his right hands on the breast.

The Flags of the Katipunan. The flags of the Katipunan symbolized the authority of the secret brotherhood. Benita Rodriguez with the help of Bonofacio's wife, Gregoria de Jesus, made the flag and was its first official flag in 1892. The red rectangular piece of cloth has a white K at the center. The evolution of the Katipunan flag became a subject of symbol of bravery and unity.

ANDRES BONIFACIO – The Great Plebian, founder and organizer of the Katipunan was born in Tondo near the Tutuban Station on November 30, 1863. He grew up in a slum environment and deprived of the benefits of a prosperous life. He had three brothers – Ciriaco, Procopio and Troadio and two sisters – Esperidiona and Maxima. The death of his father forced him to give up his studies to help the family shoulder its burden. He became the breadwinner at the age of 14, selling paper fans and bamboo canes and peddled around. When he attended the La Liga founding, Bonifacio was a business agent for the German firm Fressel and Company. Through self-study, he broadened his viewpoint and learned about the new nation state. He also read good books by the lamplight at home to improve his knowledge on the lives of leaders, penal and civil codes. He married Monica but the marriage did not last long because she died of leprosy. The young widower fell in love for the second time and married Gregoria de Jesus in the Catholic church, but later re-married according to the Katipunan rites. Gregoria was chosen the *Lakambini* (muse) of the Women's Chapter of the Katipunan.

Most of the women members were wives of the

Katipuneros who rendered valuable services to the Katipunan by guarding the important documents of the society.

Bonifacio was aware of his limitations and gave due recognition to the abilities of others. Unassuming and self-effacing though he was the founder and organizer of the Katipunan, he did not insist on becoming president of the secret society. He took over the top leadership of the Katipunan government only when the first two presidents were not as serious in their sworn duties and responsibilities. The success of the survival of the secret society ultimately was dependent on the leadership of its president and unwavering support and cooperation of its officers and members.

To safeguard the utmost secrecy of the society, they found a place in Morong (now Rizal province) the caves of Makarok and Pamitinan, a safe place and secure for hiding. Inside the cave, Bonifacio wrote on the wall with a piece of charcoal bold letters: "VIVA LA INDEPENDENCIA" (LONG LIVE PHILIPPINE INDEPENDENCE!) with the jubilation of the Katipuneros. Thereafter, launched a vigorous campaign to propagate the objectives and the ideals of the Katipunan.

Bonifacio epitomizes a decisive leader. He may have been perceived lacking in knowledge and unlettered by the middle intellectual middle class but he had insight and understanding that Spain would never grant the needed reforms demanded by the reformists. For him, the only solution to make the Spaniards realize their wickedness and foolishness and finally gain freedom and independence under the colonial government was through the use of radical and violent means. Bonifacio was the legitimate Father of the Revolution, for without him, it was absolutely difficult for the revolution to gain headway.

EMILIO JACINTO – "The brains of the Katipunan," was born on December 15, 1875 in Tondo Manila. He belonged to a poor family but this did not deter him to enroll at the San Juan de Letran College and at the University of Sto. Tomas. At the age of eighteen, he became the youngest member of the Katipunan. Endowed with superior intelligence and impeaceable integrity, he won the admiration of Bonifacio and became his trusted friend and eventually his adviser. Because Bonifacio had full trust and confidence in his abilities, the writing of the Kartilla was entrusted to him. The Kartilla embodied the teaching of the society. The Kartilla as a primer has a very vital role to play in indoctrinating all the members of the society about its lofty ideals. It consisted of thirteen teachings which all members of the society were to internalize and expected to follow. These are:

I. Life which is not consecrated to a lofty and sacred cause is like a tree without a shadow, if not a poisonous weed.

II. A good deed that springs from a desire for personal profit and not from a desire to do good is not kindness.

III. True greatness consists in being charitable, in loving one's fellowmen and in adjusting every movement, deed and word to true Reason.

IV. All men are equal, be the color of their skin black or white. One may be superior to another in knowledge, wealth and beauty, but cannot be superior in being.

V. He who is noble prefers honor to personal gains; he who is mean prefers personal profit to honor.

VI. To a man with a sense of shame, his word is inviolate.

VII. Don't fritter away time; lost riches may be recovered, but time lost will never come again.

VIII. Defend the oppressed and fight the oppressor.

IX. An intelligent man is he who is cautious in speech and knows how to keep the secrets that must be guarded.

X. In the thorny path of life, man is the guide of his wife and children; if he who guides moves toward evil, they who are guided likewise move toward evil.

XI. Think not of woman as a thing merely to while away

time with, but as a helper and partner in the
hardships of life. Respect her in her weakness, and
remember the mother who brought you into this
world and who cared for you in your childhood.

XII. What you do not want done to your wife, daughter
and sister, do not do to the wife, daughter and sister
of another.

XIII. The nobility of a man does not consist in being a king,
nor in the highness of the nose and the whiteness of
the skin, nor in being a priest representing God, nor
in the exalted position on this earth, but pure and
truly noble is he who, though born in the woods, is
possessed of an upright character; who is true to his
words; who has dignity and honor; who does not
oppress and does not help those who oppress; who
knows how to look after and love the land of his birth.

When these doctrines spread and the Sun of
beloved liberty shines with brilliant effulgence on
these unhappy isles and shed its soft rays upon the
united people and brothers in everlasting happiness,
the lives, labors, and sufferings of those who are gone
shall be more than recompensed.

Discovery of the Katipunan. The seed of a nation
through the Katipunan had nurtured and had surfaced to
protect the rights of the Filipino people; hence, its popularity
in Manila and other provinces, especially in Central Luzon
tremendously increased in membership. The spirit of
brotherhood, justice, and freedom became the driving force
to move the Filipino people forward against an abusive regime.

While the Katipunan was preparing the strategy they
were going to employ, the Spanish authorities began to suspect
the underground movement and started to observe strict
surveillance on frequent meetings of the Katipuneros. On
August 19, 1896, the Spanish authorities finally discovered the
secret society and a certain Patiño revealed its existence to
Father Mariano Gil. He told the Spanish authority that
lithographic plate was secretly hidden in the room of the Diario

de Manila and was used by the society in printing various materials used to incite the people to rise against the Spaniards.

The documents that were found were turned over to the Spanish authorities who were fully convinced of the existence of an underground society whose primary objective was to determine and overthrow the Spanish sovereignty in the archipelago.

The discovery of the secret society virtually followed arrests of Filipino suspects. Prominent businessmen and professionals who were suspected to be supportive or sympathetic to the secret movement were rounded up and charged of illegal association without due process and many of them were arbitrarily thrown in Fort Santiago. That night, the people of Manila, were engulfed with fear and anxiety and the danger by the impending arrest of the guardias civil.

Study Guides

A. Terms/Concepts to Understand

assimilation	debunk
restoration	predicament
deplorable	libertarian
fanaticism	immensely
legitimate grievances	bickering

B. Questions to Answer

1. What were the aims of the Reform Movement?

2. Who were the Filipino intellectuals that composed the Reform Movement?

3. What were the objectives of the La Solidaridad?

4. What were the contributions of the Masonry in the Reform Movement?

5. Name the prominent propagandists and describe their personalities and achievements.

6. What was the La Liga Filipina? What were its objectives?

7. Describe the Katipunan as a secret society. What were its objectives?

8. Describe Andres Bonifacio as a revolutionary leader. Identify his strength and weaknesses.

9. Do you think that without the Reform Movement, there would be no Philippine revolution? Explain your answer.

10. Was Rizal right in saying that the people of the Philippines were not yet ready for the revolution in 1896? Justify your answer.

Chapter 7

The Philippine Revolution

THE PHILIPPINE REVOLUTION (1896-1898) was a deliberate and continuous national struggle of the Filipino people against an oppressive Spanish government to obtain justice and freedom. A growing number of Filipino leaders were convinced that it was useless to secure reforms through peaceful means. With the exile of Jose Rizal to Dapitan, a new and more aggressive and determined leader rose to the occasion. He was Andres Bonifacio who grew up in a poor environment and never experienced the benefits of a comfortable life. Unlike Rizal, well-educated and cultured and was an idealist, Bonifacio was a man of action, decisive and resolute.

The discovery of the existence of the Katipunan and the subsequent arrest and execution of the reform leaders and members, some of them innocent of any connection with the secret society, left no alternative but to lead the revolution.

The Cry of Balintawak. On August 23, 1896, he gathered his men in Pugad Lawin and asked them whether they were prepared to fight to the last drop of their blood. Despite the vehement objection of his brother-in-law, Teodoro Plata, on the ground that they lack arms and were not prepared for the war, all present agreed to fight to the bitter end. Bonifacio and his followers brought out their *cedulas* (their identity papers) and simultaneously tore them to pieces as a symbolic act of defiance against Spanish imperialism and with determined efforts to take up arms against the Spanish authorities amidst the thunderous cry of "Long live the

Independence!" The Katipuneros knew that there was no turning back. The revolution was inevitable after the general call to arms was made despite Rizal's disapproval and warning that sufficient arms and mass education are needed.

The First Encounter of the Katipuneros. After the dramatic event that marked the "Cry of Balintawak" which actually took place in Pugad Lawin, Bonifacio ordered his men to be alert and be prepared for the expected assault of the Spanish forces. Aware of the inadequacy and inferior arms, the rebels decided to retreat and under cover of darkness, they surreptitiously marched head to Sitio Pasong Tamo and arrived at the yard of Melchora Aquino, known as Tandang Sora. After partaking of the food served, they stayed overnight for a restful sleep. Early in the morning, some women came rushing in and informed Bonifacio that the Guardia Civil were coming. Immediately, he deployed his men and prepared for the encounter, but a volley of fire in succession came from the approaching Spanish soldiers. In this brief encounter, the rebels lost two comrades. Because of their inferior weapons which consisted mostly of bolos, pointed bamboos and a few guns and their lack of military strategy and discipline, they decided to retreat.

On August 26, the Spaniards were dispatched to Pasong Tamo to drive away the rebels, not aware that the rebels had already left the place. After hiking the mountain trails day and night they arrived at Marikina. However, they also abandoned the place and proceeded to Hagdang Bato where Bonifacio immediately issued a manifesto. The manifesto categorically incited the Filipino people to get set for a concerted attack on the Spanish authorities on August 29. The manifesto contains the public declaration of intentions and its noble objectives, to wit:

> The manifesto is for all of you. It is absolutely necessary for us to stop at the earliest possible time the nameless oppressions being perpertrated on the sons of the people who are now suffering the brutal punishment and tortures in jails, and because of this please let all the brethren know that Saturday, the

revolution shall commence according to our agreement. For this purpose it is necessary for all towns to rise simultaneously and attack Manila at the same time. Anybody who obstructs this sacred ideal of the people will be considered a traitor and an enemy, except if he is ill or is nor physically fit, in which case he shall be tried according to the regulations we have put in force.

The planned attack in Manila and suburbs did not push through. Instead Bonifacio and Jacinto led their men to San Juan del Monte and assaulted the Spaniards who, at the time, were out numbered, but the reinforcement troops arrived. Because of their inferior weapons, Bonifacio and his comrades lost the encounter and were driven back with heavy casualties.

The revolution spread as the rebels grew in number and in strength as the towns-folk in Caloocan, Pateros, Taguig, Kawit, San Francisco de Malabon (now Genral Trias), Noveleta, San Pedro, Makati, and other towns valiantly rose and, armed with bolos and bamboo spears were ready to fight.

The San Juan Hostile Encounter. Bonifacio and his comrades attacked the powder depot of the Spaniards at San Juan which was defended by well-armed and trained infantrymen. Armed with bolos, bamboo spears and a few antiquated firearms, Bonifacio and his men hurled a frontal assault against a superior Spanish force. Because of the Spanish artillery and modern rifles, the encounter turned out to be a carnage. Bonifacio and his comrades lost the battle.

The place in San Juan where the battle was fought causing a heavy casualty among the Katipuneros, is now called "Pinaglabanan."

Reign of Terror. The flames of the revolutionary movement that seeks to change the existing social and political order gained momentum and evidently became a threat to Spanish authorities. In order to sow fear to the people and crushed the rebels, the Spanish soldiers resorted to the reign of terror entering indiscriminately houses of the suspected rebels through force in order to secure evidence against those who were directly involved in the uprising.

Meanwhile, Governor-General Ramon Blanco issued a decree on August 30, declaring the provinces of Manila, Cavite, Batangas, Laguna, Bulacan, Pampanga, Tarlac and Nueva Ecija, in a state of war and placed them under Martial Law. The decree provided that "any person accused of treachery and those against the present form of government" will be tried by the military court. The decree provided for a proviso, that "those who would surrender to the Government" within forty-eight hours after the publication of the decree" would be turned over the military court, except the leaders of the Katipunan. Some *Katipuneros* took advantage of the proviso, but they were forced at the point of a bayonet to squeal about the secret society and its members for fear of pain to be inflicted. Hundreds were arrested and incarcerated in Fort Santiago. Torture by way of hanging the suspect, or the use of electric machine whose wires were connected to the feet and hands of the suspect were employed. Suspects in the provinces were hauled to Manila to suffer inhuman punishment. Hundreds of heads of families were shipped to the Spanish penal colony in Africa to receive what the Spaniards considered their "just punishment." Several types of human violations against the Filipino people were employed by the Spaniards. There were suspected *Katipuneros* who were executed in Cavite, Bicol, and Kapis; but the most infamous injustice was perpetrated upon Jose Rizal who was executed by the Colonial government at Bagumbayan Field (now the Rizal Park) on December 30, 1896. These executions did not deter the Filipinos to fight with intense passion up to the last drop of their blood.

In spite of the Spanish terroristic policy to stop the revolution through imprisonment, torture and execution of the Katipuneros, the flames of the revolution did not stop the Filipinos to fight the Spanish tyranny.

The Katipunan in Cavite. It should be noted that even before the outbreak of the revolution, the Katipunan in Cavite were divided into two rival groups – the Magdalo Council, headed by Baldomero Aguinaldo with headquarters at Cavite del Viejo (now Kawit, and the Magdiwang Council headed by Mariano Alvarez with headquarters at Noveleta. These two insurgent groups, possessed by the spirit of patriotism and lofty ideals for their country, had successful encounters with the Spaniards. Candido Tirona led the *Magdalo* at Cavite el Viejo, which took offensive against the Spanish garrison, which was captured easily; while Emilio Aguinaldo intercepted the Spanish forces coming to Manila. The rebel efforts to repulse the Spanish troops fired the imagination of the Filipinos so that every male, young and old, carried a bolo or blunt weapon, ready to fight every Spaniard. Aguinaldo was so inspired by the unity of the people that he issued a manifesto on October 3, urging all the Filipino people to continue the struggle until freedom was won. Part of the manifesto read:

The Philippines is now a witness to a spectacle unparaled in her history, a movement for the conquest of her liberty and of her independence, the noblest and highest of all her rights, the inspiration of heroism that shall place her on a plane of equality with civilized nations.

Filipinas!... The time has come for us to shed blood in order to redeem our right to freedom. Let us march under the Flag of the Revolution whose watchwords are Liberty, Equality and Fraternity!

The skirmishes between two opposing forces continued having both casualties. The successive defeats of the Spaniards led friars to accuse Governor-General Blanco of incompetence so he was recalled to Spain for failing to stop the revolution and was replaced by General Camilio Polavieja. Polavieja is a shrewd and aristocratic chief executive. He succeeded partially in driving away several rebels from various towns in Cavite, until finally, about one-third of the province fell into their fold.

Meanwhile, the continued rivalry between the *Magdalo and Magdiwang* camps of the Katipunan in Cavite led to a series of defeat. Since, in a revolutionary movement, unity was necessary and to patch up certain issues, the *Magdiwang* faction invited Bonifacio to do something about the conflict. At the outset, Bonifacio was adamant to accept the invitation, saying that his presence in Morong where his men are deployed was necessary. However, the insistence of Artemio ricarte and Mariano Alvarez, Bonifacio acceded to the request. With his wife and brothers, Procopio and Ciriaco, they went to Cavite on the later part of December 1896. They were met by Aguinaldo and some leaders. On December 31, an assembly of revolutionists was held at Imus to decide whether the Katipunan should be replaced by another form of revolutionary movement because the *Magdalo* faction believed that with the outbreak of the revolution throughout the archipelago, the Katipunan has ceased to be a secret society. The *Magdiwang* men maintained that the Katipunan should remain the government of the revolutionists on the ground that it already has a ratified Constitution and By-laws in full operation and recognized by all. After an exchange of heated arguments full of passion to resolve the issue, the meeting virtually ended without concrete results.

The Tejeros Convention. The Tejeros Convention was primarily held to resolve the internal problems of both factions on March 22, 1897, at 2:00 o'clock in the afternoon, at the estate-house of the friars, which they abandoned and eventually fell in the hands of the rebels. The session, which was full of drama started with Jacinto Lumbreras, a *Magdiwang,* as presiding officer, and Teodoro Gonzales, also a *Magdiwang* that, to solve the problem the participants should decide whether a new government should be established to replace the Katipunan. The suggestion triggered one-heated arguments after another until both opposing factions almost came to blows. Lumbreras sensed that the situation may get out of hand and promptly called a recess to cool off the emotional passion of hotheads. After an hour, the session was resumed, this time, Bonifacio was the presiding officer and General Ricarte, the secretary. To resolve the issue, Bonifacio prudently adhered to the wish of some participants that a new government should be established to replace the Katipunan and stated categorically, the principle of the will of the majority should be respected. The next convention adopted this principle unanimously. At this juncture, since the desire of the majority is to establish a new revolutionary government, Bonifacio called for the election and reminded that those present in the convention that who should get elected to any position should be respected. The proposal was unanimously approved and the election through secret ballots followed. Elected were:

President	–	Emilio Aguinaldo
Vice-President	–	Mariano Trias
Captain-General	–	Artemio Ricarte
Director of War	–	Emiliano Riego de Dios
Director of the Interior	–	Andres Bonifacio

During the proclamation of Andres Bonifacio, Daniel Tirona, a Magdalo stood up and said: "The position of the Secretary of the Interior is an exalted one and it is not proper without a lawyer' diploma should occupy it." Bonifacio was hurt, insulted and humiliated. He immediately blurted that "the agreement before the election that whoever got elected was to be respected." With firm resolve, he demanded that Tirona retract what he said. Instead of apologizing to Bonifacio, he stood up and about to leave the convention place. Bonifacio, still fuming with anger, whipped his pistol and was about to fire at Tirona when Ricarte held his arms, thus preventing what could have been a tragic affair. The people began to leave the place while Bonifacio, still angry, declared the assembly dissolved and all that were taken up and approved were null and void, and walked out of the hall with his followers.

The second meeting at Tejeros resulted in the establishment of a new Revolutionary Government, replacing the Katipunan and the election of Aguinaldo as president. Aguinaldo and the other elected officers, with the exception of Bonifacio, took their oath of office.

Meanwhile, Bonifacio and his followers felt bad about the results of the balloting because they believed certain irregularities were committed, so they drew up a document, now called the *Acta de Tejeros* in which they gave the reasons for refusing to accept the results of the convention. The document rejected the Revolutionary Government headed by General Aguinaldo on the following grounds: e.g., 1. The Tejeros Assembly "lacks legality;" the Magdalo conspired to oust Bonifacio from leadership, and the election of officials was fraudulent.

Aguinaldo sent a delegation to Bonifacio's camp and persuaded him to cooperate with the newly constituted government, but he refused vehemently to return to the revolutionary movement headed by Aguinaldo.

The Naik Military Compact.   Bonifacio could not get over the insult and humiliation hurled on him by Daniel Tirona and the anomalous election; so he and his men, drew up another document resolving the establishment of a government, independent of and separate from, that established at Tejeros by the Magdalo faction.

The document embodied the ideals and aspirations of their objectives, to wit:

> We who sign these presents with our true names, all officers of the army who have met in convention, headed by Supreme Chief (Bonifacio), on account of the critical situation of the pueblos and the war, having discovered the treason committed by certain officers who have been sowing discord and conniving with the Spaniards, our enemies, corrupting the army and being guilty of criminal neglect in the care of the wounded, have agreed to deliver the people from this grave danger by the means herein after enumerated:
>
> *First:* All combatants shall, by persuasion or force, be incorporated in any army corps and placed under the command of General Pio del Pilar.
>
> *Second:* We shall recognize no one as being vested with full power except Right in the first place, and those courageous officers, who, since the beginning of the war and until the present moment, have never gone turned on their oath and have conducted themselves with loyalty.
>
> *Third:* Any disloyal person shall be punished on the spot, according to his faults.
>
> Such is our agreement and we swear before God and the country of our birth that we shall keep it unto the grave.

Bonifacio signed the document with Pio del Pilar, Artemio Ricarte and Severino delas Alas, to mention a few, out of the other forty-one men. The document will, in effect, affect the cause of the revolutionary movement.

The Trial and Execution of Bonifacio. Bonifacio and his wife, two brothers and a few loyal comrades left Naik and transferred to Limbon, a barrio of Indang. Aguinaldo learned about the Naik Military Compact and Bonifacio's intensions; so he immediately ordered the arrest of the Bonifacio brothers under the command of Colonel Agapito Bonzon. When the house where Bonifacio, his wife and men was surrounded by Bonzon's men, fighting followed. Bonifacio sustained wound on his neck, while Procopio was also wounded and Ciriaco was killed. Bonifacio was placed in a hammock and accompanied by his wife, wounded brother, and his followers were brought to Naik, the capital of the revolutionary government. To conduct the trial, the Council of War was created and on April 28, Aguinaldo endorsed the case of Bonifacio. After hearing the case with the plaintiff and defense lawyers presenting their arguments, the Council of War gave its decision declaring the Bonifacio brothers guilty of treason and sedition. When President Aguinaldo received the court decision, he referred it to Judge Advocate General Baldomero Aguinaldo in which he wrote the President recommending approval of the Council of War's decision affirming the death penalty of the Bonifacio brothers. On May 8, President Aguinaldo commuted the death penalty to banishment. When Generals Mariano Noriel and Pio del Pialr learned about the commutation of the death penalty to banishment, they immediately asked Aguinaldo to withdraw his order on the ground that Bonifacio's being alive, will prejudice the cause of the revolutionary movement for it will create discord among the revolutionists. Under pressure, and perhaps convinced by their position, General Aguinaldo cancelled his order.

General Noriel ordered Major Lazaro Macapagal to bring out the two brothers from jail on May 10, 1897, where he was handed a sealed letter with specific orders to read the contents only after reaching Mount Tala, about four kilometers of

Maragondon. When they reached the mountain, Bonifacio requested Makapagal to open the sealed letter, which contained the order to execute the Bonifacio brothers. Makapagal followed the order to the letter because non-compliance as a warning would be meted with harsh punishment. The pathetic condition of the death of the Bonifacio brothers smacked the dignity of man especially in giving the dead a decent burial. On account of evidence available on the literature in various prints, Bonifacio's grave was shallow having been dug by bayonets and a few twigs placed on the grave.

The Revolution Continues. General Camilo de Polavieja, tired of the endless battles, asked for his relief as Governor-General and was replaced by a former governor-general of the Philippines, Fernando Primo de Rivera. He immediately issued a proclamation that the "revolution is over," even if he knew the Filipino people struggle for freedom continues. On the other hand, when Aguinaldo arrived at Biak-na-Bato, he issued a series of proclamation informing the Filipinos about the various injustices the Spanish authorities have committed and urging them to continue the revolution until freedom is regained. With the series of proclamation, focused on the tyranny and abuses committed against the Filipinos, various new uprisings exploded in the provinces of Southern Tagalog and Central Luzon as an expression of resistance, hate and distrust on the Spaniards.

The Biyak-na-Bato Republic

President Aguinaldo issued a proclamation on July 2, 1897, in which the revolutionary demands were listed. These are: (1) the expulsion of the friars and the return of the lands to the Filipinos they appropriated for themselves; (2) representation in the Spanish Cortes; (3) freedom of the press and tolerance of all religious sects; (4) equal treatment and pay for civil servants; (5) abolition of the power of the government to banish citizens; and (6) legal equality for all persons.

The republican government at Biyak-na-Bato had its provisional constitution prepared by Felix Ferrer and Isabelo Artacho patterned after the Cuban Constitution. The Biyak-na-Bato Constitution was signed and promulgated on November 1, 1897. It provided for the creation of a Supreme Council composed of a President, a Vice-President, a Secretary of War and a Secretary of the Treasury. The Constitution also provided the basic bill of rights that the citizens should enjoy.

The Supreme Coucil had the following officers:

President	– Emilio Aguinaldo
Vice-President	– Mariano Trias
Secretary of Foreign Affairs	– Antonio Montenegro
Secretary of Interior	– Isabelo Artacho
Secretary of the Treasury	– Baldemero Aguinaldo
Secretary of War	– Emiliano Riego de Dios

The provisional government exercised control and supervision over all national and local political, social and economic affairs of the Philippines.

The Pact of Biyak-na-Bato. Pedro A. Paterno who stayed in Spain for quite sometime became the mediator between the Filipinos and the Spaniards, through Governor-General Primo de Rivera. Because he had a special concern for the welfare of Spain and the Philippines, he wanted to put an end to this dragging and destructive conflict. He negotiated with Aguinaldo and Primo de Rivera on condition that he thought that would be satisfactory and acceptable to both parties. The peace agreement was known as the Pact of Biyak-na-Bato which was signed by Paterno representing the revolutionists and Primo de Rivera, the Spanish government.

The pact is composed of three documents. The first one called "Program," provided that Governor-General Primo de Rivera would pay the rebels the sum of Php800,000 in three installments: (1) Php400,000 on the departure of Aguinaldo, and his followers from Biyak-na-Bato; (2) Php200,000 when the number of arms surrendered exceeded Php700; and the remaining Php200,000, when the general amnesty was proclaimed by the Governor-General.

The second document, called "Act of Agreement," reiterated the granting of general amnesty to the rebels who would lay down their arms. It also mentioned the financial arrangement in the Program and impliedly hinted the desire of the Filipinos for the reforms, but there was no such provision that Spain had agreed to such reforms.

The third document contains the questions of indemnity. Primo de Rivera would pay the additional sum of P900,000 to the families of the non-combatant Filipinos who were caught in the cross fire and suffered injury during the armed conflict.

To make sure that the Spanish authorities would faithfully adhered to their promise; the revolutionists demanded that the two Spanish generals were to stay in Biyak-na-Bato as hostages. While Colonel Miguel Primo de Rivera, the Governor-General's nephew, had to accompany the exile to Hongkong. The Spanish generals-Celestino Tejeiro and Ricardo Monet were the two hostages of the rebels at Biyak-na-Bato. Meanwhile, Aguinaldo and his men sailed for Hongkong with the check of Php400,000.

Failure of the Pact of Biyak-na-Bato. Perhaps, it may be inferred that the failure of the Pact was that certain provisions were not faithfully followed by both parties. The reforms, which were the primary reasons for the continuous struggle of the rebels had not been granted. Aguinaldo and his comrades continued the revolutionary Government by reorganizing the "Hongkong Junta."

The suspicious hostile attitude of both parties to each other resulted in the sporadic clashes between the rebels and the Spanish soldiers. While the skirmish raged on, one of the leaders, General Francisco Makabulos of Tarlac, established the Central Executive Committee, which was intended to be a provisional one until a general government of the Republic shall have been established again. The rebel government had also a constitution, called the Constitution of Makabulus. The Constitution provided for an executive committee composed of a President, a Vice-President, a Secretary of the Interior, a Secretary of the Treasury, and a Secretary of War. It is evidently clear that the Filipino leaders were not inclined to follow and implement the agreement in the Pact. They believed that they could use the money given to them by Primo de Rivera to buy arms and other supplies. On the other hand, the Spaniards arrested and imprisoned many civilians whom they suspected supporters and sympathizers of the rebels. These dastardly acts of the Spaniards led to the intense feeling among the Filipinos especially the rebels that the Pact of Biyak-na-Bato was but a mask to cover Spanish evil design. The mutual suspicion between the revolutionists and the Spanish authorities who acted in bad faith resulted in the resurgence of the revolution.

Study Guides

A. Terms/Concepts to Understand

oppressive	perpetrator
resolute	assault
decisive	carnage
simultaneous	categorical
manifesto	shrewd

B. Questions to Answers

1. Identify the causes of the Philippine revolution.

2. What was the effect of the discovery of the Katipunan?

3. Why did Teodoro Plata object to the immediate plan of Andres Bonifacio to fight the oppressive Spanish government by way of revolution?

4. Why did Bonifacio and his followers tear their *cedulas*?

5. Where was the first encounter of the Katipunan? Describe the dramatic event.

6. What brought about the Reign of Terror?

7. What were the watch words of the revolution?

8. Give the names of the first eight provinces to rise in arms against Spain in August 1896.

9. What was the significance of the execution of Dr, Jose Rizal?

10. Do you believe that General Aguinaldo was a better revolutionary leader than Bonifacio? Explain your answer.

Chapter 8

The Revolution Continued with the Coming of the Americans

Emilio Aguinaldo went to Singapore to confer with American consul Spencer Pratt. The subject of their talk centered on the act of persuasion from Pratt urging Aguinaldo to extend cooperation to Commodore George Dewey who was about to sail to Manila to attack and destroy the Spanish navy because war had been declared between Spain and the United States. Aguinaldo returned to the Philippines on board an American ship to continue the unfinished revolt against Spain. The Filipinos who had surrendered to the Spanish authority deserted the rebel camp.

Meanwhile, Primo de Rivera was relieved as governor-general by General Basilio Agustin. The new governor-general apparently does not have any knowledge about the actual conditions in the Philippines. General Agustin pledged that he would continue the work of his predecessor, Primo de Rivera, which hinged on pacification.

The American Plan on the Philippines. While the Spanish-American relations were turning hostile, the Cuban revolution had drawn the United States to sympathize with the Cuban rebels, because American vast economic interests in the island were paramount. At that instance, Theodore Roosevelt Sr., a very prominent and influential personality in America, longed for that war between Spain and United States to break out in order to expand the Navy. This statement was made confidentially to his sister. When he became Assistant Secretary to the Navy, he started to entertain the idea of attacking Manila in the event that war between Spain and the United States broke out. For him, there was only one man who was capable of carrying out such plan and this was Commodore George Dewey. The commander of the Asiatic Squadron, Roosevelt worked for the appointment of Commodore Dewey to get the vacant position. When the war broke out, Dewey immediately sailed to Manila to destroy the Spanish warships. It may be noted that the coming of the Americans to Philippine territory was not because of the Spanish-American war, but a deliberate plan.

The Spanish-American War.   The Spanish-American War was the result of the stories published in various New York newspapers of the alleged Spanish brutalities and mistreatment of American citizens in Cuba. This was an offshoot of who wrote a friend in Havana, Cuba, telling that President William Mckinley was weakling politician. The letter was said to be stolen and surprisingly published. The relief of the Spanish Ambassador did not appease the Americans. The instantaneous cause of this war was the blowing up of the U.S. battleship *Maine* at the Harbor of Havana resulting in the death of many Americans. The incident aggravated and triggered and outraged the Americans had and they blamed Spain for this blatant act of treachery.

On April 21, 1898, the American Congress approved a resolution declaring a state of war with Spain; and finally, Congress passed and approved a formal declaration of war on April 25, 1898.

The Battle of Manila Bay.   Upon the formal declaration of war with Spain, Dewey immediately sailed for the Philippines with seven heavily armed battle ships and entered Manila Bay shore. Meanwhile, the Spanish fleet, the longest organized unit of naval ships of Spain was along Sangley Point in Cavite ready to go into a full battle. Dewey, an intelligent and calculated U.S. admiral, ordered his men to turn towards direction of Sangley Point and on the bridge of the flagship

Olympia, he estimated the distance between the two fleets. From his mathematical estimate, his guns could hit the Spanish ships, so he ordered the captain of the *Olympia* to fire. Admiral Montojo, the captain on board the Spanish flagship *Reina Cristina*, fought gallantly, but the American fleet with superior warships were too much for the Spaniards. The destruction of the Spanish fleet was a total wreck and the Spaniards with no alternative but to bounch back, finally hoisted the white flag as a symbol of surrender. The news of Dewey's naval victory in Manila Bay reached the United States and the people in a state of euphoria rose in jubilation. This important event stirred in the minds of many people, especially the Americans to get a map or a history book to locate Manila in the Philippines.

Dewey's victory marked the end of Spain's dominant colonialism as a world power and heralded the beginning of the United States ascension to the "World Empire."

Aguinaldo in Singapore. When the Spanish-American war broke out, Aguinaldo and his men were in Singapore following the trend of events. For them, this is the time Soanish rule will most likely end in the Philippines. The division of the ranks of the exile surfaced for Isabelo Artacho, wanted the P400,000 given to Aguinaldo be divided among them but Aguinaldo vehemently refused.

Meanwhile, he had a secret interview with American consul, Spencer Pratt regarding Filipino-American collaboration against Spain. Howard Bay, an English man who had resided in the Philippines, acted as the intermediary during the Aguinaldo-Pratt interview. Aguinaldo and his men sailed for Hongkong, but unfortunately, he did not see Dewey for he had already left Manila. In another conference between Aguinaldo and Consul Wildman, the latter suggested that upon his return to the Philippines, Aguinaldo should establish a dictatorial government in the Philippines but after the peace had been restored, Aguinaldo should established a government similar to that of the United States.

Aguinaldo Returns to the Philippines. Aguinaldo considered the decision of the Hongkong Junta and left on

board the McCulloch, Dewey's ship and arrived at Cavite on
May 19, 1898. Upon his arrival, Aguinaldo and Dewey were
both delighted to see each other. Dewey expressed confidence
that the Filipinos will offer assistance against the Spaniards.
On the other hand, Aguinaldo was pleased, for he needed help
from the Americans to recognize Philippine independence.
However, the subject matter of their conference later bore no
concrete results about the United States' commitment.

Meanwhile, the struggle went on. The news of
Aguinaldo's return spread in many provinces. A number of
Filipino volunteers to the Spanish groups started to defect to
the Filipino forces and declared their loyalty to Aguinaldo.
Within a short time, Aguinaldo and his comrades were able
to repulse the Spanish forces. The Spanish attempts to win
over the Filipinos was a dismal failure.

Manila Besieged.   After the destruction of the Spanish
navy, Dewey blockaded Manila, the Walled City (now
Intramuros), to prevent thousands of Spaniards to escape; they
sought refuge and were trapped. Meanwhile, the Filipino
forces under Aguinaldo besieged Manila by surrounding and
attacking the fortified wall in such a way as to isolate it from
help and supplies, thereby making capture possible. To make
the siege effective, Aguinaldo cut off supply of foodstuffs and
even water supply. The effective design and strategy made
the people inside the Walled City – Spaniards, Filipinos and
other nationals to suffer from extreme hunger and thirst. It is
interesting to note that it was only a matter of weeks that the
Spanish authorities finally surrendered. Aguinaldo offered
Governor-General Agustin terms of honorable surrender but
he rejected. He was still waiting for reinforcement from Spain
but it never came. With the siege of Manila, the prolonged
and persistent effort of the Filipinos to overcome
insurmountable problems gained some headway.

The Filipino-American Rift. The break up of Filipino-
American relations stemmed from the Spanish-American
secret agreement. The Americans were confident that they
could drive out the Spaniards easily from the city with the
reinforcements headed by Generals Thomas Anderson, Francis

Green and Arthur MacArthur. Preparations were made for the battle that would determine the fate of Manila. For several nights there were skirmishes between some Spanish soldiers and American combatants resulting in a few casualties.

Dewey thought the surrender of Manila could be effected without the use of arms, so he negotiated with Agustin, through the Belgian consul, about the surrender of Manila. When the Spanish government came to know Agustin's plan to surrender, he was relieved as governor and replaced by General Fermin Jaudenes. Jaudenes, like Agustin, it was an exercise on futility to still fight because he believed that it was hopeless in the face of a superior enemy with the Filipino rebels. To save his honor, there should be a mock battle after which the Spanish forces would surrender. He also insisted that the Filipino rebels should be excluded from participating in the surrender of Manila and should not be allowed to enter the city. It was surprising that Dewey and Merritt accepted the terms even if it meant a deceptive move, an act of treachery to their friend, Aguinaldo. There was even a plan on Dewey to hold back the Filipino troops while the mock battle was being enacted. The agreement between Dewey and Jaudenes was so secret that no one in either camp knew of its existence.

When General Merritt arrived, he decided that the offensive against Manila be conducted along the bay side occupied by the Filipinos, so he ordered General Francis Green to request General Aguinaldo to evacuate the bay side occupied by the Filipino troops. At this point, Aguinaldo demanded that the request be put in writing. General Green assured him that such request for evacuation will be effected after they left the place. However, Green did not honor his word. Aguinaldo and other Filipino leaders started to harbor suspicious and expressed doubts about the real intentions of the Americans. It is interesting to note that what began as a friend alliance between Aguinaldo and Dewey worsened into silent hostility.

The Mock Battle of Manila.   In the morning of August 10, the assault on Manila was to begin, but bad weather delayed the planned battle. On August 7, Dewey and Merritt ordered Jaudenes to evacuate the non-combatants to safer places because the American forces would start the operations.

The morning was dark with heavy clouds and suddenly rain started to fall and drenched the soldiers. The Filipino troops, ready to assault the enemies were at the right flank of General Arthur MacArthur. General Anderson requested General Aguinaldo not to advance his troops during the fray, but he stood pat and decisive to participate in the attack of Manila. Dewey's naval guns bombarded Fort San Antonio Abad near the Bagungbayan Field, while Green advanced his attack to Malate, MacArthur's troops took Singalong. The Filipino troops moved closer to Intramuros.

At aboutr 1:00 o'clock in the afternoon, the Spaniards hoisted the white flag of surrender above the Walled City, a symbol that Manila has "fallen." There was a brief display of fireworks immediately after the hostilities ended; while American troops triumphantly entered the city, after which they prevented the Filipino troops who had helped them capture the city from entering this was very unfortunate. The Filipino generals and their troops naturally felt discriminated against and resent their exclusion in the jubilant celebration of the seizure of the city. We can infer that this incident was the beginning of the friction between the Filipino and the American animosity.

The Treaty of Paris (1898). The treaty of Paris was a very significant act between Spain and the United States for it initiated the peace agreement ending the Spanish-American war. After two months of discussions and deliberations on the terms and conditions between their respective commissioners, they came to agree with the provisions set forth in the peace treaty as follows:

1. Spain should cede the Philippines, Guam and Puerto Rico to the United States

2. The United States should pay Spain the sum of $20,000.00

3. Spain should withdraw her sovereignty from Cuba

4. The civil and political status of the inhabitants in the ceded territories was to be determined by the United States Congress

Some American writers believed that the sum of $20,000.00 paid by the United States to Spain was not a "purchase price" but given as a generous gesture to the downfall of an adversary and help to rehabilitate her country.

The end of Spanish rule marked another era of challenges ahead of the Filipinos.

Study Guides

A. Terms/Concepts to Understand

pacification   intermediary
hostile   repulse
hoisted   besieged
vehement   insurmountable
alternative   cede

B. Questions to Answer

1. Why did Aguinaldo go to Spain?

2. Why was Governor-General Primo de Rivera relieved as the Philippine-Spanish governor-general?

3. What do you think was the immediate and primary cause of the Spanish-Aamerican war?

4. What can you say about the leadership style of President William Mckinley?

5. Describe the Battle of Manila Bay.

6. Describe George Dewey as a naval American officer. Identify his strengths and weaknesses.

7. Why did Aguinaldo return to the Philippines?

8. What were the primary causes of the Filipino-American rift?

9. What is the significance of the Treaty of Paris? Identify the tangible results.

10. What was the purpose of the Mock Battle of Manila? Identify the results.

Chapter 9

The Malolos Republic

The United Stated imposed her sovereignty over the Philippines by virtue of the Treaty of Paris, in which Spain ceded the country to her. The Filipino people rejected the American sovereignty and to show their capacity for self-government, Aguinaldo established the Dictatorial Government in May and, after a month, the Revolutionary Government. They were prepared and determined to defend their freedom, which they won from Spain. In defiance of the United States to set her authority to control the Filipinos, the First Philippine Republic was established in Malolos, Bulacan, on January 28, 1899.

The Malolos Congress. In the morning of September 15, 1898, the Barasoain Church was filled with delegates and spectators while the National Anthem was being played. A few minutes later, the Malolos Cingress was inaugurated amidst the loud cry of acclamation of the people that "The Philippines is for the Filipino people." The inaugural ceremony formally began at 10:30 in the morning. Pedro Paterno was elected president of the Congress. It was attended by army officers, troopers in gala uniforms, dignitaries, foreign and local correspondents and prominent members of the community to bear witness to the historic event.

General Aguinaldo, in his message to Congress, paid tribute to the rare courage, fortitude, tenacity of spirit, patriotism and heroism which exemplified the Filipino character at its highest and loftiest measures and enjoined the Filipino people to rally behind the Malolos Congress.

The officers of the Congress were Pedro A. Paterno, President, Benito Legarda, Vice-President, Gregorio Araneta, First secretary; and Pablo Ocampo, Second Secretary. The delegates created the Permanent Commision of Justice together with the different committees; e.g., Committee on Felicitations, Committee on Messages, Committee on Internal Regulations, Committee on Style and Committee to Draft the Constitution.

The most significant act of Congress was the ratification on September 29, 1898, of the Philippine Independence proclaimed at Kawit on June 12.

The Malolos Constitution. The Committee to draft the Constitution was constituted and headed by Felipe G. Calderon and other members who belong to the Filipino intelligentia who possessed intellectual and moral integrity. The members of the committee studied carefully the three constitutional drafts for consideration – The Mabini Constitutional Plan, The Paterno Constitutional Plan and the Calderon Plan. The Mabini Plan was the Constitutional Program of the Philippine Republic, while the Paterno Plan was based on the Spanish Constitution of 1868. Calderon a noted constitutional lawyer based his plan on the constitutions of Belgium, Brazil, Costa Rica, Guatemala, Mexico and France.

After a thorough examination of the different Constitutional Plans, the Committee chose the Calderon Plan as the best subject to amendments and submitted it to the Malolos Congress for approval.

Calderon sponsored the proposed Constitution to Congress on October 8, 1898. This was followed by the distribution of printed copies to the members of Congress. The draft was presented to the floor and deliberation on every article occasionally protracted with heated debate, especially the subjects of whether or not the Church and the State should be united and the adoption of Catholic Christianity as the official religion of the State. This article was bitterly contested by opposing groups articulated by some delegates that the Filipinos as a people, up in arms against Catholic Spain, were not anti-Catholic, but merely anti-clerical practices. On the other hand, those who advocated for the separation of church and state and the freedom of religion in order to avoid the bitter lessons that occurred during the Spanish era were mostly Masonic members of the Congress.

After a few days of deliberating on the sensitive article, it was changed, thus, "The State recognizes the freedom of and equality of religion, as well as the separation of the Church and State."

The decisive decision shown by the members of Congress is an eloquent manifestation of genuine statesmanship and, in effect, became the cornerstone of Philippine democracy and showed not only nationalism and democratic orientation of those who voted for the separation of Church and State, but also their discerning and highly sensitive sense of history.

The Malolos Constitution was approved by a majority vote of the members of Congress and then forwarded to President Aguinaldo for approval on November 29, 1898.

The Constitution is the first document ever produced by the people's representatives, anchored on sound democratic philosophy and traditions. It embodied the Filipino aspirations of a government that was truly popular, representative and responsible with three distinctive branches – the executive, the legislative and the judicial. It also provided an article on the Bill of Rights that enumerated the individual rights and privileges of the citizen. It was designed to protect them against encroachments by the government, or by any individual or group of individuals. Its basis was the social importance accorded to the individual in a democratic society, that every individual has the dignity and worth which must be respected and safeguarded.

The Malolos Constitution had a unicameral legislature. It is unique in the sense that the legislature is superior to either the executive or the judicial branch. Calderon's reason for the omnipotence of the legislature was that he feared the predominance of ignorant military elements who might abuse their power because they were soldiers behind Aguinaldo.

The Malolos Constitution was the symbol of unity, freedom, equality, justice and the customs and traditions that reflect the character of the Filipino people.

The First Philippine Republic. Apolinario Mabini objected to some provisions of the Constitution; so Aguinaldo held its promulagtion until such time that Congress leaders could find the proper solution. They finally compromised with Mabini, Aguinaldo's closet adviser, by acceding to insert the needed amendments in the document. Aguinaldo formally promulgated the Constitution that embodied the ideology, belief system and values of the Filipino people on January 21, 1899. He expressed his congratulations to the members of the Malolos Congress, the Armed Forces and most especially to all the Filipino people for their cooperative efforts and sacrifices in the struggle to gain independence. He said that the aspirations of lofty ideals of a resilient race "to live under the democratic regime of the Philippine Republic, free from the yoke of any foreign domination." He concluded his inaugural address by declaring that: "Great is this day, glorious this date, and forever memorable this moment in which our beloved people are raised to the apotheosis of Independence."

On January 2, President Aguinaldo formed his Cabinet.

Apolinario Mabini	– President of the Cabinet and Secretary of Foreign affairs
Teodoro Sandico	– Secretary of Interior
Baldomero Aguinaldo	– Secretary of War
Mariano Trias	– Secretary of Finance
Graciano Gonzaga	– Secretary of Welfare, including Public Instruction, Public Works and Communications, Agriculture, Industry, and Commerce

According to Mabini, the Cabinet "belong to no party, nor does it desire to form one, it stands for nothing save the interests of the fatherland." One of the significant acts of Aguinaldo after his inauguration was to issue a decree granting pardon to all Spanish prisoners of war who were not members of the Spanish regular army and, at the same time, granting to Spaniards and other aliens the right to engage in business within the territorial boundaries of the Republic.

On Financial Matters. The Republic adopted a system similar to Spanish and other countries with some modifications. Taxes levied by the Spanish government were retained except those on cockfighting and forms of gambling. New methods of collecting revenues for public purposes were instituted. The Malolos Congress authorized the government to issue paper money of various denominations and minted coins.

The Revolutionary Periodicals of the Republic. The new Republic, as a struggling nation, had to devise a medium as a mouthpiece that should convey its ideals and aspirations to be known not only of the people of the Philippines, but also other people the world over.

Its official organ was El Heraldo de le Revolucion (Herald of the Revolution) whose first issue came out on September 29, 1898, but subsequently, changed to Heraldo Filipino, (Philippine Herald) and finally, to Gaceta de Filipinos (Philippine Gazette). The last issue came out on October 14, 1899. The periodicals published the full texts of the decrees of the government and other significant news items.

There were also privately – owned nationalistic newspapers, e.g., La Independencia (Independence), founded and edited by Pedro A. Paterno. The staff of the newspapers constituted the great Filipino writers at that time whose patriotic and nationalistic articles were written by Cecilio Apostol, Jose Palma, Fernanado Ma. Guerrero, to name a few.

In the provinces, there were also various revolutionary periodicals published by Filipino intellectuals, to keep the ideals and aspirations of the people alive; e.g., La Libertad (The Liberation), edited by Clemente Jose Zulueta; Ang Kaibigan ng Bayan, (The People's Friend) and La Federation (The Federation). While most of these local periodicals in the provinces were short-lived, their policy of continuously fighting for freedom and independence was foremost. Many headlines hailed not only the rare courage of every Filipino to fight the excesses of the repressive Spanish government, but also kept the sparks of the revolutionary movement alive which ultimately gave the Philippines her most significant, colorful and epochal peace in the history of mankind.

Education under the Republic. The destruction of many schools and the peace and order condition caught the attention of the Filipino leaders to be closed for the time being. The Revolutionary Government, through the Secretary of the Interior, ordered the various provincial governors of their respective local government jurisdiction to open classes as soon as the existing circumstances permitted. The government appropriated the sum P35,000 for public instruction. A decree creating the Burgos Institute and outlining the curriculum which included Latin grammar, universal Geography and History, Spanish literature, Mathematics, French, English, Physical Sciences and Philosophy were offered leading to Bachelor of Arts degree.

A Decree was issued on October 19, 1898 by Aguinaldo creating the Literary University of the Philippines. Subjects offered include civil and criminal law, medicine and surgery, pharmacy and notary public under well-selected professors. The first president of the University was Dr. Joaquin Gonzales who was later succeeded by Dr. Leon Ma. Guerrero. Unfortunately, the University did not live long, for the misunderstanding with Americans led its faculty and students to leave.

Diplomatic Activities of the Republic. Aguinaldo created diplomatic positions abroad through the Department of Foreign Affairs, headed by his chief adviser, Mabini, who was in charge of establishing political and socio-economic relations with other countries; most especially, to persuade foreign powers to recognize Philippine independence.

Filipino diplomatic agents were appointed to various foreign countries to represent the Republic. They were Felipe Agoncillo for the United States; Mariano Ponce and Faustino Lichauco for Japan; Antonio Regidor for England; Juan Luna and Pedro Roxas for France, and Eriberto Zarcal for Australia.

Prominent Filipino residents in Spain and France worked hard also for the recognition of Philippine independence. Agoncillo and Sixto Lopez went to the United States to work for the recognition of Philippine independence, but their attempts to have an official audience with President William Mckinley did not materialize. They also sailed to Europe to appeal to the American Peace Commissioners to give the Filipinos one more chance to consider their earnest request on the issue that deeply affected the future of the Philippines, but this likewise failed.

Literacy Pieces and Music Under the Republic. Various literacy pieces, worthy of being rememebered characterized by beauty of expression and form and by university intellectuals included Jose Palma's famous poem, Filipinas, which became the lyrics of the Philippine National Anthem; Fernando Ma. Guerrero's Mi Patria (My Country), which was a poetical masterpiece of exquisite beauty and elegance and excessively refined in treatment and character, Cecilio Apostol's famous poem, *A Rizal* (To Rizal), was the finest tribute to the Filipino Martyr and hero, worthy of its instrinsic appeal and excellence. Apolinario Mabini, the "Sublime Paralytic," lawyer, philosopher, patriot and writer and called the Brains of the Philippine Revolution because of his high intellectual endowments, composed the True Decalogue and Philippine Revolution, characterized by the expression of passionate and appealing emotion.

In the field of music, various compositions expressive of varied ideas and emotions, which were pleasing to hear and performed certain functions to release tensions were composed. Julian Felipe's Philippine National Anthem was, indeed, the greatest musical legacy of the Revolution. Other musical compositions he composed expressing patriotism and love of country were Un Recuerdo (A Remembrace), a song dedicated to the "Thirteen Martyrs of Cavite," characterized by power tone and stirring emotion and *Heneral Luna*, characterized by its piercing tone and martial pomp, a march dedicated to General Antonio Luna.

Various Filipino great musicians and composers were Julio Nakpil, a best friend of Bonifacio, who later married Gregoria de Jesus, Bonifacio's widow, composed the Katipunan hymn entitled "Marangal na Dalitang Katagalugan," "Pahimakas," a farewell song dedicated to the members of the La Liga Filipina and "Kabanatuan," a funeral march dedicated to General Antonio Luna who met his untimely death in the hands of an assassin in Cabanatuan, Nueva Ecija. One of the most popular compositions during the revolution was the *Kundiman ng Himagsikan*. The tone, pitch and melody can influence people to resort to collective expression of opposition against oppressive government to bring about change. Unfortunately, the composer of this revolutionary piece was unknown.

Study Guides

A. Term/Concepts to Understand

sovereignty	articulate
dictatorial government	encroachment
assimilation	accorded
fortitude	repressive
tenacity	nationalism

B. Questions to Answer

1. What was contained in the message of General Aguinaldo in the Malolos Congress?

2. Who was elected president of the Malolos Congress?

3. What was the most significant act of the Malolos Congress?

4. Who was the author of the Malolos Constitution? Enumerate some of its salient features.

5. When and where was the First Philippine Republic inaugurated?

6. Who were the members of the Aguinaldo Cabinet?

7. Enumerate the Revolutionary Periodicals of the Republic.

8. Describe the state of education under the Republic.

9. What were the literacy pieces and what were their tones and character?

10. Enumerate some composers and their musical compositions during the Revolution.

Chapter 10

The Filipino-American Animosity

The various incidents that contributed and eventually precipitated the Filipino-American animosity stemmed from the following factors:

1. The American insistence on the pull-out of Aguinaldo's troops of the strategic place along the Manila Bay area;

2. The refusal of the American military authorities to allow the Filipino soldiers to enter the city of Manila after its surrender; and

3. The American limitation of the areas to be occupied by the Filipino troops after the mock battle of Manila. To accelerate the unfriendly feeling was followed in the Treaty of Paris without consulting the Filipinos. In another unfortunate incident, on February 4, 1899, an American soldier standing as a guard to prevent the entry of unauthorized persons shot a Filipino soldier that resulted in the outbreak of Filipino-American hostilities. In spite of the odds to fight a mighty enemy, it took almost three years to conquer the Filipinos and finally subjugate the Philippines under American control.

The initiative came from the Americans who approached Aguinaldo in Hongkong to persuade him to cooperate with Commodore Dewey to wrestle the power from the Spaniards.

While it may not be true to conclude that Dewey promised Aguinaldo that the Americans will eventually recognize the Philippines, by implication, an informal alliance existed between Aguinaldo and Dewey to fight a common enemy at that time, the Spaniards. It was, therefore, a valid reason to say that there was a moral and legal basis for the Americans to treat Aguinaldo as an ally, but surprisingly, what happened was the opposite; because Aguinaldo and his comrades were treated shabbily. The American attitude was an explicit manifestation that they only used Aguinaldo as a mere instrument for their deceptive selfish interest. Moreover, one can infer that they came to the Philippines pretending to be an ally, but actually as a foe, masked deceivingly as a friend. It was simple naïveté not to feel the American actuations of the series of incidents that happened that led to the suspicion and bitterness of Aguinaldo and his followers that the Americans were not sincere. In such an atmosphere of anxiety caused by deception and trickery, all that could be expected was distrust and friction.

American Policy in the Philippines. The American policy in the Philippines was contained in Mckinley's "Benevolent Assimilation" proclamation on December 21, 1898, indicating the intention of the United States to stay in the Philippines by directly exercising the right of sovereignty. This meant she had the control, supervision and disposition of the Philippines.

PRESIDENT MCKINLEY'S
"BENEVOLENT ASSIMILATION"
PROCLAMATION, DECEMBER 21, 1898

In performing this duty [the extension of American sovereignty throughout the Philippines by means of force] the military commander of the United States is enjoined to make known to the inhabitants of the Philippine Islands that in succeeding to the sovereignty of Spain, in severing the former political relations, and in establishing a new political power, the authority of the United States is to be exerted for the securing of the persons and property of the people of the Islands and for the confirmation of all private rights and relations. It will be the duty of the commander of the forces of occupation to announce and proclaim in the most public manner that we come not as invaders or conquerors, but as friends, to protect the natives in their homes, in their employment, and in their personal and religious rights. All persons who, either by active aid or by honest submission, cooperate with the Government of the United States to give effect to these beneficent purposes will receive the reward of its support and protection. All others will be brought within the lawful rule we have assumed, with firmness if need be, but without severity, so far as may be possible . . .

Finally, it should be the earnest and paramount aim of the military administration to win the confidence, respect, and affection of the inhabitants of the Philippines by assuring them in every possible way that full measure of individual rights and liberties which is the heritage of a free people, and by proving to them that the mission of the United States is one of benevolent assimilation, substituting the mild sway of justice and right for arbitrary rule. In the fulfillment of this high mission, supporting the temperate administration of affairs for the greatest good of the governed, there must be sedulously maintained the strong arm of authority, to repress disturbance and to overcome all obstacles to the bestowal of the blessings of good and stable government upon the people of the Philippine Islands under the free flag of the United States.

Meanwhile, a copy of the proclamation reached the officials of the Revolutionary Government, the Proclamation was instantly subjected to severe attack followed by verbal hasty and unfavorable criticism against the United States. Antonio Luna, editor of La Independencia (The Independence) commented that the proclamation was "merely a subterfuge to quiet the people temporarily until measures could be inaugurated and applied to put into practice all the odious features of government which Spain had employed" in the Philippines. immediately, Aguinaldo also issued a counter-proclamation on January 5, a part of which is read:

> My government cannot remain indifferent in view of such a violent and aggressive seizure of a portion of its territory by a nation, which arrogated to itself the title of champion of oppressed nations. Thus, it is that my government is disposed to open hostilities if the American troops attempt to take forcible possession of the Visayan islands. I denounce these acts before the world, in order that the conscience of mankind may pronounce its infallible verdict as to who are the true oppressors of nations and the tormentors of mankind...

General Elwell Otis of the United States Army said, the Aguinaldo proclamation was tantamount to war; so, he immediately deployed the American troops. With the tense atmosphere, the Filipinos were advised to seek refuge to safer places, while Aguinaldo's proclamation drew the Filipino people together with unwavering support and determined effort to fight the "friend" turned enemy.

The Tension Escalates. Aguinaldo attempted to soften the Filipino-American strained relationship, for he was aware that such a conflict with a powerful country would require painful sacrifices on the people, considering the insufficient and inferior arms the Filipino troops had against the American troops.

A conference was held to thresh out how the "adjustment of the political interests" could be resolved. This was attended by the respective representatives of both parties. The conference did not bear any tangible results. The American panel apparently was determined to mislead the Filipino panel into believing that they (the Americans) were ready to consider Filipino aspirations; but in reality, their plan about the conference was to continue indefinitely, pending the arrival of the American reinforcements from the United States.

The Filipino military officers suspected that the Americans

were resorting to delaying tactics since the American volunteers in Manila were not enough to fight the Filipinos. Meanwhile, another meeting of the Filipino and American representatives was scheduled on January 31, but because of the mounting tension and escalating restlessness and animosity of the Filipino against the Americans, it did not materialize.

The succeeding events showed clearly that the Americans came to the Philippines, not to liberate the Filipino people from the repressive Spanish government but as imperialists to subjugate the Philippines. The Filipinos having won their freedom from Spain, were ready to fight another invading nation at all costs in defense of their country.

The Incident in San Juan Bridge. In the evening of February 4, 1899, an American soldier named Private Willie W. Grayson, with two other members of his patrol were ascertaining whether there were Filipino soldiers in the vicinity when suddenly Grayson shot and killed a Filipino soldier who was about to cross the San Juan Bridge. Investigation of the incident was not conducted on the part of the American military authorities; but instead, they ordered an all-out assault against their former allies.

News of the outbreak of hostilities reached President Aguinaldo and other Filipino military officers. Immediately, he declared war on the United States who ignited this armed conflict.

The Armed Conflict Errupted. The American army, led by General MacArthur bombared the Filipino lives with accuracy, causing many Filipino casualties. In the battle of La Loma, near the Chinese Cemetery, a valiant major, Jose Torres Bugallon was mortally wounded. To avenge Bugallon's death, the Filipino defenders killed Major McConville in Pandacan. In the fierce battle that ensued, the American superiority in war weaponry proved victorious. Meanwhile, General Luna, undaunted by his defeat, prepared a strategic plan to get back Manila; so his men set fire burning houses and created confusion in the ranks of the enemy. The American troops with fire brigades rushed to the burning areas and put the flames out, while Luna and his troops advanced, reaching Azcarraga (now Claro M. Recto Avenue), but the Americans fought back and repulsed him and his troops with heavy casualties. Luna and his comrades hurriedly retreated to Polo (now Valenzuela City) in Bulacan, where he established his headquarters.

The American Drive to the North. When the Filipino troops were driven back in Manila, the American soldiers under the command of General MacArthur, began their offensive to the north with determined and continuous intensity. Their primary objective was to seize Malolos. The Filipino soldiers bravely put a defense to repulse the advancing American troops; but they were overwhelmed with superior force of the enemy. They retreated but they burned the towns of Polo and Meycauyan and destroyed bridges by using explosives in order to delay the coming of the American reinforcements.

General MacArthur captured Malolos on March 31, 1899, Aguinaldo left Malolos and established their headquarters in San Isidro, Nueva Ecija. General Elwell Otis was jubilant, when he learned about the fall of Malolos; because he believed that the Filipino resistance had been crushed; but he was wrong, because the seizure of Malolos from the hands of the Revolutionary soldiers only heralded to intensify more intensely with determination and collected efforts of the Filipinos to resist American invasion of their territory to the last drop of their blood.

After having a short respite in Malolos, General MacArthur continued his northward military offensive until the fierce Battle of Bagbag River in Kalumpit fell into the hands of the Americans.

On the other hand, General Lawton moved southward, capturing Las Pinas, Parañaque, Sta. Cruz, Paete and other towns in Laguna. The Americans were not always victorious in their offensive thrusts because the Filipinos repulsed General Wheston in Polo and killed Colonel Egbert, an

American military officer. On April 23, the American cavalry, under Major Bell, suffered a defeat in the hands of General del Pilar in Quingua (now Plaridel), Bulacan. In this encounter, Colonel Stotsenberg was also killed, while in the battle of San Mateo, General Lawton met his fatal end. Inspite of these victories, the Filipino troops who were poorly trained, inadequately armed, poorly fed, and utterly lacked the proper military discipline, could not turn the tide against the mighty enemy.

The Resignation of Mabini. Mabini, as President of the Council of Government, was looked up to as the most powerful man behind Aguinaldo. He urged the Filipino people to continue the struggle for independence when the United States government, and the Schurman Commission formally announced the policy of extending its sovereignty over the Philippines. In a manifesto dated April 15, 1899, at San Isidro,Nueva Ecija, he said:

> And since war is the last recourse that is left to us for the salvation of our country and our national honor, let us fight while a grain of strength is left us; let us acquit ourselves like men, even though the lot of the present generation is conflict and sacrifice. It matters not whether we die in the midst at the end of our most painful day's work. The generations to come, praying over our tombs, will shed for us tears of love and gratitude, and not of bitter reproach.

The secretary of State John Hay informed the Schurman Commission, authorizing it to offer autonomy to the Philippine government, but Mabini stood for independence. Pedro Paterno and other prominent members of the Malolos Government wanted to accept the American offer of autonomy. They believed that, under the prevailing circumstances, autonomy is better than independence. These influential members of the Filipino Assembly (formerly Congress) passed a resolution asking Aguinaldo to repudiate Mabini's position on the independence issue and to relieve him as President of the Cabinet. On May 7, 1899, Aguinaldo informed Mabini of the formation of a new Cabinet headed by Paterno. In response,

Mabini congratulated Aguinaldo on his "wise political decision." With Mabini's resignation, the executive arm of Aguinaldo's government was reorganized.

The Assassination of General Luna. The best general of the Philippine Republic to fight the Americans at that time was Antonio Luna. He was the younger brother of the famous painter who painted the Spoliarium. He studied military science and strategy in Europe. Luna was born a fearless fighter, but he was hot-tempered that men fear and hate him. A disciplinarian, he saw the necessity of instilling discipline in the minds of the men, most of whom were peasants or men with no military training at all. He conceived to recapture Manila but there was no support from the Kawit Company, who only received orders from Aguinaldo that consequently, led to disastrous results. He recommended to Aguinaldo the military insubordination and disarmed the soldiers in the Kawit Company, but Aguinaldo did not approve his recommendation. Naturally, Luna was disappointed and resented Aguinaldo's decision.

There were several instances, that Luna showed his terrible temper and sharp tongue that he created animosity with people in the revolutionary movement. On one occasion, he ordered the shooting of civilians who do not follow military rules. He also ordered the arrest of members of the Cabinet who had different political orientations and decisions with him about political matters. So impulsive that, without any provocation, he slapped Felipe Buencamino, Sr., and accused his son, of cowardice. Even Mabini who personified a man of peace and sobriety, in some instances, complained about Luna's unbecoming behavior and suggested to Aguinaldo that he should be replaced.

In Bayambang, Pangasinan, while he was preparing his troops for the defense against the enemy, he received a telegram from Aguinaldo to see him at his headquarters in Kabanatuan, so he promptly left Bayambang with his aide, Colonel Francisco Roman and a few soldiers. He arrived at the convent of Kabanatuan, Aguinaldo's headquarters where one of the members of the Kawit Company whom Luna recommended for punishment stood as guard. He slapped the sentry and went directly upstairs and found Buencamino whom he disliked intensely. Suddenly, a heated and nasty exchange of words was hurled against each other. Earlier, there were talks that Luna had insulted, not only Buencamino, but also Aguinaldo who left for San Isidro to inspect the troops. All of a sudden, a rifle shot rang out and so Luna rushed downstairs to reproach severely the soldier who fired. On the threshold a group of soldiers who belonged to the Kawit Company ganged on him by throwing fist blows while others stabbed and shot him. He was able to whip his pistol and fired but he missed his target. Colonel Roman hurriedly came to help him, but was also shot. So pathetic that Luna, the sharp shooter, fell on the ground, catching his breath with mouth slightly open and muttering: "Cow......wards! As......sas........sins!" The wounds he sustained were fatal. He was buried with appropriate honors due his rank. There were no records that the assassins were investigated; nor were they punished for the unfortunate incident that caused the life of a Filipino general.

War Continued in the Visayas. The next offensive thrusts of the Americans were the Visayas and other group of islands. General Otis ordered General Miller to bombard Iloilo and demanded the surrender of the City; but the Filipino troops commanded by General Delgado refused; and instead, decided to fight against odds. Delgado ordered the burning of the city to confuse the enemy and to prevent them from using it as a strategic place for operations. Because of the superior military force of the Americans, the city of Jaro fell on February 20, followed by Sta. Barbara on the 14th, Oton on the 19th, and Manduriao on the 20th. The rage of war continued; and on February 22, Cebu City was taken by the Americans, followed by Samar, Leyte, Masbate, Marinduque, Palawan, and other cities and provinces in the South on different dates.

The Hostilities in Mindanao. The United States military continued its offensive strategy where two battalions of American troops landed in Jolo on May 19, 1899, to bring the

Muslim Filipinos of Sulu and other parts of Mindanao within the jurisdiction of American sovereignty.

Meanwhile, the Filipino patriots in Zamboanga who were determined to defend their country and its interests at all cost, captured men with large piles of machine guns and rifles from the Spanish gunboats in Basilan which they used in attacking the Spaniards in Basilan, Zamboanga.

In the provinces of Cotobato, Misamis, and Surigao, the Christian Filipinos also demonstrated their unwavering support and adherence of the Philippine Independence. Since Spain no longer had authority to rule over the archipelago, the Spanish troops left Mindanao to be occupied by the American soldiers.

The Bates Treaty

In an attempt to win the Muslims, the American authorities appointed and sent General John C. Bates to negotiate a treaty with Sultan Jamalul Kiram II by which the Muslims and Americans could co-exist peacefully. The Americans apparently had no attempt to conquer the Muslims; because they were aware that they would have a big fight to conquer them.

After the negotiation represented by both parties, the treaty was approved. The highlights of the provisions were:

1. The sovereignty of the United States over the whole archipelago of Jolo and its dependencies is declared and acknowledged;

2. The rights and dignities of His Highness, the Sultan, and his datus shall be fully respected;

3. The Muslims shall not be interfered with on account of their religion;

4. That no one shall be persecuted on account of his beliefs;

5. The domestic products of the archipelago of Jolo, were
    carried on by the Sultan and his people within any
    part of the Philippine Islands, and when conducted
    under the American flag, shall be free, limited and
    free of duty.

In addition, the American Government agreed to pay the
Sultan and his datus monthly in Mexican dollars. With
diplomatic skills, the Americans concluded a treaty anchored
on mutual understanding; and consequently, succeeded in
neutralizing the Muslims in their drive to pacify the Christian
Filipinos in the Archipelago.

Guerilla Warfare. General Aguinaldo took personal
command of the Filipino army when General Luna died. With
his assassination Filipino troops became demoralized. Without
the military discipline and expertise of Luna, the Filipino forces
suffered heavy casualties. In the war zones of Central Luzon,
Generals Mascardo, Hizon and Aquino and other commanders
were overwhelmed by their opponents. To overcome these
surmounting difficulties and to keep the spirit of resistance
alive, Aguinaldo and his men resorted to guerilla warfare. He
divided the country into military zones and commandered by
guerilla leader whose members were small independent band
of soldiers. They harassed the enemies by surprise attacks and
destroyed their communication facilities. The Filipino
guerrillas gained some headway in this strategy because they
were familiar with the terrain of the place, giving them military
advantages after some surprise attacks on American outposts
and headquarters at night and ambushing enemy patrols. In
effect, the Filipino troops employing guerrilla warfare were
successful to a certain extent and it kept the war to drag.

The Filipino Women and the War. The Filipino women,
during the dark days of our history, contributed their share to
the cause of their country. When the war broke out, many
prominent and patriotic women notably Cresencia San
Agustin de Santos served as a volunteer nurse in the hospital
of Imus, Cavite; Trinidad Tecson rendered health services in
Biyak-na-Bato; Agueda Kahabagan, woman general of Laguna

won recognition for her war exploits; and Teresa Magbanua
for her military heroic deed on Panay battlefields.

These patriotic and heroic achievements of our Filipino
women during the trying times of our country were living
testimonies of a people whose love for their fatherland is par
excellence and to be emulated.

Aguinaldo Fled to the Mountains. Running away from
the advancing American troops to escape from being captured,
Aguinaldo with his militarymen, headed by General Gregorio
del Pilar, the members of his family and some members of his
Cabinet hurriedly left Bayambang, Pangasinan on board a train
bound to Calasiao. While the American forces were moving
swiftly to all directions to trap him, Aguinaldo fled through
valleys, rivers, ravines and mountain trails, day and night,
occasionally stopping only for a brief respite. Through the
rugged hills and steep mountains of Northern Luzon, he
passed through Tirad Pass, proceeding to Cagayan Valley,
then to Palanan, Isabela, where he established his
headquarters.

The Battle of Tirad Pass. The Pass has an altitude of
4,500 feet high and commanded a good view many kilometers
around. The trail, which led to it was so narrow and steep that
only one man at a time could climb using both feet and hand
with sustained effort and difficulty. Del Pilar ordered his men
to build trenches-long narrow excavation in the ground to
serve as shelter from the enemies' fire on both shoulders of
the Pass so that they could see the movement of the enemy
below.

The American forces under Major March pursued
Aguinaldo relentlessly to capture the Filipino leader. For him,
this is the only way to end Filipino resistance against American
rule. On December 2, he went on with his comrades leading
to Tirad Pass. From atop the Tirad Pass, the Filipino troops
fired their rifles at the advancing enemies. But unfortunately,
through Januario Galut, an Igorot led the Americans and found
a secret trail to the top. Using this opportunity to advantage
the Americans surprised General Del Pilar and his men. It was

144 PHILIPPINE HISTORY AND GOVERNMENT THROUGH THE YEARS

just a matter of minutes that the Filipino defenders were overcome by the American forces. During the brief encounter, General Del Pilar was wounded in the shoulder and ordered his remaining comrades to escape. He strove to slip away to avoid being captured. As he mounted his white horse, a shot rang out and the fatal bullet hit his neck. With him died a number of Filipino defenders.

The pathetic incident left General Del Pilar's body by the way side for two days. Because of its odor some Igorots covered it with some sand and dried leaves. On his diary, and other valuable memetos which Major March found, had written:

The General Aguinaldo has given me the pick of all the men that can be spared and ordered me to defend the Pass. I realize what a terrible task has been given me; and yet, I feel that this is the most glorious moment of my life. What I do is done for my beloved country. No sacrifice can be too great.

Shortly, thereafter, the tragic encounter, Aguinaldo received the fatal news. All the followers of the Aguinaldo party said one of the soldiers in diary, "shed bitter tears and all wanted to fight the Americans."

The Capture of Aguinaldo. After the fight at Tirad Pass, the American authorities lost track of Aguinaldo's whereabouts. With the Filipino forces virtually deprived of its leader, many of them were contemplating to surrender to the enemy. Meantime, the Americans started to conduct an intensive campaign of propaganda to win over the Filipinos to their side by involving prominent Filipinos like Cayetano Arellano, Pedro Paterno, Felipe Buencamino, Pardo de Tevera, and Benito Legarda that a better solution for peaceful existence could be reached under the Americans. Some Filipino collaborators, disgusted about the prolonged battle resulting in the death of many Filipino troops and destruction to property, appealed to the guerrillas to give up their arms.

While the American peace initiatives were going on, General Frederich Funston was secretly preparing the capture of Aguinaldo. With him were American officers, two former officers of the Filipino army, Lazaro Segovia and Hilario Tal Placido and some Macabebe scouts. He quietly sailed off Manila Bay on board the warship Vicksburg and landed at dawn at Casiguran Bay, and there walked briskly through a dangerously thick forests. Funston and his American troops, pretending to be captives of the Macabebe scouts arrived at Palanan on March 23, 1901. Aguinaldo and his men met them politely and even served them food. Unaware of treacherous design, suddenly the Macabebes turned against their countrymen and without any warning Tal Placido grabbed Aguinaldo from behind, holding him helpless. At this juncture, firing ensured and Tal Placido fell, while Segovia started to fire indiscriminately like a mad man, and Colonel Simeon Villa, fearing that Aguinaldo might be shot and killed, bravely shielded him from the bullets. Aguinaldo attempted to fight back by whipping his pistol but Dr. Santaigo Barcelona instinctively held him by the arms, saying; "My General, you owe it to our people to live and continue fighting for freedom." General Funston and his American companions entered the room and arrested General Aguinaldo in the name of the United States Government. Thereafter, Aguinaldo was brought to Manila on April 1, and was courteously received by General MacArthur and some American officials where he took his oath of allegiance to the United States Government. After this dramatic historic event ending the Filipino-American hostilities, General Aguinaldo issued a proclamation on April 19, purportedly appealing to the Filipino people to accept the "sovereignty of the Philippines."

Barbaric Acts vis-à-vis War. War is a phenomenon in the history of humanity. War is waged in order to obtain economic and political goals and concessions, and to dominate. War is very destructive and its results cause too much pain and sufferings. In all types of armed conflict, in most cases brutality and various barbarous acts are practiced by opposing protagonists to weaken the enemy's resistance. The Filipino-Americans were no exception, considering that they belonged to different races and civilizations.

One type of brutality was the "cure" where a man was forced to lie flat on his back, his mouth forced open by a stick or a bayonet, and then water was poured into his mouth until his stomach expanded like a balloon. This was just one of the varieties in the mode of torture the Filipinos suffered in order to force them to reveal the movements and other strategies of the guerrillas.

In some cases, in their desperation, the American soldiers resorted to burn villages in order to force the enemy to come out. To avenge the death of some American soldiers, they indiscriminately burned to the ground houses of the natives and those suspected of sympathizing with the guerrillas were shot. These barbaric acts were not only committed by the American troops, but also committed by the Filipino guerrillas. There were some incidents were American soldiers who were captured by the guerrillas who were slapped and kicked as an outburst of their hatred.

These brutalities were unveiled from the Filipino soldiers and from eyewitnesses from the Americans themselves. In the moment of their solitude, some American soldiers could not get over with the agony brought about by the war and included in their letters and diaries the details of brutalities by way of communication to their parents and friends or in testimonies before American investigating bodies.

The End of Filipino-American War. In spite of the surrender of Aguinaldo and the Filipino soldiers to the American authorities and the American peace efforts and propaganda on a better future for the Filipinos, some Filipino commanders refused to lay their arms. General Miguel Malvar took over the leadership of the Filipino Government and relentlessly harassed the Americans by his guerilla tactics and continued the hopeless fight. In Samar, General Vicente Lukban and his troops ambused American soldiers, killing and wounding them. The relentless offensive strategy and campaign of the Americans led to the capture of Lukban on February 27, 1902 and eventually resulted in the collapse of the resistance in Samar. A few months later, the fiery and fearless General Malvar of Batangas finally surrendered to the

American authorities on April 16, 1902. Even with the surrender of General Malvar and other revolutionary officers in Luzon, some patriotic Filipinos, led by Macario Sakay, continued the resistance movement and established a Tagalog "Republic" with headquarters in Sierra Madre where they eventually surrendered to the American army.

Meantime, there were still pockets of rebellion in some parts of the Philippines keeping the torch of freedom aflame by some Filipino fighters in defense of their country and people, but their resistance were not enough to endanger the American rule.

It is interesting to note especially among historians that the capture of Aguinaldo ended an epochal period in the life of a nation, and, at the same time opened another. Aguinaldo left behind him the endearing memories of a people determined to win freedom and independence at all costs through blood and tears.

❖

Study Guides

A. Terms/Concepts to Understand

animosity	subterfuge
subjugate	autonomy
shabbily	pathetic
deceptive	odds
naivete	relentless

B. Questions to Answer

1. Enumerate the various incidents that contributed and eventually precipitated the Filipino-American animosity.

2. What was the primary policy of the Americans, after conquering the archipelago?

3. Describe the San Juan incident. What was the effect?

4. Why did the American forces drive to the North? What were the results?

5. Why did Mabini resign from the Aguinaldo government? Do you think he made the right decision?

6. Describe General Antonio Luna as a military officer.

7. Describe the death of General Luna. Did he deserve that kind of death? Explain your answer.

8. What was the Treaty of Bates all about?

9. What guerilla warfare was resorted to by the revolutionary Filipinos?

10. What could be learned from the Filipino-American animosity?

Chapter 11

The Issue on Religion

Gregorio Aglipay gained national prominence in the wake of demands within the leadership of the Revolutionary Government in 1899 for the Filipinization of the Catholic Church. Appointed Military Vicar General of the Revolution by President Aguinaldo on October 20, 1899, Aglipay used the Filipino clergy at that time to unite and ask the Pope to appoint Filipinos in all church positions from the archbishop down to the last parish priest. Aglipay agreed with and wholeheartedly endorsed a plan of Apolinario Mabini for the organization of a church administered by Filipinos. In July 1901, a radical reformists, Isabelo delos Reyes, returned to the Philippines from Rome and urged the establishment of Iglesia Filipina Independiente, marking officially the beginning of the schism with Rome. Aglipay accepted the position of Supreme Bishop of the New Church.

The story of the birth of the Aglipayan Church as a tangible result of the revolution can be attributed to the struggle of the Filipino priest to have the control in the administration of the Catholic Church in the Philippines.

The Philippine Revolution of 1896, to a great extent, was not only a conflict of political issues but also religion and races-people related by common descent and heredity. This was apparently shown in the Filipino civil service servants in the government and clerical groups against the Spanish civil and clerical segment. The friars of the Catholic Church were the primary oppressors, aided by the colonial government on the policy of repression. Mabini, in his letter, to General Otis in

149

1898, accused the Spanish friars of giving comfort to the Spanish government and taking up arms when necessity arose, against the Filipino rebels.

Upon the return of Aguinaldo from Hongkong, Governor-General Basilio Augustin and Archbishop Bernardino Nozaleda, aware of the sympathy of Father Aglipay to Spain, but belligerent to the United States became a pawn between the two forces perhaps not knowing each of them had its deliberate design. He was commissioned by Spain and the United States to confer with revolutionary leaders, particularly Mariano Trias, Artemio Ricarte and Emiliano Riego de Dios, in order to persuade them back to the Spanish government. The bait was attractive enough to entice them over to their side, it was the promise of autonomy, so Aglipay did what he was told; but his efforts were a failure because the revolutionary leaders had eventually lost their trust and confidence to the Spanish promises.

In the meantime, Aguinaldo sent Colonel Luciano San Miguel as his emissary to Aglipay to persuade him for the Filipino cause, but Nozaleda immediately countered commissioning Aglipay to win over Aguinaldo to the Spanish side. Aguinaldo did not accede and urged Aglipay to go to the North to work for the Revolutionary Government. Nozaleda, not to be outdone by the decision of Aguinaldo also, encouraged Aglipay to proceed to the North not to follow Aglipay's orders, purportedly to investigate the prevailing condition of the diocese of Nueva Segovia. Aglipay traveled and visited every parish in the northern provinces and eventually secured the release of two Jesuit priests. When he returned to Manila to report the results of his travel, he was surprised to find the entire city besieged. The surroundings had been isolated and looked like an abandoned place. With this condition staring at him, he hurriedly went to Cavite to join Aguinaldo and the Revolutionary Movement.

The Revolutionary Government, at the suggestion of Mabini, who was a lawyer, refused to recognize Nozaleda's authority. He urged every Filipino clergy from accepting any ecclesiastical responsibility from the Catholic Church or from occupying vacant parishes without the approval of the Revolutionary Government. The Revolutionary Government recognized the validity of civil marriage. The prevailing conditions and the state of political affairs were favorable for the Revolutionary Government to win the full support and cooperation of the Filipino priests in the Philippines. with the surrounding circumstances, Aguinaldo issued a decree on October 20, 1898, appointing Aglipay Military Vicar General – the religious leader of the revolutionary movement.

Friction Between Aglipay and Nozaleda. The position of Aglipay in the Revolutionary Government as Military Vicar General and another position in the Hierarchy of the Catholic Church as Ecclesiastical Governor of the Diocese of Nueva Segovia at the same time showed clearly conflict of interest. Being a Filipino he was duty bound to support the revolutionists' cause and, at the same time, being a Catholic priest he had to support the head of the church who was a Spaniard and had complete allegiance to colonial government. Aglipay, a priest of principle, moral strength and fortitude had chosen to be Filipino, first and a Catholic second. After his appointment as Military Vicar General, he issued a letter to the Filipino priests urging them to organized themselves into cohesive body or a council which would ask the Pope to appoint only Filipinos in all churches in the Philippines from Archbishop to the lowest parish priest. He also urged all the priests to rally to the revolutionary movement and consolidate all efforts for the noble cause of the Filipino priest. The ecclesiastical leadership of Aglipay made him popular and because of this, Nozaleda deeply alarmed, charged him with usurpation of power and urged the Ecclesiastical Tribunal to punish the Filipino clergy by the way of excommunication. The Tribunal issued a decree of excommunication declaring Aglipay a usurper and a schismatic with this ecclesiastical power play Nozaleda knew that excommunication was an effective instrument of the prelates to force Catholic priests to toe the line of the church hierarchy. This kind of punishment not only caused the excommunicated priest embarrassment and humiliation but also deprived him of communion and other sacraments. He will also be disqualified from ecclesiastical fellowship of the Catholic Church but Nozaleda committed a big blunder. Aglipay was a strong man of character and conviction and, instead of bending with his knees to ask for forgiveness before the Spanish Archbishop, he returned the compliment by declaring Nozaleda excommunicated. He charged him of starving the people and collaborating with the Spaniards and Americans in the latter's policy of unjust repression. Consequently, the Nozaleda excommunication decree did not have its weight with the people especially the members of the clergy.

Mabini and the Filipino National Church. Apolinario Mabini, a man of a rare courage and fortitude and an uncompromising nationalist, was aware of the necessity of having a church administered by the Filipinos. In one of his out of town sojourn, while having his summer vacation in Pangasinan, Mabini wrote a manifesto to the Filipino clergy urging them to unite themselves and organize a Filipino National Church in the Philippines. Apart of the excerpts of his manifesto said:

> Let the Filipino clergy show their zeal and love for the church; let them show their capacity to govern not only the parishes but also the diocese; let them show that the regular orders are not needed in the Philippines to maintain alive the faith in justice as a Vicar of Christ who is God, has to recognize the rights and merits of the Filipino priests. This is the most opportune occasion, which Divine Providence offers them to obtain the reparation of their grievances; those who aspire to be something more than mere coadjutors and pages must not let this occasion pass.

Mabini advocated the absolute preservation of the church, but it must upheld the appointment of Filipino clergy to all the positions. This National Filipino Church was primarily conceived by Mabini to cooperate completely with the Filipinos' quest for independence.

The Filipinization of the Catholic Church. The conception of the Filipino National Church and the call for Filipino clergy was gaining headway and this movement heartened them to believe that the time was ripe to assert their rights, not only in occupying the parishes throughout the archipelago but to direct the administration of ecclesiastical affairs. Aglipay, in his capacity as Military Vicar General, called the Filipino priests to an ecclesiastical assembly at Panique, Tarlac on October 23, 1899 and stated the primary objectives of the Filipinization of the Catholic Church, The Constitutional framework of the Provisional Constitution of the Filipino Church "explicitly outlined the vision, mission, structure and composition of the Filipino church. The nationalistic favor and temper of the Filipino clergy were expressed in the canons, which provided that foreign bishops were not allowed, except under extraordinary cases. The constitution, in effect, declared the independence of the Filipino clergy from Spanish ecclesiastical authority the control, direction and supervision. Thereafter, the assumption to negotiate with the proper ecclesiastical body in Rome did not fully develop because the Filipino Government was on the verge of falling apart and Aglipay was in the battlefield helping the cause of the Filipino rebels.

Monsieur Chapelle and Filipinization. Mons. Placido Chapelle, an American Apostolic Delegate to the Philippines, arrived on January 2, 1900 before the impending collapse of the revolutionary movement. His initial move was to drive the Filipino clergy away from Rome, because the moment he arrived in the Philippines, he arrogantly announced that he would treat Filipino clergy who opposed the friars in ecclesiastical affairs as enemies of religion and order. He even bragged that he can dominate the Filipino clergy by force, civil and ecclesiastical, for he was sent by the Pope as his representative, besides being an American. Being an American, he asserted that he can carry the authority of the United States and would use force and coercion on the Filipino clergy to make it difficult for the Spanish friars to return to their parishes. In a display of haughtiness and a feeling of superiority, he made a daring assertion that the heels of the revolutionary leaders should he cut off so that peace and order will reign. On one occasion, he stated with conviction that the Filipino priests were incompetent and only capable of holding menial position in the Church. Such an unfounded and nasty statement led the Filipinos even the rabid Catholics to dislike him. This open contempt for the Filipino clergy stirred the emotions of revolutionary leaders and eventually led them (the Filipino clergy) to close ranks and joined the religious movement purportedly seeking independence from the Vatican.

The Religious Schism. One of the contributing factors that led to separation of Aglipay and the Filipino clergy from the Catholic Church stemmed from Chapelle's undiplomatic language and his misleading perception about the Filipinos' political and religious aspirations. The unfolding developments brought about by Chapelle's hostile attitude, the Filipino clergy, insulted with contemptuous rudeness of action and speech were now determined for a Filipino church. In Rome, some Filipino priests, had sought an audience with the Pope expressing their problems. However, the Pope was inclined to listen more to the Spanish friars than to the Filipino priests. As a result, nothing concrete happened.

In the meantime, in Spain, Isabelo delos Reyes, a scholar, and nationalist radical propagandist came out with a newspaper Filipinas Ante Europa (Filipinos before Europe) and passionately wrote an article a part of which read:

Enough of Rome! Let us now form without vacillation our own congregation, a Filipino Church, conserving all that is good in the Roman Church and eliminating all the deceptions, which the diabolical astuteness of the Cunning Romanists had introduced to corrupt the moral purity and sacredness of the doctrine of Christ...

Upon his return to the Philippines in the early part of 1901, delos Reyes campaigned vigorously for the establishment of a Filipino Church. He later founded the first labor union in the Philippines, the Union Obrera Democratica (Democratic

Labor Union). Its founding gave a broad base for the religious movement because the masses were supportive of the cause of the Filipino clergy. On one occasion, Pascual H. Poblete, a radical Filipino journalist and a staunch anti-friar, scheduled a mass meeting at the Zorrilla Theater at the Azcarraga (now Claro M. Recto Avenue) and Evangelista Streets to attack the malpractices of the friars but because of inclement weather, it did not materialize. That same night, Isabelo delos Reyes also called a meeting of his Democratic Labor Union at Center of Arts attended by huge crowd and delivered an anti-friar speech and the establishment of the Filipino Church independent of Vatican with Aglipay as the Supreme Bishop. The new Church was called Iglesia Filipina Independiente (Philippine Independent Church). The founding of the New Church was enthusiastically and loudly cheered by the people when delos Reyes made the announcement. With the founding of the Philippine Independent Church, the religions schism with the Vatican began.

Isabelo delos Reyes, a man of vision and determination to give dignity to the religious movement placed in the list big names; e.g., Trinidad Pardo de Tavera, Fernando Ma. Guerrero, Manuel Ortigas and prominent lay leaders and some priests in the Executive Committee of the New Church without consulting them. These well-meaning leaders and priests, though not hostile to the movement, were not all ready to lend their names in the new church. Another misfortune that was decisively important came from Aglipay himself who did not endorse the approval of the schism for he believed that all the surrounding circumstances should be evaluated and all means should be exhausted to come to an understanding with Rome before taking any radical step. At that time, Aglipay was still busy conferring with the Jesuits, hoping that the problem can be patched up.

Delos Reyes was naturally disappointed; however, he was consoled by the fact that the masses understood the meaning of the religious movement and came to his rescue.

Many residents of Navotas, Rizal, and other towns in

Cavite and Bataan started to send their affiliation papers. Toward the end of the year, there were a number of Filipino priests who were affiliated with the new Church and soon thereafter, followed by the defection of Father Pedro Brillantes of Ilocos Sur and other priests of his province. In no time, they too embraced the new faith of religious affinity.

Aglipay and the Jesuits. Aglipay was visibly irked when his name was included as the Supreme Bishop of the new Church, because at that time he was still conferring with the Jesuits and other ecclesiastical heads of the Catholic Church in a last attempt to prevent its division into opposing groups. The Jesuits, through Dr. Leon Ma. Guerrero and Joaquin Luna, were with Aglipay in the La Ignaciana which housed the Jesuit House in Herran street (now Pedro Gil) in Sta. Ana, Manila, threshing the problem and how it can be resolved. The Jesuits chose Father Francisco Foradada, a Spaniard-astute and an eminent author of a book in the Philippines to work on the Filipino clergy.

After a few days, Foradada exerted his power and influence to persuade Aglipay to return to the Catholic church and handed a document to him for his signature. The said document obviously, was a confession of the Catholic faith that he was returning to Catholism and a clear retraction of what he had done. Aglipay read and studied the document; but when Foradada would take the document he had not signed it yet; so Foradada promised that he would be appointed bishop with a large sum of money. He was indignant and said, "I would sign this document, not for the service gallantry, but for consolidating the religious peace in my country; but can you assure me, Father, that with the publication of this document, the situation of the friars in the country will be saved? Can you guarantee at least that with the signing of this document the problem of the native priests will be solved?"

At this juncture, Foradada, over-confident and rudely arrogant blurted: "Why do you mind so much the Filipino priests, since all the world knows that they are vicious and hopelessly inefficient?" Provoked, Aglipay trembled, and with outraged fury, turned to the proud priest and held him by the nape of his neck, and shouted at the top of his voice, "Either you withdraw that odious calummy, Father Forodada, at this moment, I will forever end your slanderous impertinences."

The haughty and overbearing Spaniard, terrified at Aglipay's wrath, because of the false and malicious statements he made, fell on his knees, trembling and clasping his hands asked for forgiveness.

The commotion caught the attention of Dr. Leon Ma. Guerrero and Joaquin Luna to enter the room. Aglipay, thinking the two came to help the embattled Jesuit, turned to them saying: Do not intervene in this affair, for it is not your concern. Remember that the blood of your brother is still fresh in our fields. If that precious blood had been shed, if our Revolution took place, it was because of the tolerance of Rome in the excesses and malpractices of the friars against the Filipino people and the native priests which eventually drove them to risk all perils and sacrifice to emancipate them from the bondage of despotic authority."

Before leaving the building, Aglipay stated with conviction: "Your provocative insults took off the mask from your face." I am convinced that the ecclesiastical authorities of Rome are incapable of dealing justly with the Filipinos. By that time you will learn how to respect the character and efficiency of the Filipinos, for I will prove that we are able not only to administer dioceses, but also to establish modern churches free from all foreign interference."

There were several attempts to bring back Aglipay to the Catholic fold to repair the damage made by Foradada. Through Fr. Theo Rogers, he was invited to a conference in Intramuros with Father Joaquin Vilallonga. Vilallonga, with diplomacy urged Aglipay to forget the new church and even assured him that "anything you ask will be granted by His Holiness, on condition that you help bring to an end the schismatic movement you initiated." Aglipay expressed appreciation on the kind words of Father Vilallonga, but for him, he was only asking justice and sincere love for the Filipino people. He further stated that: "The Philippine Independent church, of which I am the head, is spreading throughout the Archipelago and its object is no other than the reestablishment of the rational worship of the only God in all His Splendor, and at the same time, to prove to the world the ability of the Filipino to enjoy an independent religious life."

All the efforts made by Father Vilallonga and the juicy positions promised Aglipay just to bring him back to the Catholic fold bore nothing. For Aglipay, "The Philippine Independent Church will go on, and neither the Pope nor all the Jesuits living now and thereafter will be able to impede it. Aglipay will live and die as poor as when he was born, but he will never betray the interests of his people."

Aglipay was consecrated as Supreme Bishop by the bishops of Cagayan, Isabela, Abra, Pangasinan, Nueva Ecija, Cavite and Manila, on January 18, 1903. The Filipino Independent Church was on its way to convert Filipinos in its homeland to a Church that was free to develop and to preach the gospel of truth and justice as it saw fit without any interference from the Vatican or his representative.

Significance of Religious Schism. The conception and birth of the Filipino Independent Church was an offshoot of the Filipino clergy to centuries of disparagement and prejudice. The Spanish prejudice stemmed from the feeling of racial superiority and the perceived incompetence of the Filipino clergy. The Spanish racial prejudice was so intense that it stemmed impossible for the friars to overcome it, for they considered the Filipinos incapable of learning. Even in the face of military defeat, the friars could not believe so they still insisted the continuation of the *status quo.* It was this stubborn refusal of the Spanish friars to accept the reality staring at their faces about the changing conditions that was responsible for the alienation of the Filipino clergy from the Catholic Church in the archipelago.

Aglipay had exhausted all means to prevent a break with the Vatican, but the nationalist movement had gained its momentum reaching its summit and there was no turning back.

The Revolution contributed two tangible results in the life of the Filipinos – the end of abuse and misrule, and the alienation of a segment of the population of Philippine society from the Catholic Church. With the establishment of the Philippine Independent Church, the Filipino people were able to demonstrate with determined effort, courage, fortitude and tenacity of spirit, which exemplified their character at its highest and loftiest measure. The political upheaval of the Revolution ended with a religious triumph.

Study Guides

A. Terms/Concepts to Understand

schism	usurpation
descent	excommunication
belligerent	ecclesiastical
virtual	haughty
besiege	servile

B. Questions to Answer

1. Why is religion a universal institution?

2. How does religion affect the lives of the people?

3. Is there a separation of church and state in the Philippines? Explain your answer.

4. Why did Gregorio Aglipay gain national prominence during the Philippine Revolution? Explain your answer.

5. What were the factors that contributed to the issue on religious schism?

6. Describe the friction between Bernardino Nozaleda and Gregorio Aglipay.

7. Describe the Filipinization of the Catholic Church.

8. Who was Isabelo delos Reyes? What significant role did he play during the Philippine Revolution?

9. Describe Father Francisco Foradada as a Catholic priest.

10. What two tangible results did the Revolution contribute in the lives of the Filipinos?

Chapter 12

The Philippines under the American Rule

The American rule in the Philippines lasted from 1898 to 1946. During her rule, she trained the Filipinos in self-government and prepared them for independence.

Step by step, the Filipinos gained experience in the rudiments of good government and the principles of democracy. On July 4, 1901, the Civil Government was established, replacing the Military Government. A year later, on July 1, 1902, the United States Congress passed the Philippine Bill and established the Philippine Assembly.

The provisions of the Philippine Bill of 1902 were: (1) extension of the Bill of Rights to the Filipino people, except the right of trial by jury; (2) appointment of two Filipino resident commissioners to Washington; (3) establishment of an elective Philippine Assembly, after the proclamation of complete peace, and after the publication of a census; (4) retention of the Philippine Commission as the upper house of the legislature, with the Philippine Assembly acting as the lower house; and (5) the consultation on the natural resources of the Philippines for the Filipinos.

The American Policy on Filipinization. The United States adopted the policy of gradual substitution of American with Filipino personnel in the government service as one of the governing principles of American colonial policy.

Taft Commission and Filipinization. President McKinley instructed the Philippine Commission to prepare the guidelines for the gradual Filipinization of the government. The members of the Commission were tasked to devote their time to the establishment of municipal governments in which the Filipinos would have the opportunity to run their own civil affairs subject to the supervision and control of the Americans. The Taft Commission was also ordered by President McKinley through the recommendations of the Schurman Commission to consider the extension of a system of primary education, which shall be free for all. This was one of the administrative policies of preparing the Filipinos for self-government. Since there was diversity of Philippine Languages, the Commission was advised by the President of the United States to give special attention to the dissemination of the English language as a medium of instruction.

The resistance of the Filipinos to the imposition of American sovereignty convinced the Americans to formulate a policy of government that would reduce the opposition. Filipinization, as an administrative policy of the United States, was dictated by political and economic factors.

The uncertainty of American tenure in the Philippines was another consideration for Filipinization.

The motivations of Filipinization saw to it that Americans still controlled the strategic positions in government, especially positions which had to do with the formulation and implementation of important policy decisions. The governor-general remained under the control of an American who enjoyed the confidence of the president of the Unites States. The United States president rejected the demands of the Filipino leaders that the office of the governor-general should be given to a Filipino in 1920. The Department of Public Instruction remained in American hands until the establishment of the Commonwealth Government in 1935. The Americans allowed the Filipinos to participate in the legislature process; the Congress of the United States reserved its prerogative the sole power and authority to nullify laws enacted by the Philippine Legislature.

Training for Self-Government. The training for self-government included the reorganization of the municipal government, on January 31, 1901, in accordance with McKinley's instruction that the Filipinos should be allowed to manage their own municipal governments.

The Provincial Code (Act No. 83), enacted by the Philippine Commission on February 6, 1901, placed the provincial government under a board composed of a governor, a treasurer and a supervisor. Qualified Filipinos were elected to the office of governor for a term of two years by municipal councils in the province.

Filipinization of National Government. In spite of the inadequacy of the administration of justice and charges of incompetence against judges who were trained in the Spanish colonial judicial system, the American authorities first prioritized the judicial branch of the government by issuing a number of orders, which served to reorganize the judicial branch system in the Philippines. The Supreme Court, the highest judicial body composed of nine justices, six of whom were Filipinos, was created in May 1899. Cayetano Arellano, a native of Orion, Bataan, was appointed the first justice of the Supreme Court, which he held until his retirement. Other Filipino jurists who rendered exemplary service in the Supreme Court during the first decade of the American rule were Victorino Mapa, Florentino Torres and Manuel Araullo.

The Jones Law (1916). The Jones Law was the first American formal and official commitment to grant independence to the Philippines. The Jones Law, in its preamble, proposed "to withdraw the American sovereignty over the Philippine Islands and to recognize their independence as soon as a stable government can be established." To achieve this purpose, the preamble declared it "desirable to place in the hands of the people of the Philippines the control of their domestic affairs so they may be better prepared to assume fully the responsibilities and enjoy the privileges and blessings of complete independence. The Jones Law became a virtual constitutional compact between the American and the Filipino peoples. Under the Jones Law, the Filipinos controlled the Legislature, but not

the executive and judicial branches of the government. The
Governor-General, the Insular Auditor and majority of the
justices of the Supreme Court were Americans. They were
appointed by the president of the United States.

The Philippine Legislature under the Jones Law. The
Jones Law gave the Filipinos complete control of the
Legislature. The Philippine Legislature under the Jones Law
was inaugurated at Manila on October 16, 1916. Manuel L.
Quezon was the President of the Senate, while Sergio Osmena,
was elected Speaker of the House of Representatives.

The first important law was the reorganization of the
executive departments. The six departments were: (1) Interior,
(2) Finance, (3) Public Instruction, (4) Justice, (5) Agriculture
and Natural Resources, and (6) Commerce and
Communication. Each of these departments was placed under
a secretary.

The heads of the executive departments constituted the
Cabinet, which acted as an advisory body to the Governor-
General.

The Council of State was created by virtue of an Executive
Order dated October 16, 1918, by Governor Harrison. The body
consisted of a Governor-General, the department secretaries,
the Speaker of the House of Representatives, and the President
of the Senate. The chairman of the Council was the Governor-
General; the Vice-Chairman was the Speaker of the House.

The functions of the Council of State were: (1) to advice
the Governor-General on matters of importance; (2) to prepare
and approve the budget before the Governor-General
submitted it to the Legislature; and to determine the policies
of the various executive departments.

National Civil Service. On September 19, 1900, the
Philippine Commission enacted the Civil Service Act (No. 5),
which placed all classified employees in all divisions and
agencies of insular, provincial and municipal governments
under the administrative control of the Bureau of Civil Service.
The Civil Service Law required all prospective government

employees to submit a competitive examination that would give them eligibility.

The civil service in the Philippines, as envisioned by the Civil Service Act, should be free from in the intervention of the Church and the intervention of politics or the "spoils system," whether Filipino or American.

The Harrison Administration. Francis Burton Harrison succeeded William Cameron Forbes and paved the way for the rapid Filipinization of the civil service. The Filipinos gained greater autonomy and control in practically all branches of government.

Harrison's first administrative reform was to make the Filipinos the majority in the Philippine Commission. The executive bureaus became Harrison's next objective of Filipinization. He affected Filipinization by reducing the number of highly paid officials, most of whom were Americans.

The enactment of the Civil Retirement Act No. 2589 in February 1916, further accelerated Filipinization. Harrison had transformed a government of Americans "assisted by Filipinos to a government of Filipinos aided by Americans." Harrison gave the cabinet full liberty of action and refrained from interfering in the affairs of the various departments.

In the affairs of the Council of States, Harrison "endeavored to give to the Filipino executives all possible opportunity to exercise their own discretion, and even forced upon them responsibilities of decisions and action as frequently as possible." All decisions of the Council of State were ratified by the legislature.

Results of Filipinization. The radical changes Harrison introduced in his administration did not make many Americans happy. According to some Americans, the appointment of untrained and inexperienced Filipinos resulted in the inefficiency and incompetence in government service. While Harrison admitted that Filipinization had impaired, to a certain extent, the efficiency of government, he maintained that in many ways, efficiency was gained because the people's support and cooperation made the task much easier. Despite marked inefficiency in administration, both the Filipino rank and file employees and their administrative heads made significant progress in the art of self-government. Valuable lessons in self-government could not have been gained had not the Filipinos been entrusted the science and the art of managing the affairs of government.

The *System of Government under Harrison.* Sergio Osmeña , epitomizes the Filipino virtues of statesmanship as a political leader, emphasized and articulated that: "Our systems of government is truly ours, products of our policies and the progressive evolution of the various institutions of our country, the natural outgrowth of our achievements in self-government. Whatever gaps and contradictions there may be, they merely showed that the progress we have attained showed after a tenacious and persistent struggle between the people that demanded liberty and the representatives of the sovereign power that had naturally resisted popular impatience. The organization of the departments with responsibilities clearly defined, with the heads amenable to popular control; the Council of State, as a symbol of solidarity of our participation in the government as a medium of coordination and harmony between the powers of the government, the budgetary system that insured an efficient administration of our finances and effective control over the same; the Filipinization of the government as a whole as the tangible expression of our autonomy and as a proof of our political capacity – are the outstanding features of this government of ours, which showed our determination fearlessly to assume responsibility for the management of our affairs while we awaited the concession of promised freedom."

The *Wood Administration.* The Wilson-Harrison policy effected political changes in the Filipinization of government. It may be inferred that in seven years under the Harrison Administration, the Filipino leaders, by local legislation and his cooperation, perfected a "new government," fashioned in accordance with Filipino "counsel and experience." The

Americans and the Filipinos knew that the return of the Republican Party to power, which was known to be unsympathetic to Filipino aspirations, could not change the course of Philippine independence which was began by Wilson's administration.

The Wood-Forbes Mission arrived in the Philippines and was cordially received by the Filipinos. After completing its works, the Mission returned to the United States and submitted a report to President Harding. When the report was published, the Filipino leaders were displeased because it recommended the postponement of the grant of independence for the following reasons: 1) the poor financial conditions of the Philippines and 2) the instability of the Philippine government.

Wood returned to Manila on October 5, 1921 as the new governor-general replacing Harrison. He was coldly received by the Filipino leaders because of his unfriendly attitude toward Philippine Independence. Wood was an able administrator, efficient and honest, but he lacked the genial personality of Taft and the understanding style of leadership of Harrison. He checked graft and corruption in government, stabilized the finances, and improved transportation and communication and public works. But he was frank, strict and tactless and consequently antagonized the leaders of the Philippine Legislature. The growing tension between Wood and the Filipino leaders flared up dramatically on July 23, 1923, when Senate President Quezon, Speaker Osmena and the Filipino members of the Cabinet resigned from the Council of State resulting in the "Cabinet Crises." Governor Wood abolished the Council of State and governed the Philippines without the cooperation of the Philippine Legislature.

The conflict between Wood and the Filipino leaders stirred the nationalistic spirit of the people. The opposing political parties, the Nationalista and the Democrata, joined forces in to common cause against Governor Wood and a coalition, called National Supreme Council was formed. The following year Governor Wood went to the United States for a vacation. He died there on August 7, 1927.

Meanwhile, General Wood was succeeded by three Republican Governor-General who successively governed the Philippines for short periods, e.g., Henry L. Stimson (1928 – 1929), Dwight F. Davis (1929 – 1932), and Theodore Roosevelt, Jr. (1932 – 1933). In their administration, they pursued a policy "between the liberalism of Harrison and the conservatism of Wood administrative style and restored the era of good feeling between the seat of executive powers and the Philippine Legislative.

Murphy, the Last American Governor-General. Governor Frank Murphy arrived in Manila on June 15, 1933 and was warmly welcomed by the Filipino people. In his inaugural address, he promised to give them a "simple, honest and effective government" and to secure the "peace and contentment of every Filipino – a promise which he faithfully kept and translated to meaningful reforms, he humanized our penal code by way of introducing the probation system and the indeterminate sentence by reviewing and by revising the parole system. He helped the Filipino people in their campaign for independence; for he believed that they had the ability to maintain a stable democratic republic.

The Independence Mission. The promise of independence envisioned in the preamble of the Jones Law gave impetus to the independence campaign. But because of the First World War (1914 – 1918), the Filipinos temporarily suspended their independence campaign. After the war, they resumed their independence drive and effort with greater intensity and vigor.

On November 7, 1918, the Philippine Legislature created the Commission of Independence to study all matters relating to "the negotiation and organization of independence" of the Philippines.

On February 23, 1919, the First Philippine Independence Mission headed by Senate President Quezon left Manila for Washington. He was accompanied by a number of prominent Filipinos representing the various institutions – political, economic and social elements of the country. The mission presented the Filipino case for independence before the United States Congress.

President Wilson, in his farewell address to the United States Congress on December 20, 1920, recommended favorably the granting of Philippine independence. Unfortunately, the Republican Party at that time controlled Congress, so that the recommendation of the outgoing Democratic President was not considered. In the subsequent years, there were other independent missions that were sent to the United States to press for Philippine independence but they were dismal features.

The OS - ROX Mission. In 1931, the independence drive gained momentum. Quezon presented three alternative proposals to solve the independence issue. He suggested immediate independence with free trade for ten years with sugar allowed free entry up to 1,000 tons and labor immigrants to the United States.

The Philippine Legislature sent another mission headed by Sergio Osmeña, Senate President Protempore, and Manuel Roxas, Speaker. By this time, the powerful American farm, dairy and labor interests under the impact of the wide great depression and widespread unemployment, favored the granting of Philippine independence, because they wanted to close America's door to Filipino exports and laborers that were competing with American products and laborers.

Of the numerous independence bills submitted by the delegates of the Independence Mission to the United States Congress for consideration, the Hares-Hawes-Cutting Bill was the only one favored by the OS-ROX Mission.

The Hare-Hawes Cutting Act. The Hare -Hawes Cutting Bill provided for a ten-year transition period, at the end of which the United States would grant and recognize the independence of the Philippines. The bill called for the immediate establishment of a Filipino Constitutional Convention, subject to the approval of the President of the United States, to formulate a Constitution for the Commonwealth.

The Commonwealth would be autonomous in its domestic affairs, but the bill reserved to the President of the United States the power to approve or disapprove all constitutional amendments. The bill also authorized the United States to retain land or other property designated by the President of the United States for military purposes.

On the economic aspect, the bill established an annual quota of fifty immigrants during the ten-year transition period effective upon the acceptance of the law by the Philippine Legislature. The bill also allowed the free entry of American goods to the Philippines but provided for quantitative limitations on the free-duty importation of Philippine products.

The bill was passed by Congress in December, 1932, vetoed by President Herbert Hoover, and repassed over the presidential veto on January 17, 1933; and thus, the H-H-C Bill became a law.

The passage of the Hare-Hawes-Cutting Act was fitting climax to the long and acrimonious battle that had began in 1898 between the advocates and the opponents of Philippine independence

It must be noted that the H-H-C law divided the Philippine political parties and the Filipino people into opposing groups – the Antis and the Pros. The ensuing conflict was not only between issues but also between two opposite and powerful personalities. The controversy over the acceptance of the law became inextricably intertwined with the question of control of the Nacionalista Party and the government. The Antis, led by Senate President Quezon, opposed it because of its objectionable features. On the other hand, the pros headed by Senator Osmena and Speaker Roxas, defended the law, on the ground that it was the best independence measure that could be obtained from the United States Congress.

The Philippine political landscape was convulsed by a bitter political war between the Antis and the Pros. With the reorganization of the Legislature, the Antis gained control of the political situation. On October 17, 1932, the Philippine Legislature, which was controlled by Quezon, rejected the H-H-C Law. A few months later, the legislature then appointed Quezon to head another mission to the United States to seek a more favorable independence measure.

The Tydings-McDuffie Law (1934). Quezon went to the United States in early December 1933 and following a series of conferences with President Franklin D. Roosevelt and various congressional leaders in Washington; he was able to win the members of the United States Congress to his side. A new independence act called the Tydings-McDuffie Law, sponsored by Senator Millard E. Tydings and Representative John McDuffie was passed into law and signed by President Roosevelt on March 24, 1934. It was a revised copy of the rejected H-H-C Law of 1933. The only differences from the H-H-C Law were the change in title, the elimination of military reservations and the modification of certain, ambiguous provisions.

The important provisions of the Tydings-McDuffie Law were the following: (1) a ten-year transition period under the Commonwealth of the Philippines preparatory to the grant of independence on July 4, 1946; (2) a graduated tariff on Philippine exports to America beginning with the 6th year of the Commonwealth; (3) an annual quota of fifty Filipino migrants to America; (4) control of Philippine currency, coinage, foreign trade, and foreign relations by America; (5) representation of the Commonwealth in the United States by a Filipino Resident Commissioner; and (6) representation of the United States President in the Philippines by an American High Commissioner.

With the passage of the Tydings-McDuffie Law and its subsequent ratification by the Philippine Legislature, Quezon won a triumphant victory over his opponents and virtually retained supreme leadership over the Nacionalista Party and the government.

The Framing of the Constitution. The Tydings-McDuffie Law contained explicit provisions on the various steps and conditions, which must be fulfilled before the establishment of the Commonwealth. The first requisite was to hold a constitutional convention to formulate and draft a constitution, which should be submitted to the President of the United States for approval. Upon the President's approval, a plebiscite would be held for ratification or rejection of the Constitution. After the plebiscite had been approved, the Filipino people were to elect officers of the Commonwealth government in a general election. After the ten-year transition period, the United States would relinquish her sovereignty over the Philippines and finally, recognize its independence.

The Constitutional Convention met in an inaugural session at the Hall of the House of the Representatives on July 30, 1934 and formally opened by Senate President Quezon. The delegates elected the officers and Claro M. Recto was elected president.

The convention was carried out on a non-partisan basis. Quezon who was convinced that the Commonwealth should be established with the cooperation of the majority in the legislature was urgently needed in solving the serious economic and social problems of the country.

The Constitution of the Philippines was approved by the delegates of the convention on February 8, 1935. The signing of the 1935 Philippine Constitution by the delegates was held on February 19, 1935, amid simple but impressive ceremonies. One delegate signed the historic document in his blood. He was Gregorio Perfecto, a delegate from Manila.

Since the Tydings-McDuffie Law required that the Constitution be approved by the President of the United States, the Constitutional Mission composed of Senate President Quezon, Convention President Recto and delegate Roxas went to the United States to have an audience with President Roosevelt.

On March 23, 1935, President Roosevelt approved the Constitution of the Philippines. The news of approval was received by the Filipino people with the great pride and joy. The Constitution "embodies the ideals of liberty and

THE PHILIPPINES UNDER THE AMERICAN RULE

democracy of the Filipino people."

Meanwhile, in the election held in September 1935, Quezon won convincingly over his aging rivals, General Emilio Aguinaldo and Bishop Gregorio Aglipay. Osmena won the vice-presidency.

On November 15, 1935, the Commonwealth was inaugurated with Manuel Quezon and Sergio Osmeña as its president and vice-president, respectively. The administration of government, with the exception of its currency and foreign relations, were now completely in the hands of the Filipino people. In his inaugural address, President Quezon declared with hope and optimism, that this was only "a means to an end. It is an instrumentality placed in our hands to prepare ourselves fully for the responsibilities of complete independence."

Preparation for Independence. President Quezon, in his inaugural address focused on the political process of change. Full of optimism for the future, he declared that:

> "We are bringing into being a new nation. We are witnessing the final stage in the fulfillment of the noblest undertaking ever attempted by a nation in its dealings with a subject people. We shall build a government that will be just, honest, efficient and strong so that the foundations of the coming Republic may be firm and enduring – a government, indeed, that must satisfy not only the pressing needs of the hour but also the exacting demand of the future."

Quezon's visions for the Commonwealth as a transition period during which the government would make adjustment in the political, social, economic, and cultural dimensions in preparation for complete independence. Quezon inherited insurmountable problems from the Spanish and American periods. He needs the unwavering support of the Filipinos to prove to the world that the Philippines was capable and deserving of independent national existence in a free world of nations.

The pressing problems of the Commonwealth government were the need for political stability, national security, peace and order, and an underdeveloped economy.

The Problem of National Security. The need for installing an adequate and maintained defense system in the Philippines should be given priority. The fear of external foreign aggression, led the Commonwealth government to consider the problem of national security an urgent one. It is in this premise that the first law of the National Assembly was the enactment of the National Defense Act, which provided for the establishment of national defense for the Philippines. President Quezon requested the services of General Douglas MacArthur in formulating the Philippine defense system. MacArthur's defense plan envisioned the organization of a citizen army composed of two forces – a regular force of the Philippine Constabulary and a reserve force that train twenty-four year old able-bodied men for a period of five and a half months. The defense plan also involved, the establishment of a modest Philippine Navy.

The National Language. The constitution provides that "the National Assembly shall take steps toward the development and adoption of common national language." In compliance with this constitutional mandate, the National Assembly enacted Commonwealth Act No. 184, which established the Institute of National Language. The Institute conducted studies on the Philippine language and dialects all over the archipelago. On the basis of the study, it recommended to the President that the Tagalog language be used as the basis of National Language of the Philippines.

On June 7, 1940, the President approved Commonwealth Act No. 570, declaring the National Language (Tagalog) one of the official languages in the Philippines.

On Economic Problems. In 1937, President Quezon and the U.S. President agreed to establish a joint Philippine-American committee to study the economic problems of the Philippines and to recommend a program for economic adjustment. The Joint Preparatory Committee on Philippine

Affairs (JPCPA) was created on April 14, 1937 and hearings were held in Washington, San Francisco and Manila for over a year. The JPCPA recommended the grant of political independence to the Philippines on July 4, 1946, and the extension of free trade relations between the United States and the Philippines up to 1960.

The National Assembly created the National Economic Council to advise the government on economic and financial questions. The government strengthened the National Development Company, which supervised and managed government-financial and operated corporations to bring about economic improvement in the country. The National Development Company proposed to bring about expansion of credit facilities for agricultural and commercial activities; the installation of hydroelectric power plants; and the creation of abaca and other fiber corporations.

The government attempted to wrest control of the retail trade from Chinese and other foreign traders. The National Economic Protectionism Association (NEPA) and the consumers' Cooperative League of the Philippines campaigned for public support of native retail trade.

On Social Justice. The Constitution provides that the "promotion of social justice to insure the well-being and economic security of all the people should be the concern of the State." The State shall protect labor, especially working women and minors, shall regulate the relations between landowners and tenants, and between labor and capital in industry and in agriculture. The Minimum Wage Act provided laborers to be paid minimum wage of one peso for working eight hours daily. The Public Defender Act was created for public defender (qualified lawyers) for purposes of depending in court the rights of poor laborers.

On Education. According to the Constitution, the government must provide at least free public elementary education, and "schools shall aim to develop moral character, personal discipline, civic conscience and vocational efficiency. The National Council of Education was created for the purpose of studying the needs and problems of the nation. The Adult Education program was created to help the adult illiterates to read and write. The Office of Private Education was established to supervise all private schools, colleges and universities throughout the country. Education is the best weapon against ignorance.

On Social Problem.   Social discontent among the masses was caused by the perpetuation of feudal practices whose origins may be traced to the Spanish regime. Usurious practices increased the misery of the peasant farmers. Small and self-sufficient farmers, unable to cope with the expenses of large-scale cultivation became share tenants.

The Sakdal uprising further exposed the growing unrest among the tenant farmers. The Sakdal movement campaigned against misdistribution of property, excessive taxes and the concentration of landownership, especially in the church.

Results of the American Occupation.   The United States introduced a regime of democratic partnership. The policy, while not satisfactory enough from the point of a Filipino nationalist, was nevertheless an improvement over that of Spanish rule. Universal education was given importance, public health and welfare programs were carried to the remote places; commerce, industry, and trade were given impetus; basic individual rights and freedom are protected; means of communication and transportation were improved; and the political consciousness was developed through the introduction of American political institutions and practices.

While there were a number of positive results, the American occupation had contributed negative results; e.g., partial loss of racial heritage, the continuance of the colonial mentality and a distorted sense of values.

On Development in Education.   Perhaps one of the greatest contributions of the United States to Philippine civilization is the system of public education. Directly opposed to the Spanish system, which emphasized the study of the Catholic religion, the American educational system focused on democratic traditions and the practical application of laws and principles. The Spanish authorities in the Philippines discouraged the Filipinos from learning Spanish, while the Americans compelled the Filipinos to learn the English language. American schools were established. The first public school teachers were the American soldiers who were later replaced by the "Thomasites," American teachers who came to the Philippines on board the S.S. Thomas. The American educational system prepared the Filipinos for administrative civil service, an advantage in the Filipinization of government.

Higher education was provided by the establishment of the state-supported University of the Philippines in 1908. Other educational institutions, owned and operated by private individuals and corporations were established. The results of this system increased Filipino literacy. Adult education was also introduced; eventually this became a movement.

The Americans believed that education should be free for all and that the primary purpose of education was to prepare the individuals for present-day living. Thus, every child should be given the opportunity to finish at least elementary education.

Efforts were also exerted by the Americans to humanize laws, equalize the distribution of wealth and ensure economic stability for all.

On Public Health and Welfare. The Americans' contribution in the area of public health and welfare was the introduction of a scientific program to look after the health of every Filipino. The creation of the Board of Public Health signaled the intensified campaign against the spread of cholera, small pox, dysentery, malaria, tuberculosis and other deadly diseases. Dispensaries, leprosaria and hospitals were established to take care of the sick people.

The result of the development of health and welfare programs did not only decrease mortality, but also improved the standard of living.

On Trade, Commerce and Industry. The economic

development of the Philippines greatly improved because of the free trade relations with the Americans. Under the Payne-Aldrich Tariff Act, all Philippine exports, except rice, were allowed to enter American markets free of duty within certain quota limits. On the other hand, American exports to the Philippines were unlimited and duty-free.

Domestic trade also developed. Textile and cigar and cigarette factories multiplied. Sawmills, coconut oil factories, fishing and fish canning, alcohol distilleries and sugar centrals were established. Mining, one of the most important industries became the backbone of Philippine economy.

On Transportation and Communication. Bridges and roads were established. The means of transportation improved. The bull carts, carretelas and rigs existed, while cars, tracks and railway cars sped up the means of transportation. The government extended the railroad lines to the north and south of Luzon; thereby, bringing the far-flung provinces nearer Manila; the political, cultural and commercial center.

Water transportation was also developed to connect the islands of the south with the provinces of Luzon. To protect domestic coastwise shipping, the Philippine Legislature passed a law in 1923 providing that only ships owned locally could engage in inter-island shipping.

Development in communication was evidently felt. Telephone lines were introduced linking together by telephones, telegraph lines and radio.

On Individual Freedoms. The recognition of individual freedoms, the very foundation of any democratic system was enjoyed. Such freedoms include freedom of religious worship, freedom of the press, freedom of assemble peaceably for redress of grievances, freedom of domicile, and freedom of speech.

The freedom enjoyed by writers found expression in drama and theatre arts. As the conditions of peace and order improved, the repression of civil liberties was removed.

Filipinos enjoyed all the basic freedoms in their relations with one another.

On Political Consciousness. Filipinos began to understand the intricacies of modern politics. With the gradual political consciousness, the Filipinos became aware of the political problems brought about by man and his political activities. They also participated in decision-making through public hearings on political issues of national significance that directly affect their lives. Filipinos realize the importance of the sanctity of the ballot during elections. They came to know the value of clean, honest, orderly, credible and orderly election. They became aware of their political rights and obligations as citizen of a democratic society.

On Negative Results. While there are many beneficial results that the American occupation contributed to the development of the Philippines, there were also negative results. Some of these are: The conditioning of the Filipino mind to the American standard of living has made them economically dependent on the United States. The result is the utter neglect and consequent death of Filipino industries. They have been replaced by American goods. If the goods are stateside, they are the best. If they are made in the Philippines, they are inferior. The mental attitude of the Filipinos despises one's own and loves anything foreign was the root cause of colonial mentality. While the Spaniards almost killed the Filipinos by maltreatment, the Americans, on the other hand, showed them "kindness," their love for their language and culture had been replaced by the adoration of the American language and culture. The American posture of materialism found expression in the ordinary Filipino mind. Success is measured in terms of material possessions. A Filipino is perceived to be successful if he made millions through corrupt practices; he is successful if, in spite of his scanty education; he wins a congressional seat. It seems that the Filipinos, as a rule, have lost their sense of values.

The American movies, to a great extent, influenced the Filipino minds. Gangsterism, juvenile delinquency, racketeering, graft and corruption, promiscuous love affairs, betrayal and various type of violence – all these have been brought to the Philippines through Hollywood.

It may be inferred that many social problems that plague Filipino society today, are as much the results of American "movies" shown indiscriminately in our movie houses.

Study Guides

A. Terms/Concepts to Understand

self-government	intervention
rudiments	epitomize
Filipinization	indeterminate
dissemination	alternative
preamble	autonomous

B. Questions to Answer

1. How did the Americans train the Filipinos for self-government?

2. What were the provisions of the Philippine Bill of 1902?

3. What were the American policies on Filipinization?

4. Enumerate the important steps that led to the training for self-government.

5. What is the significance of the Jones Law in the lives of the Filipinos?

6. Discuss the important features of the Jones Law.

7. What is the role of the civil service as envisioned by the Civil Service Act?

8. Describe the status of education under the American rule.

9. What is the Hare-Hawes Cutting Act? Discuss its significant provisions.

10. Discuss the importance of the Tydings-McDuffie Law.

Chapter 13

The Philippines under the Japanese Occupation

While the ten-year preparatory period was gaining ground for the Commonwealth government, it was abruptly interrupted when the Japanese naval bombers at dawn attacked Pearl Harbor in Hawaii in December 8, 1941, Feast of the Immaculate Conception.

On December 6, President Roosevelt of the United States addressed a personal appeal to Emperor Hirohito of Japan in a last-minute effort to stop the impending American-Japanese conflict. It was unfortunate the reply to this appeal was the sudden treacherous attack on Pearl Harbor. The American naval and military losses at Pearl Harbor were very big and unimaginable to comprehend. The tragedy struck deep into the hearts of the Americans and drove them to emotional outrage. People in all walks of life swelled around the White House in Washington D.C., eagerly waiting for President Roosevelt's message to Congress. At 12:25 in the afternoon, Monday, a joint session and a few minutes later, President Roosevelt, his face grim and stern, delivered his message. "Yesterday, infamy, the United States of America was suddenly and deliberately attacked by naval and air forces of the Empire of Japan." At the end of the message, urged U.S. Congress to declare war.

Meanwhile, Prime Minister Winston S. Churchill of England also announced to the world that Great Britain would declare war on Japan.

The Japanese Offensive Attack. The Japanese offensive naval and air attack was focused at the rich Dutch and British possessions in Southeast Asia, especially Malaya and Dutch East Indies (now Indonesia). To effect this strategy, the Japanese forces had to destroy the American Pacific Fleet at Pearl Harbor, and then, attack the Philippines so that communication of American lines in the Pacific will be cut off.

While Pearl Harbor was being attacked, the Japanese war planes and naval guns were aggressively shelling simultaneously in Davao, Baguio, Tarlac, Zambales and Tuguegarao. Clark Field in Pampanga was violently attacked by dropping bombs where American Air Force Arsenal and facilities suffered heavy loss. Sangley Point and Nichols Field were also attacked and suffered incalculable destruction.

On December 9, the silence of the night was broken by the sounds of the zooming warplanes that attacked Port Area and the ships at the piers in Manila. Manila was declared an open city by General Douglas MacArthur on December 29, 1941 to be spared from further destruction. The Japanese did not respect Manila as an open city, because they still dropped bombs in Intramuros destroying San Juan de Letran and the Central Bank Building, Sto. Domingo Church and Sta. Catalina College. The Philippines Herald Building was also destroyed.

The following days, marked destruction of human lives and property in some parts of the provinces because of indiscriminate bombing of Japanese air squadrons, the experience the war brought; in spite of these utter destruction, they remained calm.

The Japanese Invasion Begins. The Japanese preparation for the war, was deliberately and calculately planned, particularly the attack in the Philippines. After the Pearl Harbor attack, the Japanese landed at Aparri and Vigan without any resistance. In the south, similar landings were made in Davao and Jolo. While invasion forces made a beachhead at Legaspi. On December 22, the Japanese moved swiftly and landed at Lingayen, Pangasinan, Damortis and Rosario and then headed on to Central Luzon. Similar landings were made at Lamon Bay: at Mauban and Atimonan under the command of Lt. General Masaharu Homma. While the Japanese troops were landing at various points of the Philippines, these airplanes were bombing military camps and installing actions even in civilian evacuation centers. When Nichols Field and Fort McKinley were raided, Captain Jesus Villamor and two gallant pilots bravely put up an aerial fight. Villamor shot down one Japanese airplane and because of his exemplary courage and bravery, he was awarded the Distinguished Service Cross by General MacArthur.

The air skirmish in Batangas airfield continued and Captain Villamor and five Filipino airmen attacked two enemy formations of 27 planes each. Unfortunately, Villamor lost two of his men – Lt. Cesar Basa and Lt. Geronimo Adan after two Japanese planes blown into flames during the dogfight.

Bleak Christmas. For many Filipinos, Christmas is an occasion of joy and merrymaking and the anticipating of the coming of the Lord Jesus. Christmas of 1941 was a bleak one. There were no traditional *misa de gallo* in the Philippines Churches. Many people in the provinces left the town and sought refuge to the mountains and other places where they could be safe while fighting raged with fury on both sides.

The war condition began to rise as an impending event unfolded ominously hopeless for the USAFFE, because General Homma's forces were inching closely to Manila. Realizing that defending Manila, as a last-ditch stand would be an exercise in futility, General MacArthur immediately ordered the transfer of valuable military equipment and supplies of the USAFFE to Corregidor and Bataan, and those that could not be moved and transferred were virtually destroyed. For General MacArthur, it was obvious that the only alternative strategy to save his army was to take the military contingent to the Bataan Peninsula where he planned to hold back the advancing Japanese forces. The military field commanders receiving orders from MacArthur retreated to Bataan.

On December 24, 1941, Christmas Eve, President Quezon, his family and members of his Cabinet moved to the island fortress, Corregidor, on board S.S. Mayon, where the Commonwealth Government was transferred. Those who accompanied him were Vice-President Sergio Osmeña, Secretary of Justice Jose Abad Santos, General Basilio Valdes, and Colonel Manuel Nieto. Jose P. Laurel, Acting Chief Justice of the Supreme Court wanted to go with Quezon, but the President said: "No, Laurel, someone will have to meet the Japanese. The people must be given the necessary protection. A big man is needed for the job. You must stay." Justice Jose P. Laurel, a man of wisdom, fortitude and his abiding faith to God and his country men, stayed behind together with other high-ranking officials in the government to look after the general welfare of the people during the critical times.

The Retreat to Bataan. Bataan is a peninsula on western Luzon surrounded by mountain ranges and long irregular coastlines along Manila Bay. The retreat to Bataan by MacArthur and his army was brilliant maneuver as a military strategy for he outwitted General Homma, the Japanese Commander-in-Chief with his superior ingenuity who failed to encircle the USAFFE. MacArthur and his army succeeded in maneuvering their military offensive in a limited territory by keeping intact and well coordinated. On several occasions, the Japanese launched their offensive assault against MacArthur's stronghold only to be repressed with heavy losses. Many times, the Japanese land and sea forces aided by continuous air attacks, were driven back because the Bataan line of resistance stood its ground heroically.

To demoralize the USAFFE, the Japanese airplanes dropped leaflets on Bataan specifically in war zones, urging the Filipino soldiers to surrender and to desert the American comrades-in-arms, but the courageous Philippine army just ignored the Japanese propaganda.

The battle of Bataan exemplified the Filipino-American troops heroic stand and resisted with rare courage. Day and night, the fierce fight between the Japanese forces and the defenders of Bataan raged with fury. The flaming battleground of Bataan peninsula billowed by smoke, drenched with blood and tears of Filipino-American soldiers, fighting side-by-side, became a hallowed ground to immortalize their extraordinary courage and fortitude in a new epic in the annals of war.

As days and months dragged on, the Filipino-American defenders were faced with grim situation. The air and naval support from the United States seemed impossible because the Japanese navy had the complete control of sea lanes in the Pacific. With this predicament, the Bataan defenders were gradually being demoralized for without the needed arms, ammunitions, food, medicines and other supplies, to sustain their effort to continue fighting seemed to be utterly hopeless. By the early part of March 1942 rations from the United States was cut and as a result led to malnutrition of soldiers causing various diseases, e.g., diarrhea, dysentery and malaria.

General MacArthur, cognizant of the difficulty of continuing the fight against overwhelming odds and the impending defeat of the USAFFE, on orders of President Roosevelt, left Corregidor for Australia on March 11, 1942, and was succeeded by General Jonathan Wainwright as commander of the USAFFE, President Quezon, his family and the members of his cabinet were earlier picked up on the night of February 18 by the submarine *Swordfish* and successfully eluded through the Japanese blockade and reached Panay, then to Negros and finally, to Mindanao where they were fetched by a plane for Australia. From Australia, Quezon and his party crossed over to the United States and upon reaching San Francisco on May 8, 1942, a train brought them to Washington, where President Roosevelt and other high ranking American official met them.

Meanwhile, General Macarthur took command of the newly formed Southwest Pacific Area upon his return to Australia. It is interesting to note that, before he fled for Australia amidst and hard-pressed Filipino-American soldiers in Bataan and Corregidor who were bearing the brunt of Japanese invasion, they were electrified by his pledge, "I SHALL RETURN!" This promise made the Filipino-American soldiers' spirit alive.

The Fall of Bataan. Under the circumstances of an

inevitable defeat, the hungry, physically exhausted and sick Filipino-American defenders continued to fight, but their continuous struggle was a hopeless cause. The much-awaited convoy from Australia carrying reinforcements, ammunitions, food and supplies never came and the gallant Bataan defenders had no other alternative than to surrender.

On April 3, 1942, Good Friday to the Catholics, General Homma relentlessly unleashed the full fury of an all-out Japanese offensive in Bataan peninsula, to pressure the Bataan defenders to give up. Thousands of Japanese infantry in full battle gear with bayonets, rifles, grenades, mortars and machine guns supported by artillery, bolster their offensive operations and pounded the Filipino-American last line of defense. From the sea, the Japanese war ships continued shelling the defenders' positions to annihilate the enemy.

On April 9, 1942, General Edward P. King, commander of the forces on Bataan, surrendered to prevent further injury of the helpless defenders, while some 78,000 infantry forces under General King were included in the island of Corregidor and other surrounding mountains in Bataan.

From the deep tunnel of Corregidor, the VOICE OF FREEDOM, radio station of the USAFFE, with a feeling of grief, but proudly told the world: BATAAN HAS FALLEN, but the spirit of valor and heroism the Filipino-American soldiers will forever stand – a beacon to all the liberty-loving peoples of the world.

The Infamous Death March. The infamous death march started in Cabcabin, Mariveles on April 10, 1942. The surrendered Filipino-American soldiers were forced at gunpoint to March from Mariveles, Bataan to San Fernando passing through the towns of Bataan – Limay, Orion, Pilar, Balanga, Abucay, Samal, Orani, Hermosa, and Lubao, Pampanga under the scorching heat of the sun. Those who could not march because of physical weakness due to hunger, fatigue and sickness were either shot down or bayoneted. So inhuman that defied human sensibility, the pathetic event had been called "Death March."

In San Fernando, Pampanga, the weary, hungry and sick marchers were herded like animals into army trucks and were transported by railway to Capas, Tarlac. Before reaching their destination, many prisoners died due to suffocation and physical exhaustion. From Capas' railroad station, the war prisoners were forced to march on foot to the prison camp at Camp O'Donnell. Only, about 58,000 prisoners reached the Camp alive on April 15, 1942 after enduring the harrowing ordeal. The prisoners' camp was even worse than the battlefield in Bataan. The records of the War Crimes Commissions, which tried the surviving Japanese, showed that about 22,155 Filipinos and 2,000 Americans died in Camp O'Donnell. Death March forged the steel in the spirit of a whole generation of Filipinos.

With the surrender of Bataan, the Japanese stepped up their continuous offensive day and night against Corregidor. The impregnable and defiant Rock-Corregidor, guarding the entrance to Manila Bay continued to resist the Japanese forces, from Cavite, the island fortress was subjected to intense fire by successive bombings. At night, the people could see flashes like lightning that heralded the booms of the Japanese artillery pounding relentlessly with deafening sound at the historic fortress.

In a last-ditch effort to defend Corregidor, General Wainwright and his valiant soldiers tried, but in vain. In the early morning of May 6, 1942, General Wainwright addressed a message to General Homma through the "VOICE OF FREEDOM" offering to surrender the forces under his command. In the afternoon of the same day, General Wainwright met with General Homma to discuss the terms and conditions of the surrender. General Homma demanded the surrender of the entire USAFFE forces in the Philippines, but General Wainwright hedged to surrender only soldiers directly under him. Homma with his voice firm and demanding insisted on the surrender of all and stood up to leave. At this juncture, Wainwright had no alternative than to give in the enemy's demand.

The war was over as far as the American forces in the

Philippines was concerned; however, for the Filipino people, the war was still on. Many Filipino military officers and ordinary soldiers vehemently refused to give up their arms as a sign of surrender. Instead, they fled to the hills with their arms, and with the help of the civilians, they waged relentless guerri¹la warfare against the Japanese invaders in various parts of the archipelago.

The falls of Bataan on April 9, and the fall of Corregidor in May 6 of the same year, 1942, were deeply mourned not only by the Filipino people but also the Americans and other peace-loving people of the world.

The execution of Chief Justice Jose Abad Santos in the hands of the Japanese, because of his refusal to take an oath of allegiance to the Japanese authorities was an eloquent manifestation that the Filipinos were ready to die for their fatherland.

Justice Abad Santos, faced with serene courage and fortitude the Japanese firing squad and died in the finest moment of history rarely afforded to everyone.

The execution of Justice Abad Santos sparked the flame of the resistance movement for the Filipino guerrilla leaders pursued vigorously to fight the Japanese intruders. Among the Filipino guerilla leaders who stood to fight during the dark days of our history were Guillermo Nakar in Northern Luzon; Macario Peralta, Jr. in Panay; Wenceslao Vinzonz in Camarines Norte, and Reperto Kangleon in Leyte to name a few who rendered valuable services to the resistance movement.

The support extended by the civilians in various towns and villages contributed immensely to the guerrilla warfare.

The Japanese Military Government. The Commander-in-Chief of the Japanese Imperial Forces, General Masaharu Homma, in his proclamation announcing the end of the American occupation and the Japanese expedition in the Philippines, was "to emancipate the Filipinos from the oppressive dominion of the United States of America, and letting them establish the Philippines for the Filipinos as a member of the Co-Prosperity Sphere in Greater East Asia and making you enjoy your own prosperity and culture."

It should be noted that during the first few weeks of the Japanese occupation, the status of the provinces and the charted cities remained practically the same as during the Commonwealth years. However, by February, the Japanese started to institute radical reforms in the administration of the government. General Homma issued an order to Jose B. Vargas directing him to be the Chairman of the Executive Commission. The Central Administrative Organization was composed of six administrative departments: Interior, Finance, Justice, Agriculture and Commerce, Education, Health and Public Welfare, and Public Works and Communications. Each department was headed by a Commissioner who was responsible for the objectives and operation of his department. Each department had a Japanese adviser. The organization and functions of each department and the courts of justice remained the same as prescribed by the Commonwealth, provided that the essential features be approved by the Commander-in-Chief of the Imperial Japanese Forces. A Council of State was also created as an advisory body to assist the Central Administrative structure. On the provincial and municipal levels, the order was to maintain the *status quo*.

Educational Policy. The Japanese educational policy focused on educational reorientation. The basic features included the propagation of Filipino culture, the dissemination of the principle of the Greater East Asia Co-Prosperity Sphere, the spiritual rejuvenation of the Filipinos the teaching and propagation of Nippongo, the diffusion of vocational and elementary education, and the promotion of love of labor. It may be inferred that the motive and motivation behind this educational policy was to create an atmosphere friendly to Japanese intentions and also to erase from the minds of the Filipinos the American cultural influence.

The schools were reopen where pupils, teachers and school officials were made to pledge to support the new educational policy. The reopening of the elementary schools was given priority, obviously because the Japanese believed that the minds of the young boys and girls could be easily shaped or molded into the patterns of the Japanese design. The reopening of vocational and normal schools as institutions of higher learning, offering various degree courses were reopened, except law, because the Japanese military authorities thought that, under the prevailing conditions lawyers' services were useless.

It might be observed that, at the outset, there was not much enthusiasm on returning to the schools. First, the Filipinos were suspicious about the Japanese intentions, and second, children were preoccupied selling anything or helping their parents to look for something in order to survive. The lack of interest and enthusiasm to go to schools under the Japanese occupation was reflected in the meager enrollment.

The Japanese-sponsored Republic. The Japanese authorities resorted to channel their concerted efforts to propaganda strategy in order to win the sympathy of the Filipinos and made them believe the Japanese intention to see the Philippines become a Republic.

Premier Hideki Tojo, in an address before the Imperial Diet on January 21, 1942, underscored that the Philippines would be granted independence, provided that the Filipinos would cooperate in the establishment of the "Greater East Asia Co-Prosperity Sphere." This promise was repeated on January 28, when he again addressed the Imperial Diet. He said: "Substantial progress is being made in the degree of cooperation rendered to the Japanese Empire by the people of the Philippines as well as in the restoration of peace and security. Under these circumstances and on condition that further tangible evidence of cooperation is actively demonstrated, it is contemplated to put into effect the statement made previously on the question of Philippine Independence in the shortest time possible."

The Filipinos took it with a grain of salt; however, there was a bit of rejoicing over the announcement of Philippine "independence." Jose B. Vargas pledged support of the Filipinos in the attainment of independence, and on February

8, 1943, pledged a rigged demonstration of gratitude to the Japanese authorities for the promise of independence. The Council of State issued a manifesto on February 26, urging the people to cooperate and exert all efforts towards the realization of independence.

On May 6, Premier Tojo addressed the Filipino people at the Luneta, stating that Japan would help them, "emerge from the chaos and turmoil of the past regime into the glorious national existence of the new." When he returned to Japan, the Premier told the Imperial Diet that the Philippines will be accorded independence.

The KALIBAPI. On June 18, the KALIBAPI (Kapisanan sa Paglilingkod sa Bagong Pilipinas) was instructed to form the Preparatory Commission for Philippine Independence. Thereafter, it was organized on June 20, with Jose P. Laurel as President and Benigno S. Aquino and Ramon Avancena as Vice-Presidents. The Commission prepared the draft of the proposed Constitution, and was approved on Sept. 4, and ratified by a "popular" convention by the delegates. The Constitution provided for a unicameral National Assembly.

On September 25, the National assembly elected Jose P. Laurel President of the Republic. On October 14, 1943, the Declaration of Independence was read and subsequently inaugurated, the induction into office of President Laurel.

Amidst the simple and solemn ceremonies, President Laurel concluded his inaugural address with these words:

> Thinking of a common effort to save our country from the tragedy that had fallen it, I am sure people will rise as one to meet the challenge. We shall encounter difficulties greater than any we have even faced in our national history. We shall have to adopt ourselves to the strange stimuli of the new environment and undergo the travails of constant adjustment and readjustment. With God helping us, we shall march with steady, resolute steps forward, without doubt, vacillation or fear. There shall be no tarrying on the way, no desert from the ranks, no stragglers left behind.

Together we shall work, work hard, work still harder, work with all our might and work as we had never worked before.

The inaugural address of President Laurel was full of meaning with determined effort to demolish all impediments, including the Japanese interference standing in the way in the pursuit of genuine independence of the Filipino people.

Economic Conditions. The economic activities during the occupation were limited. Commerce and trade suffered a set back. Industries, banks and factories were on a stand-still. Work animals decreased and agriculture became weak in terms of production. Horses, cars, tracks and other means of transportation were confiscated by the Japanese. Many rice fields and big *haciendas* remained idle for a time. Rice production sank very low, resulting in prohibitive price of rice. Suddenly, the farmers who were looked down by the *bourgeoisie,* rose to prominence and importance.

It was not surprising to see vendors on Azcarraga (now Claro M. Recto Avenue) selling dresses, polo shirts, and pants that were stolen from the interred dead at La Loma Cemetery and other graveyards. In Dulong Bayan Market, men and women, called out aloud: "*Baka may gintong ngipin kayo riyan na ipinagbibili.*" Do you have gold teeth for sale? The acute demand of gold at that time led some unscrupulous people to dig the graves or destroy the tombs of the dead in the cemeteries hoping to find gold. The buy and sell business flourished. It seemed that the Japanese encouraged this kind of trade by printing what the Filipinos called "Mickey Mouse" money that consequently resulted in inflation. It was an ordinary sight to see people carrying a *bayong* or a small sack full of "Mickey Mouse" money to buy a few gantas of rice. Goods were sold at very high prices. To cushion the impact of the occupation on the economy, the Japanese military authorities distributed goods to the people at prices determined by the government. The price of cigarettes were astronomical. Smokers who could not afford to buy at such prices manufactured their own cigarettes out of dried papaya leaves.

For coffee, uncooked rice was toasted to dark brown pounded, then boiled and served hot. The sap of banana plant and papaya tree were cut to small pieces and crashed and cooked for human consumption.

Because of the scarcity of food, President Laurel urged the Filipinos to plant vegetables in their backyards. The aquatic *Kangkong* that grew in low and watery places became the favorite vegetable food for the family. Food production campaign was intensified. The Economic Planning Board organized the *Bigasang Bayan* (BIBA) to control the procurement and distribution of rice and other cereals. Cooperatives were created to allow private initiative to insure equitable distribution of prime commodities at reasonable prices. These steps were all designed to alleviate the people's sufferings brought about by the acute shortage of food; but in spite of this problems that seemed insurmountable, the Filipino people remained steadfast and loyal to the ideals of their country.

Social Conditions. Life under the Japanese occupation was full of fear and anxiety. Its impact on the psychological and physical nerves of the Filipinos were terrifying and dangerous. The Filipinos had to grapple with the Japanese military, diseases, hunger, the guerrillas and the Japanese-paid Filipino spies. The most terrifying moment was to contend with some Filipinos employed by Japanese authorities to obtain secret information concerning guerrilla activities from the civilians. Suspected civilians sympathetic to the guerrilla movement meant severe punishment. The *Kempeitai,* the dreaded Japanese Military Police had total disregard of human lives. In Manila, and its suburbs, houses with unregistered radios were raided and the male adult occupants were thrown into the dungeons of Fort Santiago in Intramuros where they experienced inhuman punishment. Hanging a suspected guerrilla by both hands and hitting him with a piece of wood or lead pipe seemed ordinary in the dungeons. In most cases, the Japanese soldiers made a punching bag of the prisoner's body. Another type of brutal punishment was the "water cure" where the prisoner was forced to lie flat on his back, his mouth forced open, and then water was poured into his mouth until his stomach was filled with water expanding like a bursting balloon. Another type of inhuman torture which the Japanese enemy used was through the use of electric wire into the flesh of the helpless prisoner's naked body. There were a number of men and even women who died in Fort Santiago; these were not recorded. A few of the prisoners who were no longer able to withstand the excruciating pain inflicted by the Japanese soldiers they had been undergoing almost every day, were forced to cry out the names of the guerrillas and where they could be found. As a consequence, guerrillas who were captured were executed by having their heads cut off with the razor-blade deadly *Samurai* sword.

There were also cases where a number of innocent women were raped by the Japanese military men. During the darkest days of the occupation, it seemed that no one could sleep soundly, because at any moment the Japanese soldiers could forced the door to open to arrest men in the house. The *zona* in Mabatang, Abucay, Bataan and other parts of the province, the Japanese soldiers indiscriminately arrested men and herded them like cattle and eventually were tortured. There was no safety. The climate of fear enveloped the community.

The Japanese sentries strategically located at street corners and foot of bridges slapped men and women, and even children for failure to bow their heads before them. It should be noted that the most feared Japanese word was *kura*. This word *kura* was a communication which had two meanings depending upon the movement of the Japanese hand: a *kura* with an inward wave of the hand suggesting action, meant "Come here," when signified with a slap or a kick; a *kura* with an outward wave of the hand meant, "scram!" and one was spared. Cases of slapping was a common scene. These include the improper bowing before the sentry, failure to bring the residence certificate, for having a face the Japanese did not like, trivial behavior of the Filipinos. For Filipinos, slapping was a sign of condescension and an insult. They would prefer to be boxed, to be slapped because slapping for them is a sign of inferiority as men.

Another threatening danger Filipinos had to contend were the Filipino spies who were loyal to the Japanese. They squealed the names of their guerrillas and their activities, as well as those who supported the resistance movement. Once you were pointed by these spies that were supporters of the underground movement, you will be arrested, imprisoned and tortured to death. Some of these spies were members of the worst and notorious collaborators – the MAKAPILIs.

Side by side with the danger posed by the Filipino spies were guerrillas coming down from the hills asking food from the civilians in some villages. If the Japanese soldiers, by chance or accident, sensed that there were guerrillas around, shooting were likely to occur and the helpless civilians were caught in the crossfire. The guerrillas were quick to liquidate Filipinos whom they suspected of being Japanese spies.

Because of the economic crises and the scarcity of food, many Filipinos died of malaria, tuberculosis, malnutrition and other diseases. Medicine was very scarce. It was a common sight to see men, women and children suffering from extreme hunger with hundreds of flies feasting on the large fresh wounds. Young and starved-looking children scrounged around garbage cans in public markets searching something edible for survival.

This appalling condition inevitably aggravated social problems. Crimes against persons and property rose high. Burglary and hold up even in broad daylight were common occurrences.

It should be noted, however, that persons caught stealing during the occupation were paraded on an open vehicle around the town accompanied with Japanese soldiers as a punishment, with a big sign attached to their bodies: "KAMI AY MAGNANAKAW, HUWAG NINYO KAMING PAMARISAN." The type of punishment did not serve as a deterrence to curve stealing because of survival.

Cultural Aspects. All was not bleak. There were still light and music. Aside from comedies presented before pleasure-hungry audience, there were theatres where pre-war

American films were shown after they were censored by the Japanese authorities. There were also Japanese films whose stories glorified the Japanese way of life. The Dramatic Philippines, Inc. brought to the stage some popular plays in English that were translated into Tagalog. Acclaimed plays were *Golden Boy, Sa Pula, sa Puti and Isang Kuwaltang Abaka.*

Good music by Filipino classical composers presented several concerts at the Metropolitan Theatre. These concerts provided the people – the elites, the middle class and the masses with delight and enjoyment that they forgot temporarily the pain brought by war.

Filipino literature in English was in a state of extinction. The Japanese authorities discouraged the Filipinos from writing in English. The only Tagalog weekly magazine in circulation was the *Liwayway.* There were also a few writers who began to write short stories similar to Japanese *haiku.*

There was absolutely no freedom of expression. Writers were just limited in their subject matter. The favorite topics were mostly every day life situations occurring in the rural areas. In spite of the restrictions on freedom of expression, Filipino writers were able to produce good literary pieces that the Japanese civilian authorities were impressed and created a committee to choose the best stories. Consequently, an anthology entitled *Ang 25 Pinakamabuting Maikling Kathang Pilipino ng 1943* (the Twenty-five Best Filipino Short Stories in 1943), published in 1944.

The Japanese published the Philippine Review and Pillars both containing propaganda materials about Japan. The cultural scene, although to a great extent, did not flourish, the Japanese in effect, encouraged the development of Tagalog. One may inferred that whether their primary purpose was selfish or not, it remained to be seen. The fact remains that the Japanese purpose in encouraging Filipino writers to write in Tagalog, rather than in English, helped to a great extent these writers in Tagalog to rediscover the beauty and the promise about the potentialities of his native language-FILIPINO.

198 PHILIPPINE HISTORY AND GOVERNMENT THROUGH THE YEARS

The Commonwealth Government-in-Exile. President
Quezon, a man of vision, fortitude and rare courage thinking
of his death, issued an executive order naming Colonel Manuel
A. Roxas, President of the Commonwealth in the event that
he and Osmeña died. On March 26, two American bombers
took Quezon and his party to Australia. Almost a month later,
on April 19, they left for the United States on board the ship
President Coolidge. While in the United States with the
Commonwealth Government as an exile, Quezon appointed
members of his Washington Cabinet. They were: General
Basilio Valdez, Secretary of National Defense; Manuel Nieto,
Secretary of Agriculture and Commerce; Jaime Hernandez,
Secretary of Finance; and Joaquin Elizalde, Resident
Commissioner. The failing health of Quezon and officials of
the government-in-exile could not do more than raise the
morale of the Filipinos miles and miles away across the very
great area and extent of the Pacific.

Meantime, while the Filipinos were full of agony and
anxiety under the Japanese regime, the Commonwealth
Government was functioning in Washington, D.C.. Quezon
participated in the Pacific War Council of which he was a
member and subsequently, signed the agreement providing
for the creation and organization of the United Nations.

Because of the abnormal condition and the prevailing
circumstances brought about by war, Quezon felt that he
should continue to serve as President even beyond the eight-
year limit the Constitution prescribed for the office of the
President and Vice-President, respectively. On the issue of the
term of office, Senator Millard Tydings, co-author of the
Tydings-McDuffie Independence Act, pointed out by virtue
of the operation of the Philippine Constitution of 1935,
President Quezon's term of office would expire on November
15, 1943. It can be gleaned from Quezon that he still wanted to
continue as President even beyond the term provided by the
Constitution; however, some of the members of his cabinet
felt that Osmeña should succeed him in accordance with the
fundamental and highest law of the land. Osmeña, a man of
patriotism and humility, thought that at this hour of our

history, there must be unity in the ranks. Cognizant of the fact that Quezon still wanted to continue as President, he prepared a resolution to the American Congress, requesting that the provisions on succession embodied in the Philippine Constitution be waived, in effect, making Quezon President of the Philippines even beyond the eight-year limit. Such as genuine gesture is unprecedented in the annals of the Philippine politics.

The resolution was passed and approved by the United States Congress on November 9, 1943 which President Roosevelt signed on November 12, 1943, three days before the expiration of the term of the office of President Quezon. Thus, Quezon continued as President of the Commonwealth Government. Because of his health almost a year later, on August 1, 1944, he died at Saranac Lake Sanitarium, New York. In the afternoon of the same day, Sergio Osmeña succeeded him and became the President of the Philippines.

Study Guides

A. Terms/Concepts to Understand

indiscriminate   predicament
skirmish   scorching
bleak   atrocity
annal   impregnable
maneuver   fortitude

B. Questions to Answer

1. Why was the Philippines involved in the Second World War?

2. Why does our Philippine Constitution renounce war? Explain your answer.

3. What incident sparked the outbreak of war in the Pacific?

4. Describe the bleak Christmas of 1941.

5. Relate the Fall of Bataan.

6. Do you think it was correct for the Filipinos to fight against Japan during the Second World War? Explain your answer.

7. What changes were made in our national government under the Japanese control?

8. Describe the Japanese educational policy. What was the main focus of the educational program?

9. Describe the infamous "Death March."

10. Describe the social and cultural conditions under the Japanese occupation.

Chapter 14

The Liberation of the Philippines

The guerrillas carried out missions that were of great importance to the Allied war efforts in the Pacific. Undoubtedly, they played a significant role in the eventual liberation of the Philippines from the Japanese invaders. They supplied the most-needed information that MacArthur should have in planning his return to the Philippines. He knew exactly where to land and what to expect from their enemy who were holding their ground and fighting with tenacity. It should be noted that, aside from the valuable information and intelligence reports they gathered, such as size of the combat troops and their movements and the activity of the Japanese Military Administration, the guerrillas performed other functions like abusing Japanese patrol and liquidating Filipino spies.

The Battle of the Philippine Sea. By August 1944, impending hostile encounter between the American and the Japanese forces was inevitable. Slowly and deliberately, the American naval and marine forces were approaching the Philippine sea. Saipan Island was bombarded by the American naval fleet while mariners landed in Guam, an island belonging to the United States.

Meanwhile, the Japanese fleet, composed of battleships cruisers and destroyers, moved hastily toward the Marianas to relieve the Japanese garrison where their big troops were stationed. On the other hand, Admiral Raymond Spruance, commanding the American fleet were eagerly waiting for the enemy west of the Marianas, simultaneously, he sent heavy-bomber airplanes to attack Iwo Jima to neutralize the Japanese bases in the islands. On June 1944, the Battle of the Philippine Sea began. This was fiercely fought between the protagonists primarily an air fight. The air battle began in Guam, with Admiral Mare Mitchel and his task force pushing relentlessly the attack. The result of the air combat over Guam was the total destruction of four hundred and two airplanes as against seventeen American airplanes lost and four battle ships damaged. With the massive destruction of the Japanese airplanes, battleships, and cruisers, the American bombers subsequently captured the islands.

Objective Leyte. With the knowledge of President Roosevelt, the landings in the Philippines were to be carried out by the forces under General MacArthur. The liberation forces of General MacArthur meant the adequate battleships, escort carriers, mine craft, amphibian tanks, landing craft and cargo ships to encounter the stubborn resistance of the Japanese forces led by Lt. General Tomoyuki Yamasita.

Almost every day in the first two weeks of October 1944, the Americans intensified their air and sea attacks in the Philippines. The relentless attacks of the American forces were carried out through air strikes, while at the same time, similar air raids were directed to Formosa in order to paralyze Japanese offensive. In desperation, the Japanese suicide pilots known as *Kamikaze* engaged in dog-fight against American pilots. Luzon was also attacked, while American navy troops moved over the seas in the Visayas to block the Japanese navy from their offensive operations in Leyte.

In October 1920, the Leyte beaches were severely bombarded by the American fighter planes and thereafter, beachheads were made, and at the same time, moving swiftly to counter attack the Japanese naval ships to drive the enemy. After the successive wave of assault, General MacArthur, together with Vice-President Osmena, General Carlos P. Romulo, General Valdes and some American troops waded ashore, at "Red Beach." They landed at Palo, Leyte, on October

20, 1944. The Americans had returned amidst speculation by skeptical Filipinos that it would be difficult for them, but General MacArthur fulfilled his promise: "I SHALL RETURN!"

Prelude to the Landing at Lingayen Gulf. The Battle of Leyte Gulf, considered one of the greatest battles in history, was fought simultaneously by both the opposing forces with intense ferocity in three places from October 24 to 26. These three places were the Battle of Surigao, Strait, the Battle of Samar, and the Battle of Cape Engano. These battles were fought by both the contending forces using, airplanes, battleships and carriers determined to demolish the enemy. Both suffered heavy losses in this hostile and non-stop war engagement.

On January 9, 1945, the American forces escorted by airplanes carriers and torpedoes, landed unexpectedly at Lingayen Gulf, because the Japanese were caught off guard, they could not offer stiff resistance. Their airplanes apparently dwindled in number and their battleships sank; and the Americans landed at San Fabian, Pangasinan. Meantime, the Japanese, in a desperation effort, retreated to the nearby hills. With the enemy disconcerted, the American forces moved without any resistance to Central Luzon, while the Japanese prepared a last-ditch battle in Manila.

The Liberation of Manila. MacArthur's plan and strategy after landing at Lingayen, was to move down South, for Manila has excellent harbor facilities. Meanwhile, the offensive operations were carried out in Batangas and San Narciso, Zambales. The move was deliberately designed to cut off the Bataan Peninsula so that the American troops can proceed to Subic Bay. On January 30, Subic Bay was in the hands of the American forces.

The Japanese forces in Manila started series of atrocities. They burned private homes, government buildings, churches and other landmarks. Men found in the streets were forcibly taken and compelled to work in Japanese garrisons and airfields. Trucks, cars and carts were confiscated by the Japanese from the civilians to be used for transporting soldiers and supplies from one place to another. They indiscriminately destroyed valuable documents, books, sculptured saints and other art objects. Hundreds of civilians – men, women, and even children were massacred in cold blood. Similar atrocities were perpetrated in the provinces by the Japanese, apparently as a revenge against the civilians for not collaborating with them. Houses and buildings were burned. Bridges were blasted to prevent the American forces from their offensive operation.

In Tarlac, the American forces moved rapidly to Pampanga, Bulacan and finally the outlaying border leading to the City of Manila. General MacArthur and the American forces entered Manila on February 3, 1945, spearheaded by tanks. The Filipinos welcomed the American soldiers as they yelled: "Victory, Joe!" making a "V" sign with their fingers as the jeeps and tanks sped by the streets of the city. The American armored units promptly moved with accelerated speed to the University of Sto. Tomas campus and saved the American and allied prisoners.

The Japanese forces, pushed against the wall, continued fighting and as they retreated, they set on fire buildings in Sta. Cruz, Binondo and Quiapo. Manila became a city of raging fire. They also blasted the bridges. After the dark billows of smoke, Manila lay prostrate amid the ruins of her once magnificent and imposing buildings.

The Battle of Besang Pass. The Besang Pass was about 5,000 feet high and commanded a good view for the enemies coming below. This mountain trail led to Cervantes, Ilocos Sur, which General Yamashita had strongly fortified. The long, narrow elevation of land and heavy artillery were installed, ready to assault the enemy. Colonel Russell V. Volckman of the United States Armed Forces in the Philippines, North Luzon (USAFIL, NL) was given the dangerous mission by the United States Sixth Army to assault and seize Besang Pass. The Battle of Besang Pass may be considered one of the fiercest and most dangerous battles between the American forces and the Japanese soldiers because the fury was day and night and continued over five months, resulting in heavy casualties on both sides. As the fury continued to surge furiously, the

American troops with heavy artillery and combat planes supported the fighting guerrillas until the enemy collapsed.

The Battle of Besang Pass characterized by courage and heroism, as well as bloodshed, ended on June 14, 1945, and immortalized the bravery of the Filipino soldiers.

The End of Hostilities. General MacArthur determined to carry out the war right at Japan's door; launched hundreds of B29's, the superforts; the U.S. heavy, long-ranged, four engine bomber dropped bombs in mainland Japan ports and cities like Tokyo, Nagoya and Osaka night and day.

On July 26, 1945, the Three Allied Powers – Great Britain, China and the United States, through President Truman and Prime Minister Churchill, issued the Potsdam Proclamation urging Japan to surrender unconditionally or face "prompt and utter destruction," but instead of heeding the unconditioned surrender, Japan, still proud and arrogant of her strength, through Premier Kantaro Susuki, refused to surrender, saying that the Imperial Government of Japan would take no action of the ultimatum.

The August 6, 1945, the United States Air Force dropped the deadly uranium bomb on the Japanese City of Hiroshima. It destroyed over half the city, killed about 60,000 persons outright and wounded 100,000 others. On August 9, of the same year, another bomb that fell on Nagasaki three days later was actuated by the fission of plutonium, an artificial radioactive element derived from the bombardment of uranium by neutrons in atomic reactors built for that purpose in the United States. It flattened a square mile of Nagasaki and took a heavy toll of life. With the most incomprehensible destruction of the atomic blast in the history of mankind, Japan finally lost its will to resist. Faced with total annihilation, Japan unconditionally accepted the demand for surrender on August 15, 1945. On September 2, 1945, Japan signed the terms and conditions of surrender on board the battleship USS *Missouri* at Tokyo Bay. General MacArthur, newly appointed Supreme Commander of the Allied Powers (SCAP) in Japan, presided over the historic ceremonies, finally ending the war.

Meanwhile, Lieutenant General Yamashita, referred to as the "Tiger of Malaya" because of his conquest of Malaya, a British protectorate in 1942, surrendered to Major General Leavery, Deputy Commander and Chief of Staff of the Armed Forces in the Western Pacific region.

The Restoration of the Commonwealth Government. Immediately after almost the entire part of the archipelago fell in the hands of the Americans, General MacArthur, upon his return to the Philippines with President Osmeña, who succeeded the late President Quezon, the Commonwealth Government was temporarily established in Tacloban, Leyte, on October 24, 1944, and later it was established in Manila.

On the ninth anniversary of the Commonwealth Government, on November 15, 1944, President Osmeña delivered his address to the Filipino people full of endearing words about the bravery, ideals of democracy and freedom. A part of his address read:

> "The cause of democracy and liberty, the right of every people to govern itself and to be secure against aggression, the great moral issues of justice and righteousness and human dignity, are being fought in the Philippines today. I am proud of the way the American soldier is fighting the battle. I am also proud of the way the Filipinos are abiding in that fight."

General MacArthur, a man of foresight and wisdom, turned over the administration of the civil government to President Osmeña which he had previously taken over as Military Administrator.

In a simple ceremony on February 27, 1945 regarding the turn-over of the Commonwealth Government to President Osmeña, General MacArthur declared:

> ....God has indeed blessed our arms! The girded and unleashed power of America, supported by our Allies turned the tide of battle in the Pacific... culminating in the redemption of your soil and the liberation of your people. My country has kept the faith!

President Osmeña, was deeply touched by the simple but meaningful message of General MacArthur on the significant event of the life a nation and he pledged with firm resolve and determination to do his best in rehabilitating our country which had been ravaged by war.

The proclamation of the liberation of the Philippines from the Japanese Imperial forces was on July 4, 1945, amidst the euphoria and jubilation of the Filipino people. Thus, the END of the WAR.

The Task Ahead. President Osmeña, as the head of the duly constituted government, was challenged by the gigantic task of rehabilitating the country as a result of war.

The complete restoration of the Commonwealth of the Philippines – the executive and judicial branches will be reestablished with utmost vigor and dispatch. The duly elected members of Congress who had remained steadfast in their allegiance to our government during the dark days of the Japanese occupation must be ready to meet in Manila as soon as conditions allowed them to for the reestablishment of the Legislative branch. Cognizant of the various problems of national significance that must be dealt with, were the reorganization of the government-national and local levels, the reestablishment of agencies that should be responsible for law and order, the reopening of schools, the construction, rehabilitation and repair of school buildings, hospitals, bridges and other important infrastructure that had to be rehabilitated or indemnified. The legitimate claims of common laborers, small farmers and fishermen who had lost their tools, work animals, and fishing nets must be given preferential attention and priority.

This war had not only caused untold misery and suffering to our people, but it had also brought about wanton destruction to lives and property, economic dislocation and financial bankruptcy. Farms and industries had to be rehabilitated, banks and credit facilities had to be reopened.

As head of the duly constituted government, President Osmeña appealed to the Filipino people to remain united and urged them to forget petty political bickering and differences; bury the hatred and animosities engendered by the struggle; obey the rule of law, justice and reason; and to remember that the Philippines belongs to the Filipinos.

The Congress of the Philippines met for the first time after the war and Senator Manuel A. Roxas was chosen President of the Senate, while Senator Elpidio Quirino was chosen President Pro-tempore.

The Speaker of the House of the Representatives was the Representative of Iloilo, Jose C. Zulueta and Speaker Pro-tempore was Representative Prospero Sanidad. The newly constituted legislative body passed various resolutions and legislative enactments concerning the rehabilitation and reconstruction of the Philippines.

The Transition of the Commonwealth to Republic. It should be noted that the term of office of President Osmeña was soon to expire. On April 23, 1946, the last national election under the Commonwealth Period was held. Manuel A. Roxas and Elpidio Quirino were elected President and Vice-President, respectively. On May 26, 1946, Roxas' assumption to office was inaugurated in simple but impressive ceremonies as the last President of the Commonwealth. A mammoth crowd witnessed the outgoing President Osmeña, accompanied by the in-coming President Roxas. The change of national leadership from May 26, 1946 when Roxas was inaugurated as the last President of the Commonwealth to July 4, 1946, the date of the proclamation of Philippine Independence was to close.

On July 4, 1946, the Republic of the Philippines was inaugurated at the Luneta amidst the jubilant Filipinos rejoicing the regained freedom. During this historic event, round of cheers and applauses; loud sounds from gun salute and from church bells were heard as foreign high-ranking officials and dignitaries witnessed the simple but solemn occasion. Representing the United States were Honorable Paul V. McNutt, last United States High Commissioner and First American Ambassador to the Philippines and Senator Millard

E. Tydings, co-author of the Philippine Independence Law. From Tokyo, General Douglas MacArthur came by a chartered plane to witness and to take part in the ceremonies.

President Roxas, after taking his oath of office, delivered his inaugural address, a part of which read:

"The Republic of the Philippines has now come into being, under a constitution providing a government which enthrones the will of the people and safeguards the rights of men. Our independence is our pride and our honor. We shall defend our nation with our lives and our fortunes."

Study Guides

A. Terms/Concepts to Understand

tenacity   hostile
simultaneous   collaborator
prelude   immortalize
beachhead   heavy artillery
skeptical   radioactive

B.   Questions to Answer

1. Who liberated the Philippines from the Japanese?

2. Describe the economic condition of the Philippines before the liberation.

3. How did the guerrillas carry out their missions? Explain your answer.

4. How did the World War end? What were the results?

5. Describe the liberation of Manila.

6. Describe the Battle of Besang Pass.

7. Do you justify the atomic bombings of the cities of Hiroshima and Nagasaki which caused so much destruction of human lives and properties? Explain your opinion.

8. How did General Douglas MacArthur carry out the war against the Japanese?

9. When and where did the terms and conditions of Japanese surrender happen?

10. Describe General MacArthur as a military man. What do you think were his good qualities as a soldier?

Chapter 15

The Republic of the Philippines as a Sovereign Nation

On July 4, 1946 the Republic of the Philippines was inaugurated in the City of Manila and Philippine independence proclaimed to the world by Harry S. Truman, President of the United States of America. It is the third Philippine Republic in our history, the first was the Malolos Republic (1899-1901) and the second, the Japanese-sponsored Philippine Republic (1943-1945). Despite the horrible destruction of our country during the war, our young Republic, firm and resilient, bravely marched to fulfill its noblest ideals.

Since 1946, our Republic has made considerable progress in the field of politics, economy and culture. Being the first Malayan Republic to emerge from the ahes of war, its record of development and achievement can be considered at par with developing countries. From 1946 up to the year 2002, ten Presidents had been administering the affairs of our country. They were Manuel A. Roxas (1946-1948), Elpidio Quirino (1948-1953), Ramon Magsaysay (1953-1965), Carlos P. Garcia (1957-1961), Diosdado Macapagal (1961-1965), Ferdinand E. Marcos (1965-1986), Corazon C. Aquino (1986-1992), Fidel V. Ramos (1992-1998), Joseph Ejercito Estrada (1998-2001), and Gloria Macapagal-Arroyo (2001-present).

Problems of the New Republic. Having risen out of the ashes of World War II, the new Republic that came into being was beset with tremendous problems it had to contend. One of the most serious problems was the peace and order issue

211

which came to escalate because of the agrarian unrest in Central Luzon and the existence of armed dissidents, especially in the rural area. It seemed that the government was helpless because of lawlessness that plagued not only Manila and other cities but also in some provinces.

The second serious problem was the financial condition because the Philippine economy was virtually destroyed by the war. Factories and industries had no production and agricultural lands had been idle for a quite a long time. The financial crisis was even aggravated by monetary inflation. The price of prime commodities soared high and the existence of millions of unredeemed guerrilla currency and billions of worthless Japanese war notes contributed immensely to the financial burden of the new-born republic.

The third problem was the acute shortage of fruitstuffs, consumer goods and construction materials. The prices of basic essentials, e.g., rice, corn, and canned goods became prohibitive. Cement, steel bars, lumber and galvanized iron sheets were very costly. Thousands of families lived in small shanties made of scraps called *barong-barong* and were undernourished was a common sight everywhere.

The other problem that needed attention was rehabilitation of schools, hospitals, churches, government buildings, roads and bridges that were destroyed during the war.

The unemployment and underemployment problems affect the lives of many Filipinos because of a malfunctioning economic system. Poverty, which is one of the effects of unemployment contributed tremendously to related social problems like squatting, criminality, mendicancy and malnutrition.

Manuel A. Roxas (1946-1948). Manual A. Roxas was the last president of the Commonwealth and the first president of the Republic of the Philippines. At the outset of his administration, the government's thrust was to set out its effort to solve the tremendous problems brought about by war. With the support of Congress and his Cabinet he pursued vigorously the rehabilitation and industrialization of the Philippines. The blueprint and the agenda of his economic programs were anchored on the various studies such as the Joint-Philippine-American Finance Commission Report of 1947, and the Hiben Technical Memorandum of 1947. It was noted that he made good beginnings in the areas of rehabilitation of our agriculture, industries, trade, transportation, communication and health care.

One of the serious political problems of the Roxas administration was the Hukbo ng Bayan Laban sa Hapon (HUKBALAHAP) movement. This was a social unrest characterized by restlessness and increasing disorder of peasant farmers in Central Luzon who felt that they were being exploited by the landlords. To aggrevate the volatile situation when Luis M. Taruc, the leader of the movement who was elected congressman in Pampanga was not allowed to take his seat in Congress. The Roxas government adopted a strong "mailed fist" policy against the HUKS with the objective of suppressing them. The Armed Forces of the government engaged in many battles against the HUKS but failed to check the socio-political menace.

The HUKBALAHAP Movement. The Hukbalahap Movement had its deep roots in the Spanish *enconmienda* system which began and developed into a system of exploitation. The numerous injustices, cruelties and abuses perpetrated by the *enconmienderos* upon the Filipino peasants led to the uprising that failed because of lack of unity and strong leadership, until agrarian became a national issue.

The founding of the Hukbalahap stemmed from the socialist-communist orientation of the Central Luzon peasants led to a more aggressive and militant peasant and labor movement. To carry out their action plan, the peasant leaders adopted a three-point platform: economic, political, and military. The economic phase of the peasant underground struggle consisted in the development of all means of providing the people with sustenance and at the same time, sabotage Japanese efforts to "loot the country." The political phase consisted of discrediting the "puppet regime" and in destroying its influence. The military aim was to harass the Japanese.

With the policies and principles laid down, the peasant leaders met and discussed the possible problems of the movement and thereafter, unanimously agreed to call it Hukbo ng Bayan Laban sa Hapon or HUKBALAHAP. Luis Taruc was chosen chairman of the committee.

The high command of the movement imposed an iron discipline on all its members. The unity and the discipline of men and women under the influence of HUKBALAHAP made Central Luzon and a few other provinces a HUK territory.

The sharp and constant fighting between the HUKs and the Military Police (MP's) civilian guards wrought havoc on the agricultural economy of Central Luzon. The people, placed in the crossfire of two contending forces, lived in misery, fear and hunger because seasonal harvests decreased tremendously resulting in the spiraling of the prices of essential commodities. For almost two years, the Roxas administration tried to quell the HUK resistance movement but to no avail.

The Death of Mrs. Quezon.   Frequent and sharp clashes between the MP's and the HUKS occurred throughout Central Luzon. This serious condition reached its climax when, on April 28, 1949, Mrs. Aurora Aragon Quezon, the wife of the late President Quezon, her daughter,Baby and other members of the group were ambushed and shot to death mercilessly in Bongaban, Nueva Ecija.

It can be said that the significance of the Huk Movement culminated the *enconmienda* system characterized by greed, brutality injustice and abuses, and consequently, redeemed the peasant degradation, loss of respect and abject poverty.

The Huk movement was both a lesson and a warning to the government. It can forestall the resurgence of dissidence only if it initiates genuine reforms in the Philippine agrarian system, which had remained feudalistic up to the present time, in order to establish permanent peace and order in our country.

The Death of Roxas. Roxas, whom the Huks labeled as the willing tool of American and Filipino vested interests, died of heart attack at Clark Field on April 15, 1948, after delivering a speech to the officers of the United States Air Force. The news of his untimely death shocked the Filipino people.

Important achievement of Roxas administration was the approval of Republic Act No. 35, which gave the tenants a more equitable share in the rice harvest, that 70% for tenants and 30% for landlords. Financial recovery was achieved by the promulgation of measures of lowering the cost of living, the establishment of the Rehabilitation Finance Corporation (RFC), the redemption of the Philippine National Bank notes and the guerrilla currency, the sale of war surplus property turned over to the government by the United States government, and the fiscal and balancing of the government budget for various operations.

There were two events of historical significance that happened during the Roxas administration. The first was the plebiscite of March 11, 1947, which approved the "parity amendment" to our Constitution, which provided the Americans to have the right to dispose, exploit, develop, and utilize "all agricultural, timber, and mineral lands" of the Philippines.

The second historical event that was significant was the return of the mortal remains of the late President Manuel L. Quezon to Manila on July 27, 1946, on board the United States aircraft carrier Princeton. Amidst the tears and prayers of the mourning nation, the Filipino people paid their last respect to their beloved president. President Quezon – Statesman, Freedom Fighter and exponent of Social Justice, was laid to rest at the North Cemetery of Manila on August 1, 1946.

Elpidio Quirino (1948 -1953) Second President of the Republic of the Philippines. Vice-President Quirino took his oath of office as President of the Republic of the Philippines on April 17, 1948. His official act as head of the government was the proclamation of a state of mourning for the late President Roxas. On April 28, 1948, his mortal remains were laid to rest at the North Cemetery while thousands of Filipinos mourned.

Quirino completed the unexpired term of President Roxas in 1949. During the Presidential election on November 9, 1949, he ran for Presidency as the official candidate of Liberal Party, with Senator Fernando Lopez as his running mate. He won the election and served from 1949 to 1953.

Some of his important achievements were: (1) the breaking of the backbone of the Huk movement and the restoration of the relative peace and order; (2) the creation of President's Action Committee on Social Amelioration (PACSA) to help the poor families; (3) the establishment of rural banks to facilitate credit facilities in rural areas; (4) the establishment of the Agricultural Credit Cooperative Financing Administration (ACCFA) to help farmers market their crops; and (5) the adoption of a new economic policy called "Total Economic Mobilization Policy" to develop our trade and industries.

Ramon Magsaysay (1953 -1957) Third President of the Republic of the Philippines. Magsaysay succeeded Quirino. The presidential election held on November 10, 1953, saw the downfall of the Liberal Party where President Quirino ran for reelection and lost. Ramon Magsaysay, the Secretary of National Defense in President Quirino's Cabinet and Senator Carlos P. Garcia, National Party candidates for President and Vice-President respectively, were elected.

Ramon Magsaysay, an able and honest man, Secretary of National Defense before he was elected president brought about an official change of attitude toward the problem of dissidence. Regarded as plain banditry compounded of communism, the Huk movement, which was, in essence agrarian in nature, gradually lost its support when Secretary Magsaysay came to them and listen to their problems with an open heart and convinced many of them that their future lay in peace and honor.

Magsaysay's Charismatic Leadership. Magsaysay became President because he was loved by the common *tao.*

True to his promise, he worked hard to uplift the lives of the masses in their communities. He involved various government agencies and civic organizations in the vast undertakings of bringing progress to every barrio. He approached the rural problem along three lines of objectives: (1) the improvement of the land tenure system; (2) easy-term credit to the farmers, the building of roads and other facilities for the benefit of the rural folk, and giving technical advices to the farmers on how to improve farm operations, and an (3) intensive community development through self-help as a basic strategy.

The remarkable achievements of Magsaysay administration were:

1. Restoration of the Filipino people's faith in democracy.

2. Communication threat was checked by defeating the objectives of the Hukbalahap.

3. Improvement of the barrios and the vigorous implementation of the Presidential Assistant on Community Development (PACD) program all over the Philippines.

4. Promotion of positive nationalism through the use of native attire (barong tagalog and balintawak) during social and political functions, and the encouragement of the use of the Filipino language.

5. Ratification by the Philippine Senate of the San Francisco Treaty ending the war with Japan on July 16, 1956.

6. The construction of artesian wells and water systems in order to give the rural folk clean and potable drinking water.

7. Improvement of health and sanitation.

8. The creation of the Presidential Complaints and Action Committee (PCAC) in order to help make the Government "truly a government of the people."

It may be of interest to every Filipino that during his incumbency as President of the Republic of the Philippines, he opened Malacanang Palace to all the people, especially the common *tao.* He believed that the Palace was built and being kept with the taxpayers' money.

President Magsaysay died in an airplane crash in a mountain in Cebu on March 17, 1957. With him died twenty-five companions on board the ill-fated plane, including Dr. Gregorio Hernandez, Jr. the Secretary of Education. The only survivor of the plane crash was Nestor Mata, a newspaperman.

His funeral procession was mourned and witnessed by thousands of Filipino people from all walks of life in the long stretch street from the Legislative Building in Manila up to the North Cemetery under the scorching heat of the sun to catch a glimpse of the funeral cortege of their beloved idol, the late President Magsaysay, man of integrity and simplicity, man of the masses.

Carlos P. Garcia (1957-1961) Fourth President of the Republic of the Philippines. On March 18, a day after the death of Magsaysay, Vice-President P. Garcia took his oath of office at Malacanang as the Fourth President. Garcia completed Magsaysay's unexpired term in 1957. He ran for President as the official candidate of the Nationalista Party, with Speaker Jose Laurel, Jr. as running mate. His opponents were Jose Yulo of the Liberal Party with Diosdado Macapagal as running mate. The Presidential election was held on November 1957. Garcia won the presidency, but Laurel lost the vice-presidency. He took his oath of office as president of our Republic and Vice-President Macapagal took his oath of office on the same day.

Garcia Administration. With the serious economic problems that confronted the country, President Garcia, anchored his program of government in austerity. Appealing to the people to support his program, he said that austerity as a policy means "temperate spending". It signifies more work, more thrift, more productive investment and more efficiency. It means less imports and less extravagant consumption. It is a challenge to our resiliency as a people to change our past habits and make thrift and economy our everyday way of living.

Among the achievements of the Garcia administration were:

1. The promotion of economic independence through the adoption of the Filipino First policy.

2. The establishment of Filipino dignity as a free people by dealing with foreign powers in terms of sovereign equality.

3. The achievement of a balanced economy by providing equal impetus to agriculture and industry.

4. The promotion of social justice and general welfare of the people, especially the masses.

5. The revival of Filipino culture by way of encouraging Filipino historians to pursue intensive researches in the Philippine arts.

Carlos P. Garcia lost the presidential election on November 14, 1961 while Vice-President Diosdado Macapagal was elected President, with his running mate, Emmanuel Pelaez.

Diosdado Macapagal (1961-1965), Fifth President of the Republic of the Philippines. President Macapagal came from a poor family from Lubao, Pampanga. Macapagal is best remembered as a man of intellectual and moral integrity. His dedication to public service as president helped propel our economy in the early 1960's to second position after Japan.

When he assumed the presidency, he promised to champion the cause of the common man. To bring about a "New Era," he adopted a five-year socio-economic program and a determined policy of moral regeneration.

Among the significant achievements of Macapagal Administration were:

1. The land reform program, which aims to abolish the century-old tenancy in our country.

2. The propagation of Filipino, as our national Language. The language was used in diplomatic credentials, passports, stamps and traffic signs and landmarks.

3. The changing of our independence from July 4th to June 12th.

4. Greater participation in world affairs. He was responsible for the establishment of MAPHILINDO (a Confederation of Malaya, Philippines, and Indonesia). To maintain peace in Asia, he tried to mediate in the U.S.-Cambodia crises and the Malaysia – Indonesia conflict.

Study Guides

A.   Terms/Concepts to Understand

sovereign	monetary inflation
horrible	HUKBALAHAP
ideals	puppet regime
rehabilitation	social-communist orientation
quell	degradation

B.   Questions to Answer

1. Who served as President of the Philippines upon the restoration of the Commonwealth government?

2. Who was the last President of the Commonwealth?

3. Enumerate the various problems besetting our country after World War II

4. What was the worst political problem of the Roxas administration?

5. How did the Hukbalahap movement start? What were the factors that contributed to its support?

6. Who was Luis Taruc?

7. What could be learned from the HUKBALAHAP movement?

8. Identify the accomplishment of the Quirino administration.

9. Why was Magsaysay loved by the Filipino masses? State the reasons.

10. Identify the significant accomplishments of the Macapagal administration.

Chapter 16

Martial Law and the New Society

Article VII, Section 10, of the 1935 Constitution of the Philippines provides that the President shall be the Commander-in-Chief of all armed forces of the Philippines and whenever it becomes necessary, he may call out such armed forces to prevent or suppress lawless violence, invasion, insurrection, or rebellion. In case of invasion, insurrection or rebellion, when the public safety requires it, he may, suspend the privilege of the writ of habeas corpus or place the Philippines or any part thereof under Martial Law.

A question may be asked. What is the meaning, basis, object, and duration of Martial Law? Martial Law in its comprehensive sense, includes all laws that have reference to and administered by the military forces of the State. They include the military laws enacted by the law-making body for the government of the armed forces and the rules governing the conduct of military forces in times of war and in place under military occupation. However, in its strict sense, it is that law which has application when the military arm does not supersede civil authority but is called upon to aid it in the execution of its vital functions. The Constitution refers to this meaning of Martial Law.

As to the basis, the right to declare, apply and exercise martial law is one of the rights of sovereignty. It is as essential to the existence of a nation as the right to declare and carry on

222

war. The power is founded on necessity and is inherent in every government.

The object of martial law is the preservation of public safety and order. Unless the right and power to exist, peace, order and security – government itself may be destroyed and obliterated, when mob becomes so powerful that it can not be contained by the civil authorities.

Some political analysts and observers inferred that history will be able to record in its final and proper perspective that some over-ambitious politicians and rapacious wealthy anti-Marcos, to a certain extent, actually did democracy a disservice in the Philippines. They provided Marcos with the final excuse to declare Martial Law with their ban of Marcos resolution of 1976. Perhaps, if some of the Marcos political opponents who subjected the President to expose to public ridicule at every turn and were only united in their efforts in their criticism who may have their own selfish personal objectives to serve had a little more patience and gave him more time to reflect, he might consider an accommodation. After all, he was only another mortal like all politicians, he would also fade and die.

Prelude to the Declaration of Martial Law. While the political bickerings between opposing major political parties escalated, the unfolding drama of the militant student activities intensified their demonstrations and rallies with inflammatory rhetorics against the Marcos administration. The wave of dissent included workers, intellectuals and even members of the religious groups.

The spade of lawlessness and violence erupted with a series of incidents; e.g., the bombing of Joe's Department Store on busy Carriedo Street in downtown Manila and the constitutional site at Quezon City Hall, the Manila Water Works and Sewerage Authority (NAWASA), and the City Hall building of Manila were badly damaged. The sporadic bombings in Metro Manila seemed like a nightmare for many peace-loving Filipinos. To aggravate the problems, assassination, sabotage, urban terrorism, armed robbery, carnapping, illegal traffic in prohibited drugs, smuggling of arms, murder and armed clashes between the military and the enemies of the government became prevalent and were undermining the security and stability of the state. As a result of these incidents, economy began to stand still.

The most tragic drama was the bombing of Plaza Miranda, which exploded in the face of the nation in the evening of August 21, 1971, where the proclamation rally of the opposition candidates of the Liberal Party for local elections scheduled on November 8, 1971. Two Vietman-war type fragmentation grenades were lobbed by unidentified persons and exploded on the stage where the entire Liberal Party leaderships except Senator Benigno B. Aquino who was not present during the horrible night. Among those wounded were Senator Gerardo Roxas and his wife, Senator Jovito Salonga, Sergio Osmeña, Jr., Eva Estrada-Kalaw, Congressman John Osmeña, Ramon Mitra, Jr., Ex-Congressman Eddie Ilarde, Congressman Ramon Bagatsing, and Laguna Governor Felicisimo San Luis. The outrageous Plaza Miranda carnage stirred the indignation of the Filipino people.

The opposition political leaders alleged that those terror-bombing incidents were perpetuated by the military, but President Marcos blamed the Maoist New People's Army. The opposition further allegedly accused the Marcos administration of fabricating incidents in order to destroy the people's faith in their existing form of government and thereby weaken their opposition to, or accept as an only viable alternative to a nationwide anarchy, the imposition of Martial Law. Whether the accusations were true or not, it was evident that the country was on the verge of social upheaval.

Suspension of the writ of Habeas Corpus. President Marcos issued Proclamation No. 880, suspending the privilege of the writ of habeas corpus "in order to maintain peace and order, secure the safety of the people, and preserve the authority of the State." It should be noted that President Elpidio Quirino also suspended the writ of habeas corpus on October 22, 1950 to suppress the Hukbalahap rebellion escalating in some provinces, especially in Central Luzon.

Despite the suspension of the writ of habeas corpus, the local elections of 1971 was held on November 8, 1971, where six out of eight senators of the Liberal Party were elected and two Nacionalista Party candidates won. The six LP senators were Jovito Salonga, topnotcher, Genaro Magsaysay, John Osmena, Eddie Ilarde, Eva Estrada-Kalaw and (NP, but guest candidate of the LP) Ramon Mitra. The two NP senators elected were Ernesto Maceda and Alejandro Almendras.

In the months following these elections of 1971, the menace of communist insurgency became less in intensity, so Marcos restored the privilege of habeas corpus on December 4, 1971 in some provinces and cities and later, on January 11, 1972, the whole archipelago.

The restoration of the writ of habeas corpus gave the entire nation the opportunity to enjoy once more the valuable human right and freedom which is the essence and well-spring of democracy. However, the threat on the security and stability of the State was again put to a precarious situation. The government claimed that dissidents were receiving military support from a foreign source with the interception of military men on the landing of combat weapons, ammunitions and equipment along the Coast of Digoyo, Palanan, Isabela on July 2, 1972. The ambush of the official car of secretary of National Defense Juan Ponce Enrile provided for the implementation of the proclamation of Martial Law. On September 21, 1972, President Marcos by virtue of Proclamation No. 1081, placed the entire Philippines under martial law. In a nationwide radio and television broadcast, he gave two objectives in utilizing the power, namely: "to save the Republic and reform our society." "We will eliminate the threat of a violent overthrow of our Republic" and "at the same time, we must now reform the social, economic and political institutions in our country." He abolished Congress of the Philippines, the law-making body under the 1935 Philippine Constitution.

While Martial law existed, civil rule prevailed in the country. The officials and employees of the national and local governments continued in office and discharged their duties. General Order No. 3, issued on September 22, 1972, provided that "all executive departments, bureaus, offices, agencies and instrumentalities of the National government, government-owned or controlled corporation, as well as all government of all provinces, cities, municipalities, and barrios throughout the land shall continue to function under their present officers and employees. Moreover, all courts, from the municipal courts up to the Supreme Court, continued to try and decide cases, in accordance with existing laws."

Immediately upon signing Proclamation No. 1081, thousands of anti-Marcos politicians, student activists, columnists, newspaper men who were critical to his administration, were arrested and herded into military stockades. Among them were Senators Benigno Aquino Jr, Jose W. Diokno and Ramon Mitra and other politicians. The Constitutional Delegates included Napoleon Rama, Enrique Voltaire Garcia and Jose Mari Velez (anti-Marcos radio-television commentator), Joaquin "Chino" Roces, publisher of Manila Times, Jose Lacson, publisher of Philippine Free Press, Journalists Maximo Soliven, Amando Doronilla and other communists and newspaper men. Some professors in the universities who were critical to the administration were thrown to jail.

The President's military choked hard at the throats of writers, editors and publishers. Constabulary troopers sealed newspapers, radio and television facilities. Those arrested were confined either at Camp Crame or at Fort Santiago. Provincial Constabulary barracks served as jails for provincial journalists. All mass media – print and broadcast were subjected to strict censorship.

The only newspaper, which never closed its door was the Daily Express. Its sister facility, television Channel 9, and allied radio stations of Kanlaon Broadcasting System, also were opened. Before the end of the year 1972, the Times Journal and the former Manila Daily Bulletin were allowed to re-open under the new name Bulletin Today. These newspapers and TV channel 9 were perceived to be owned by Marcos cronies.

Vital public utilities and industries, e.g., the MERALCO

(Manila Electric Company), the Philippine Long Distance Telephone Company, and the Iligan Integrated Steel Mills were seized and subsequently placed under control.

All student demonstration and rallies, public meetings and assemblies and labor strikes were strictly not allowed. Curfew was imposed. No person was allowed to go out the curfew period without a pass or a permit from the military authorities. Travel ban was imposed on Filipino citizens who wanted to leave the country. Exempted from this ban were Filipino immigrants to the United States and Canada, Filipino diplomats on foreign diplomatic missions, consuls assigned to other countries with the approval of the Office of Foreign Affairs and Filipino delegates to attend conferences to other countries.

The drive to surrender firearms and other explosives was vigorously enforced. Heavy penalties were imposed on persons confiscated with firearms. The Philippine Constabulary reported the total of 528,618 firearms that were surrendered during the first months of Martial Law.

The Government Under Martial Law. The government to govern the country was euphemistically called an authoritarian constitutional government. The President exercised extra-ordinary powers. Combining the executive and legislative powers, he made new laws called presidential decrees, general orders, proclamations and letters of instruction, and executed them himself. The Congress of the Republic of the Philippines, the legislative organ under the 1935 Constitution, was abolished. The Supreme Court, and other lower courts, including the quasi-judicial courts continued to exercise their judicial functions. Martial Law had brought a new stimulus and experience to the conduct of government in the Philippines.

The President introduced new changes embodied in the Reorganization Plan. These were:

- Creation of new executive departments, e.g., Department of Public Information,

- Department of Local Government and Community Development, Department of Trade, Department of Natural Resources and Department of Tourism,

- Renaming of the Department of Education to Department of Education and Culture, where three separate bureaus were created – Bureau of Elementary Education, Bureau of Secondary Education and Bureau of Higher Education,

- Creation of the National Economic Development authority (Neda),

- Changing of the Bureau of Immigration to the Commission of Immigration and Deportation,

- Abolition of the Court of Industrial Relations, the National Economic Council (NEC), the Presidential Economic Staff, the Code Committee, the Office of Agrarian Counsel, the Anti-Dummy Board and the government offices performing duplicate functions.

- To check the abuses of the military officers and other military personnel, he established special military courts called "military commissions" which tried cases and punished them after they were found guilty for committing abuses against the civilians. Civil service personnel who were notoriously undesirable and inefficient were terminated from the service.

The first few months of the declaration of Martial Law, peace and order was evidently better because crime rate was relatively reduced. Life in Greater Manila and in the provinces returned to normal.

Marcos' New Society. The President's vision was not only to save the Republic but also to form a new society – a society that is disciplined, self-sufficient, orderly, peaceful, and self-reliant. For Marcos, the New Society had brought a new kind of governance that incited actions, feelings and thoughts. Much effort had gone to social reform, the maintenance of peace and order, mobilization of government resources for land reform, the accumulation of foreign reserves, economic

MARTIAL LAW AND THE NEW SOCIETY

investment, educational innovation, socialized housing, and promotion of health.

The barangays or the citizen's assemblies were revitalized and evolved to effect participation through consultation with the people and headed by Imee Marcos, National Chairman of the Kabataang Barangay.

The reforms he conceived and instituted for his New Society was anchored on seven areas with the acronym PLEDGES with the underlying programs of governance, as follows:

P – Peace and Order
L – Land Reform
E – Economic Development
D – Development of Moral Values
G – Government Reforms
E – Educational Reforms
S – Social Services

To translate these programs full of ideals and promises, President Marcos created various "Task Forces" and "Do Tanks." At the early part of existence, peace and order as a component was evidently felt, perhaps because of the new stimulus, there was a climate of fear due to an authoritarian rule. The government programs were pushed through presidential decrees and assumed broader responsibilities in economic planning, technological training, transport development, conservation and management of oil and power resources, human settlements and environment control, housing, agriculture, water resources, management effective land use and educational innovations and alternatives.

On Agrarian Reform Program. Perhaps one of the achievements of the Martial Law was the land reform, which emancipated the tenant farmers from the land they till that belonged to the oligarchic feudal land system. On October 21, 1972, he issued Presidential Decree No. 27, entitled Emancipation of Tenants from the Bondage of the Soil, Transferring to Them the Ownership of the Land They Till and Providing the Instruments and Mechanism Thereof.

Pursuant to this Decree and its implementing rules, through the Department of Agrarian Reform confiscated from the landlords, their rice and corn lands, whose area exceeded seven hectares, and distributed them in smaller farm lots to the landless tenant farmers. The tenant farmers were awarded seven hectares per family, and the amount to be paid by the Land Bank on installment basis payable in 15 years. The farmers were liberated from the bondage of the soil. They finally became owners of the agricultural lands, which they and their ancestors had been tilling for their landlords for many years.

On Economic Development. President Marcos established the National Economic and Development Authority (NEDA) which will formulate the viable economic policies and the "task of formulating and overseeing the national economic development program" of the New Society. Economic development programs purportedly promised to bolster and accelerate development were the Philippine geothermal plant in Tiwi, Albay, Mount Makiling and Mount Banahaw in Laguna. The government boasted that oil was discovered on the west coast off Palawan (Nido-Cadiao Malintoc oilfields) and in the succeeding years, the Nido oil wells will start to produce oil in commercial quantity.

The construction of the first nuclear plant in the Philippines that will supply adequate power was constructed in Morong, Bataan; but unfortunately, the Philippine government had not benefited from this economic investment. What is worse, a big amount of the debt service in the annual budget had to be appropriated to pay for the interest loan annually.

The construction of various infrastructure projects, e.g., water ports, airports, bridges, dams, irrigation and communication facilities and school buildings contributed to the economic image of our country. The longest bridge in the Philippines, San Jaunico Bridge, that links Samar and Leyte is indeed a landmark. The Light Rail Transit (LRT) that stretched from Bonifacio Monumento in Caloocan City up to Baclaran, provides transportation system to our people.

Prominent among the buildings, that were constructed were the Philippine Heart Center, the Philippine International Convention Center, the Film Center, the Folk Arts Theatre, Palace in the Sky and Coconut Palace. While some of these big magnificent buildings are being used today, the Film Center and Palace in the Sky are not.

On Development of Moral Values. The Department of Education and Culture was tasked to provide and promote values education at all levels of the educational system. Its goal was the development of the human person committed to the building of a "just and human society" and an independent and democratic nation. The primary objectives were directed towards the proper implementation of the program that will develop Filipinos who are self-activated, integrally developed human beings imbued with a sense of human dignity.

On Government Reforms. Through the Reorganization Plan, the President introduced new modes of restructuring and creating new departments mentioned in the preceding topics. For purposes of better administrative control and supervision, the decentralization scheme was instituted by dividing the archipelago into twelve administrative regions, each headed by a regional director.

He also created the Metro Manila of the manager-type form of government (P.D. No. 824) to coordinate, unify and integrate the planning and delivery of common essential local government services and functions and has proven to have truly harnessed the Area's potentials and resources to arrest the physical deterioration of socio-economic decline of the nation's premier metropolis.

Corollary to this manager-type form of government was the Metro Manila Commission, which sought to formulate an overall comprehensive development framework plan for Metro Manila.

On Educational Programs. The educational reforms emphasized both academic studies as well as technological and vocational courses. To remedy the oversupply of graduates in various academic courses like business education, liberal arts and law, resulting in the serious problem of "white collar" unemployment the technological and vocational courses were the main thrusts of the educational reforms. To remedy the misconception and eliminate the cultural bias on technological and vocational courses, the President issued the Educational decree No. 6-A which defined the objectives of the national educational system, relating them more directly to the national development goals. This provided that the guidelines for the planning of the Ten-Year Educational Program. This educational reforms include:

- Adoption of the national College Entrance Examination (NCEE) for all high school graduates who would pursue bachelors degree in higher education in colleges and universities.

- The introduction of the Youth Civil Action Program (YCAP) requiring students to render services like cleaning the school surroundings, town plazas and streets and planting trees, to install in their minds the value and dignity of labor.

- Introduction of the bilingual method of instruction in Filipino and in English as the medium of instruction in selected subjects to be implemented gradually from elementary, secondary and college levels. Filipino is used as a medium of instruction in Social Studies, Character Education, Health Education and Physical Education, while English is used in Mathematics and Physical and Biological Sciences.

- The restoration of the traditional 3R's (reading, 'riting and 'rithmetic) in the elementary school curriculum.

- The massive printing of textbooks for public elementary schools through a $25 million loan from the World Bank. This huge textbook project was undertaken by the Educational Development Project Implementing Task Force (EDPITAF).

- Filipinization of all schools in the country.

- The creation of the National Manpower and Youth Council tasked to develop skill-training programs on technical and vocational education.

On Social Services. The Ministry of Social Services and Development was tasked to identify social problems; conceptualized programs and provide alternative strategies and solutions. Among the social problems include poverty, population and crime, health, squatting, juvenile delinquency, alcoholism, drug abuse and dependency, effects of drug abuse, prostitution and sexually transmitted diseases, child prostitution, battered women and street children. In one of the programs was included former rebels and dispatched persons and these were given assistance. Corollary with its functions, the medical facilities of the Philippine Medical Care Commission extend health care through barrio midwives and paramedic personnel, helped roving doctors and nurses bring health care to communities that could not use medical services.

Other social agencies involved in uplifting the social condition and general welfare of the people are the Social Security System, Government Service Insurance System, Pag-ibig and other social agencies and organizations.

On Philippine Tourism. Many countries of the world, e.g., Italy, Spain. Portugal, France, United States and other European countries give tourism special attention and priority as development programs because this industry gives promise to accelerate income for the government. Presidential Decree No. 189, created the Department of Tourism to promote and supervise the tourist industry in the Philippines.

One of its programs was to encourage living abroad, especially those in the United States, Canada and Australia to visit their native country. This program called Balikbayan (Homecoming) offers certain incentives and benefits, like reduced plane ticket, hotel discount and other motivations in kind.

Other programs that were launched to attract tourist to come and see the Philippines include the holding of Miss Universe Beauty Pageant in Manila, the "Thrilla in Manila," the heavy weight boxing championship between Mohammad Ali and Joe Fraiser and other international activities such as Chess Tournament, basketball competition and cultural shows.

The Government and the Labor Market. President Marcos signed the Labor Code on may 1, 1974 which protected the rights of labor; promoted peaceful settlement of capital-labor disputes; prohibited labor strikes in vital industries; and laid down the principle of "one-industry one-union."

Because the unemployment and underemployment conditions in our country have increased in an alarming rate, and consequently, afflict the lives of many Filipinos, the government established the Overseas Employment Development Board and the National Seamen Board to help Filipino workers secure overseas jobs. To train jobless laborers, the government created eleven regional skills training centers under the supervision of the National Manpower and Youth Council. The exodus of skilled workers and professionals in the field of nursing, health care and medicine, engineering and teaching, consequently led to the phenomenon popularly known as "brain drain." The Labor statistics service of the Department of Labor and Employment has reported tens of thousands of Filipino overseas contract workers in various countries all over the world, especially in the Middle East. This role of the government on overseas employment and maximizing foreign job contracts as a national policy to ease unemployment and underemployment pressures in our country.

A Policy for our Muslim Brothers. The President launched various political, social and economic and cultural reform programs to uplift the lives of Filipino Muslims. He ordered the use of the local Muslim dialect in the elementary schools attended by Muslim children; offered various scholarships in colleges and universities for qualified and deserving Muslim youth; reorganized Muslin religion, laws, customs and traditions; and appointed qualified Muslims to public office.

The government under Martial Law spent millions of

pesos for the various infrastructure projects for the development of Mindanao. The annual Filipino-Muslim Pilgrimage to Mecca, Islam's holy city in Saudi Arabia was given aid and protection by the government.

It may be interesting to note that a Golden Mosque was built for our Muslim brothers for their spiritual meditation and nourishment in Quiapo, Manila. A Muslim village, called Maharlika, was established in Bicutan, Taguig, Rizal. An Islamic Studies Institute was opened at the University of the Philippines and the Islamic Affairs Ministry was created. The President also proclaimed Sultan Kudarat, a distinguished Maguindanao sultan, a national hero of the Philippines. He created the Muslim Provinces – Sultan Kudarat, Maguindanao, North Coatbato, and Tawi-Tawi, on October 1973. In compliance with the Tripoli Agreement on December 23, 1976, President Marcos proclaimed on March 26, 1977, an autonomous region on the Muslim Mindanao. These 13 Muslim provinces are composed of Basilan, Davao del Sur, Lanao del Norte, Lanao del Sur, North Coatabato, South Coatabato, Sulu, Tawi-Tawi, Sultan Kudarat, Palawan, Maguindanao, Zamboanga del Norte and Zamboanga del Sur.

In a plebiscite to determine the status of the autonomous region for the 13 provinces, both Christians and Muslims voted in favor of the autonomous government under Republic of the Philippines on April 17, 1977.

The Barangay. The creation of the barangay as a basic political unit that will serve as a forum wherein the collective views of the people may be expressed, crystallized and considered and where disputes within its jurisdiction may be amicably settled was another government reform under Martial Law. President Marcos issued Presidential decree No. 86 establishing the "citizens assemblies" in all cities, provinces and towns all over the archipelago. The Kabataang Barangay (Barangay Youth) was created by Presidential Decree No. 684, on April 15, 1975, to broaden the participation in the democratic process of the youth on national issues affecting them. Its primary functions dealt primarily with planning and implementing unit of government programs, projects and development activities in the community. The Pambansang Katipunan Ng Mga Sangguniang Bayan was also created. One of the administrative structures of the barangay is the Katarungang Pambarangay (Barangay Justice) to relive judicial courts of numerous petty cases submitted for adjudication. The administrative body of the barangay is headed by the barangay captain. The Lupong Tagapamayapa is authorized to hear petty cases brought to the Lupon and settle amicably disputes among the members of the barangay.

The government also launched the Barangay Brigade Development programs with different components such as barangay tanod, barangay traffic brigades, barangay disaster brigade, barangay women's auxiliary brigade and barangay volunteers brigade. The philosophical concept of these barangay brigades was to make all barangays in the Philippines to be self-reliant so that they would not depend totally on the national government on certain petty problems on their community and other public services which they could do on the barangay levels.

Like any development programs of the government amidst great fanfare at the launching ceremony there were lots of enthusiasm, but later on, the attitude and tenacity of purpose was lost.

Framing of the 1973 Philippine Constitution. Since the political independence of the Philippine on July 14, 1946, there had gradually developed a sentiment among the Filipinos that finally ripened into a consensus that the 1935 Constitution should be examined; and if there was a need to overhaul it, a constitutional convention was necessary.

The idea of calling a Constitutional Convention to propose amendments grew and more intense so fast, and as a consequence, Congress decided to call a convention for the purpose of proposing amendments. Republic Act No. 6132, approved on August 24, 1970 called the Constitutional Act of 1971, paved the way to the framing of the 1973 Constitution.

There were several reasons for calling a constitutional convention.

The 1935 Constitution was made by a colonial power – then, the mother country, United States. The Filipino people would have a chance to decide for themselves whether the 1935 Constitution was still adequate and satisfactory for their purposes.

The Constitutional Convention was set on June 1, 1971, with 320 delegates apportioned among the representative districts on the basis of proportional population representation. The qualified electors of every representative district were qualified to vote for the number of delegates corresponding to their districts.

The public support for the task of Constitution-making received by all sectors of society in our country – political, religious, economic, educational and civic, had fully cooperated in awakening the people of the importance of the historic task of constitution-making and of the election of the best minds to the convention. The general appeal for the election to the convention of men and women of ability, dedication and integrity became an issue. A candidate for delegate should have the qualifications required of members of the House of Representatives: Senators and representatives if elected delegates, could not hold the position without forfeiting their seats as legislators.

It was interesting to note that the 1971 Constitutional Convention was a representative of Philippine society. Dominated by a big number of lawyers, the Convention included in its membership businessmen, industrialists, physicians, educators, religious ministers, labor leaders, and men and women of the media. Two of them had been President of the Philippines – Carlos P. Garcia and Diosdado Macapagal.

The delegates brought with them to the convention a wealth of experience and information from the legislative, executive, judicial, departments: from local governments, from labor and industry; from education and religion; and from science, agriculture and culture.

The inaugural ceremonies held at the Manila Hotel were opened with senate President Gil Puyat and Speaker Cornelio

Villareal of the House of Representatives, jointly presiding. The chairman of the Commission on Elections, Jaime Ferrer called the roll of the delegates. The President of the Republic of the Philippines, Ferdinand E. Marcos, addressed the Convention.

Originally, the convention venue was the Manila Hotel. After holding its session for more than a year, it was moved to Quezon City Hall on August 3, 1972, where it held its sessions until the completion of its task on November 30, 1972.

Delegate Carlos P. Garcia, former President of the Philippines, was elected President of the Convention. Upon his death three days later, President Pro-Tempore Sotero H. Laurel took over the powers and functions of the presidency until the convention elected, as president, Delegate Diosdado Macapagal, likewise a former President of the Philippines, who continued to serve until the final adjournment of the Constitutional Convention.

The important issues that were heated by debate among the delegates were:

- Should the government be parliamentary or presidential?
- Should the national language be Filipino, or English?
- What should be the concept and theory of private property?
- Should compulsory voting be adopted?
- Should the voting age be reduced from 21 to 18 years?

After the deliberation on the vital issues that will affect the future of the country, the delegates came to a consensus to resolve the issues. A few days later, with a number of amendments, the delegates unanimously endorsed the approval the Convention adopted the Constitution on November 29, 1972, with two hundred seventy-three delegates who voted in favor of the Constitution, and fifteen who voted against the same; and one abstained. The Constitution was then signed by the delegates on November 30, 1972.

The Plebiscite Issues. On September 21, 1972, while the Convention was still in session, President Marcos placed the Philippines under Martial Law. The following day, he issued General Order No. 1, wherein he proclaimed that he would govern the nation and direct the operation of the entire government in his capacity as Commander-in-Chief of all the Armed Forces of the Philippines. Subsequently, he issued other decrees of the nature of legislation. From the attending circumstances, it appeared that perhaps for some time, Congress would not meet to pass the necessary ratification measure.

On November 22, 1972, while the delegates were working, expecting that their work would be finished before long, they approved a resolution proposing to the President that a decree be issued calling a plebiscite for the ratification of the proposed New Constitution on an appropriate date so he could determine and provide the necessary funds. The resolution did not prescribe the procedure to be followed in the ratification process.

On December 1, 1972, the Constitution was formally submitted to the President and on the same date, he issued Presidential decree No. 73, submitting to the Filipino people for ratification the proposed New Constitution and setting the plebiscite on January 15, 1973. The decree provided further that the provisions of the Election Code in 1971, insofar as they were not inconsistent therewith, should apply to the conduct of the plebiscite. In other words, the voting should be by secret ballot, and by then qualified voters who must be at least 21 years of age.

Constitutionality of the Decree. The constitutionality of the decree was challenged with the Supreme Court on December 7, 1972, by Attorney Charito Planas on the grounds that the said decree had no force and effect as law because the calling of such plebiscite, the setting of guidelines for the conduct of the same, prescription of ballots to be used, the questions to be answered by the voters, and the appropriation of public funds for the purpose, were matters within the exclusive jurisdiction of Congress. Besides, there was no sufficient time left to inform the people of the contents thereof. There were other similar actions filed by other petitioners.

The President abandoned the implementation of Presidential Decree No. 73; instead , the Commission on Elections immediately took steps to submit to a plebiscite for ratification of the New Constitution through the citizen assemblies. On December 23, 1972, he announced the postponement of the plebiscite. No date was announced.

On December 31, 1972, President Marcos issued Presidential Decree No. 86, creating "citizen assemblies" to broaden the base of citizen participation in the democratic process and to afford ample opportunities for the citizenry to express their views on important national issues. On January 5, 1973, he issued Presidential Decree No. 56-B defining the role of the barangays in expressing their views on national issues from time to time; that the initial referendum should include the matter of ratification of the 1973 Philippine Constitution.

The Supreme Court failed to resolve the Planas case and other similar cases, but pending judicial resolution of these cases, the process of ratification by the barangays went on from January 10 to January 15, 1973. The Daily Express published reports about this and it appeared that the political process on the matter was even going faster than the judicial process.

The Supreme Court explained later the reason for the postponement of final action on the cases filed by Charito Planas and others, said:

"In view of these events relative to the postponement of the aforementioned plebiscite, the courts deemed it fit to refrain, for the time being, from deciding the aforementioned cases, for neither date nor the conditions under which said plebiscite would be held were known or announced officially. Then, again, Congress was, pursuant to the 1935 Constitution, scheduled to meet in regular session on January 23, 1973, and since the main objection to Presidential

Decree No. 73 was that the President does not have legislative authority to call a plebiscite and appropriate funds therefore which congress unquestionably could do, particularly in view of the formal postponement of the plebiscite by the President – reportedly after consultation with, among others, the leaders of Congress and the Commission on Elections, the Court deemed it more imperative to defer its final action on these cases."

The President announced proclamation of the ratification of the Constitution on January 17, 1973. After making some remarks, he signed in the presence of the Katipunan ng mga Barangay (Federation of the barangay councils), a proclamation to the effect that the New Constitution had been ratified by the Filipino people (Proclamation 1102) stating further that as of today at 2:00 noon, the New Constitution was in force.

Supreme Court Hearing on January 17, 1973. While the Planas case was being heard on January 17, 1973, the Secretary of Justice, then Jose Abad Santos, called on Chief Justice Roberto Concepcion, informing him that upon the instructions of the President, he was delivering a copy of Proclamation No. 1102, which had just been signed by the President. Immediately, Chief Justice Concepcion returned to the Session Hall and announced to the Court, the parties in G.R. No. L-35948 – inasmuch as the hearing in connection therewith was still going on, and the public therein present that the President had, according to information conveyed by the Secretary of Justice, signed Proclamation No. 1102, earlier that morning. Thereupon he read Proclamation No. 1102.

Meanwhile, the Supreme Court justices deliberated on the aforementioned cases. On January 22, 1973, five days after the Presidential Proclamation of the ratification of the New Constitution, the Supreme Court dismissed the Plebiscite cases.

On Ratification Cases. On January 20, 1973, Jose Javellana filed a case in the Supreme Court questioning the constitutionality of the New Philippine Constitution. There were others who filed similar actions on January 23, 1973 and on February 12, 1973. These cases revolved about the constitutionality of the procedure adopted by the President for ratifying the New Philippine Constitution; e.g., by barrio assemblies wherein Filipino citizens including those between 15 and 20 years of age, participated in the voting and by raising their hands. They cited that under Article XIV of the 1935 Constitution, as amended, and the implementing election law, only Filipino citizens at least 21 years of age could participate, and by secret ballot, in an election called for the purpose of ratifying proposed amendments to the Constitution.

In view of the various approaches and views expressed during the deliberations, the members of the Supreme Court agreed to synthesize the basic issues at bar in broad general terms in five questions for purposes of taking the votes. These basic issues were:

- Was the issue of the validity of Proclamation No. 1102 a political question, and, therefore, the Supreme Court had no power to pass upon it and decide the same?

- Had the Constitution proposed by the 1971 Constitutional Convention been ratified validly (with substantial, if not strict compliance) conformably to the applicable constitutional and statutory provisions?

- Had the proposed 1973 Constitution been acquiesced in (with or without valid ratification) by the people?

- Were the petitioners entitled to relief?

- Was the proposed 1973 Constitution in force?

It should be noted that on the first issue, six of the ten justices heed the issue of the validity of Proclamation No. 1102 presented a non-political question, and consequently, the Court had the power to pass upon and decide the same.

On the second issue, six of the ten justices held the Constitution had not been validly ratified in accordance with Article XV, section 1, of the 1935 Philippine Constitution which provided only one way for ratification; i.e., in an election or plebiscite held in accordance with law and participated in only by qualified or duly registered voters.

With regard to the third issue, the Court had reached no majority vote.

On the fourth issue, six of the ten justices voted to dismiss the petition; hence, the petitioners were not entitled to relief.

On the fifth issue, four members of the Court held that it was in force by virtue of the people's acceptance. Two members voted that the Constitution was not in force. Four members cast no vote on the premise that they could not state with judicial certainty whether the people had accepted or not the constitution.

Finally, the results of the ratification cases showed that a majority of six justices, of the ten, voted to deny the petition for relief, all the ratification cases were dismissed. In the words of the members of the Supreme Court, "This being the vote of the majority, there is no further judicial obstacle to the New Constitution being considered in force and in effect."

Postscript. The 1973 Constitution of the Republic of the Philippines was not submitted to the people for ratification in accordance with the procedure prescribed in Article XIV of the 1935 Philippine Constitution. Hence, the Planas, the Javellana cases and other petitioners in the Supreme Court.

It had been contended in the Planas case that only the law-making body could prescribe the guidelines for the plebiscite; and in the Javellana case, that the new constitutional provisions should not be implemented because the new Constitution had not been ratified in accordance with the 1935 Philippine Constitution.

In retrospect, it may be said that Article XIV of the 1935 Constitution of the Philippines would apply to the amendments to the Constitution.

Contrary to the instructions to the Congressional resolution and in the Constitutional Convention Act, the Constitutional Convention adopted a New Constitution. In doing this, in effect, assumed the role and power of a revolutionary convention. Such being the case, it had the power to prescribe that the President submit the ratification of the New Constitution to the people without specific instructions on the matter.

The President, in the absence of such instructions, thought it best to submit the constitution for ratification by the people in citizens' assemblies. Having been ratified by a majority of the people. The New Constitution should be deemed in force.

The Planas plebiscite case and the Javellana ratification case had stirred the minds of legal luminaries, opinion political writers and columnists, political scholars and analysts and even students in the College of Law about the historic decision of the Supreme Court. For them, the existence and operation of the Supreme Court was the best argument against Martial Law in the Philippines. But, unfortunately, for them the Supreme Court that was supposed to uphold the majesty of the land and is considered the guardian of the Constitution and defender of democracy did not live up to expectations.

The question to be resolved by the judiciary, if at all should be: Was the method adopted by the President for the ratification of the Constitution in accordance with the law? According to Lord Bryce, a British jurist –

"Nothing more clearly touches the welfare and security of the average citizens that his sense that can relay on the certain and prompt administration of justice. The test of good government depends on its judiciary. The law is respected and supported when it is trusted as the shield of innocence and the impartial guardian of every private civil right. But if the law be dishonestly administered, the salt has lost its savor; if it be weakly or unfaithfully enforced, the guarantees of order fail; for it is more by the certainty than by severity of punishment that offenses are repressed. If the lamp of justice goes out in darkness, how great is that darkness."

It is interesting to note that the lone woman member of

the Supreme Court during the Martial Law era, Associate Justice Cecilia Muñoz-Palma, could not help being alluded to the prostrate figure of justice in a well-applauded speech on Labor Day, which coincided with the third anniversary of the observance of Martial Law in September 19, 1975. The lady justice called the judges and the members of the Philippine bar to "muster the will, the boldness, the resources and the perseverance to work collectively and decisively for the maintenance of an independent judiciary." Such courage and fortitude to face extreme dangers and difficulties without fear, that a local political opinion writer remarked: She is the only member of the Supreme Court of the Philippines "wearing pants."

Salient Features of the 1973 Constitution. The 1973 Constitution of the Philippines had different features not found in the 1935 Constitution. For the first time, in the history of the Philippines, the Parliamentary System of government was established, with the Prime Minister as the real head of the government and the President as symbolic head of state. Both were to be elected by the members of the National Assembly. The Prime Minister would exercise both executive and legislative powers. The legislative power was exercised by the unicameral National Assembly composed of assembly men elected by district by qualified voters. The voting age for Filipino was reduced to 18 years to give wider participation especially among the youth. The civilian authority was supreme over the military at all times. The Supreme Court has the power to exercise administrative supervision over all courts and their personnel. Under the 1935 Constitution this power was vested in the Department of Justice. The National Economic and Development Authority (NEDA) was created, an economic body headed by the Prime Minister. The Sandigang Bayan, a special court was created specifically to try cases involving graft and corruption committed by officials and employees of the government. The Office of the TanodBayan (Ombudsman) shall investigate complaints against the government officials and employees and prosecute them in Court with probable cause. The 1973 Constitution prescribed the study of the Constitution as part of the curricula of all schools. It provided for the development and adoption of a common national language to be known as the Filipino language.

In view of its historical record of adaptability and successful performance in Asia and many countries with diverse cultures, political maturity, religion, race and climate, the proponents of this parliamentary form of government believed that it will succeed in the Philippines.

Before this 1973 Constitution could be freely implemented various amendments had taken place, as follows: An Interim Batasang Pambansa was established, composed of 120 members, including the incumbent President of the Philippines, the regional representatives elected in different regions, the sectoral representatives, and those to be appointed by the President from his cabinet, instead of the National Assembly.

The members of the Interim Batasang Pambansa shall have the same powers, privileges, responsibilities, rights, and disqualifications as those of the National Assembly, which was replaced. The incumbent President of the Philippines shall, within 20 days from the selection and election of the members, convene the Interim Batasang Pambansa and preside over its sessions until the Speaker is elected. The incumbent President shall be the Prime Minister and shall exercise the power of the President and the Prime Minister. The president (Prime Minister) together with his cabinet shall exercise all the powers and functions. The President, if he so desires, may appoint a Deputy Prime Minister. The incumbent President shall continue to exercise his legislative powers until martial law is lifted. In the event that the Batasang Pambansa cannot cope with emergency or threat to the government, the President may issue the necessary decrees, orders, or letters of instruction, which shall form part of the law of the land. The barangays and sanggunians shall continue in their compositions, but their powers and functions may be altered by law. All provisions of this Constitution not in consistent with any of these amendments shall continue in force and effect. The amendments shall take effect after the incumbent

President shall have proclaimed that they have been ratified by a majority of votes cast in a referendum.

President Marcos proclaimed the ratification of the amendments to the 1973 Constitution on October 27, 1976 and became effective.

Philippine Foreign Policy under Martial Law. Philippine foreign policy had evolved from colonial status, to special relations, to complete independence and self-reliance. Before the New Society, Philippine foreign policy was largely shaped by "special relations" with the United States. The close identification with the United States was regarded with suspicion, and sometimes with hostility, by newly emerging states. Moreover, socialist states viewed the Philippines as unfriendly. Isolated from countries with whom we share more common problems and characteristics, we became embroiled in the conflict and rivalries of the Big Powers and partisan to their quarrels.

The guiding principles of the new foreign policy of the Republic of the Philippines were: The foreign policy must be geared to Philippine aspirations to national development and progress. That there is need to maintain fruitful and beneficial ties with other nations must be based on mutual respect, mutual benefits, and mutual regard for each other's independence. 1) The Philippine foreign policy identifies itself with the movement to reform the international economic order; 2) The foreign policy reflects the conscious exercise of national independence and sovereignty on every issue, and every initiative; 3) To strengthen the Association of South East Asian Nation (ASEAN) as a regional organization and foster bilateral relations with its individual member nations; 4) To maintain harmonious relations with communist countries, including the Soviet Union and the People's Republic of China; 5) To support Arab countries in the Middle East and expand Philippine diplomatic and trade relations with them; 6) To promote economic and cultural relations with countries of Western Europe; 7) To seek closer relations with countries of the Third World, with whom we have similar interests; 8) To continue the beneficial relationships with Japan; and 9) To support the

United Nations in its objectives and activities for international friendship for world peace.

The changing realities in Asia and the world signaled the need for reorientation of the Philippine foreign policy. The national interest demands that the foreign policy be non-ideological, non-aligned and development-oriented. Aligned with these principles, the Republic of the Philippines abolished the American "parity rights" in the 1973 Constitution and ended the Laurel-Langley Agreement when it expired on July 3, 1974.

In asserting its independence as a sovereign nation, it signed the United States on January 7, 1979, a six-point amendment to the Philippine-U.S. Military Bases Agreement on March 14, 1947. the important amendment contained the six-point policy on U.S. military bases on the Philippines: 1) a reaffirmation of Philippine sovereignty over the bases; 2) installation of a Filipino Commander in every base; 3) significant reduction in the base areas for the use of the United States; 4) assumption by Philippine Armed Forces of the responsibility for perimeter security; 5) assurance of unhampered military operations of the United States; and 6) a thorough review of the agreement every five years, including its objectives, implementation, and duration.

Corollary with the amendment, the United States, pledged $500 million in military assistance and $700 million in economic aid and loan for five years.

This, in effect, the Republic of the Philippine foreign policy premised on dynamic pragmatism for national survival and development.

The Crises Government Gradually Returns to Democracy. The crises government under martial law was an authoritarian form of government because the President assumed total control of administration of government in his belief "to save the Republic and to reform society." Gradually, as the conditions of the country seemed normal, President Marcos restored some basic features of a democratic government and one of these was a clean, honest, peaceful

MARTIAL LAW AND THE NEW SOCIETY

and orderly election. He was fully aware of the lessons of history that no Martial Law government or despotic leader ever lasted forever in any country of the world. History, attested that dictators who were shrewd, ruthless, vindictive, fascistic, extravagant, whimsical, capricious and greedy for power who would not give up power and authority willingly and restore it to the people died and were relegated to oblivion. The likes of Francisco Franco of Spain, Benito Mussolini of Italy, Joseph Stalin of Soviet Russia and Adolf Hitler, Nazi Dictator of Germany who wanted greatness for their nations and peoples, all fell and their people discredited them.

On September 10, 1976, President Marcos issued Presidential Decree No. 995 creating the Batasang Bayan (Legislative Advisory Body) composed of 132 members to help him make laws, but later on replaced by the Interim Batasang Pambansa (Provisional National Assembly) preparatory to the lifting of Martial Law and eventual restoration of the democracy.

To implement the establishment of the interim Batasang Pambansa, he promulgated Presidential Decree called the Election Code of 1978, providing for the election of its members and setting the election date on April 7, 1978. This was the first national election for the legislature where 200 members (including President and then Prime Minister Marcos) of the Interim Batasang Pambansa, 165 elected in different regions; 10 cabinet members appointed by the President; 14 sectoral representatives – youth, agricultural and industrial workers were elected.

Among the political parties in this national election under martial law was Kilusang Bagong Lipunan (KBL) Lakas ng Bayan, Pusyong Bisaya, Mindanao Alliance and Konsensiya ng Bayan.

As expected, the results of the legislative election, majority of candidates of the KBL headed by Imelda Romualdez Marcos won. Only a few opposition candidates won. The opposition alleged that the election was a mockery of democratic process – sham and comical.

On June 12, 1978, the 80th anniversary of the Declaration of Philippine Independence, the Interim Batasang Pambansa held its inaugural session at the newly constructed building on Constitution Hill in Quezon City were elected assembly men were to be proclaimed. The inaugural session was the State of the Nation Address by President and Prime Minister Marcos in which he presented the achievements of the administration under Martial Law, spelled out his program of government for the years to come.

Another local election was held on January 30, 1980, where Filipino voters went to the election precincts to cast their votes. As usual, majority of the KBL candidates won while a handful candidates of the opposition survived.

The End of Martial Law in the Philippines. President Marcos signed Proclamation No. 2045 on January 17, 1981, ending the eight years and four months of martial law in the Philippines. There were, however, certain conditions embodied in his proclamation, as follows: 1) that the Armed Forces of the Philippines shall continue to prevent and suppress lawless crimes, insurrection, rebellion, or subversion in the country; and 2) the suspension of the privilege of writ of habeas corpus shall continue in the two autonomous regions of Mindanao – Region IX and Region XII.

Results of Martial Law. According to the Civil Liberties Union of the Philippines chaired by the late Jose W. Diokno, after eight years and four months of the Martial Law, shatters the theory that only an authoritarian government can solve the nation's persistent problems, and finally move the economy forward; instead, martial rule virtually ruined the country's political, economic and social institutions, and even became worse.

An over emphasis on exports and tourism, to the neglect of the people's basic needs for better and cheaper food, clothing and shelter, and a dependence on foreign capital, have resulted in an economic growth that had not benefited either laborers or consumers; had prejudiced national capital, judged by its reduced share in the economy; and had impoverished the nation, which today is more deeply in debt, internally and externally, than ever with our national resources gradually being transferred to foreign hands.

Although peace and order improved markedly at the early part of martial law, crimes had increased. Violence against persons by civilians had lessened; but this had been replaced by unreasonable searches and seizures; indiscriminate arrests, indefinite detention without known charges, and tortures of prisoners; repression of some minorities like the Bontocs and the Kalingas; and reprisal against unarmed Muslims. Corruption had not been eliminated nor evidently reduced; the old dishonest politicians were gone; but new mandarines had taken place. What was worse, they were not accountable to the people.

Labor policies sought to create a labor force that was comparatively cheap, abundant, trained and docile. Wracked by inflation, shackled by the strike ban; the process of collective bargaining weakened by compulsory arbitration under executive, rather than judicial, controlled labor, cannot improve the working conditions nor make wages and salaries keep up with soaring prices.

Land reform held out much promise; but performance had been too little and too slow. No tangible improvements had resulted in the lot of landless peasant farmers. The problems were so grave, the situation so urgent, that only through a united and concerted effort of all people can we hope to find and to achieve a lasting, just and real solution, not out of the barrel of a gun.

Martial Rule is Dictatorship. Martial rule denied the people any meaningful participation in making public decisions that shaped their lives and their livelihood. Martial Law, "Philippine Style," was dictatorship, pure and simple. It respected no constitutional rights, no civil liberties. It was subject to no effective checks or balances.

Martial Law can not reform society because our social, political and economic problems are so grave and deeply rooted that no one man is wise enough to solve them or good enough to be entrusted with unlimited power to do so; yet that was what Martial Law did; it created a dictatorship and entrusted unlimited power to one man – the President.

It was absurd, because to revolutionize society was to eliminate the privileges of the few so that the rights of the many may be respected; but martial law eliminated both the privileges of the few and the many in order to concentrate absolute power in one man, and privileges only on those he had chosen to reward.

Martial Law was absurd, because to reform society was to eliminate corruption, but, "power corrupts, and absolute power corrupts absolutely," and it created a dictatorship of absolute power.

Martial Law, as the President himself said, "connotes the power of the gun, meant coercion by the military, and compulsion and intimidation" but guns can not kill, nor coercion by the military liquidate, the poverty, the inequality and the injustice that were the most serious of our economic and social problems.

Martial Law had brought about changes in political system. Democracy "Philippine style" was far from perfect, but martial law "Philippine Style" was not any better. It had not only failed to solve our problems, it had aggravated them.

Martial Law was antithetical to a free press – it cannot coexist and it had not coexisted in the Philippines during the past years of martial law. Like all other freedoms, which are our birthmark under the constitution, it can never be truly restored as long as martial law continued. The mass media was docile and timid. Media became an exclusive propaganda outlet of the government. Media ownership was in the hands of the President's cronies.

Failure of Martial Law Not Unique to the Philippines. Political scholars and analysts viewed that the failure of Martial Law was not unique to the Philippines. There were numerous other dictatorships, in Latin America and Asia, that had given up political democracy and destroyed civil liberties and yet had not achieved either economic democracy or cultural liberation.

Dictatorship never benefited the people in the long run; and seldom, in the short run – even when the dictator came as a Messiah, untarnished by the crises he vowed to save the people from. When the dictator himself created or contributed to the mess, when his credibility to begin with was low, the chances of effecting meaningful change were immeasurably small.

While Martial Law had introduced some innovations purportedly premised to improve the general welfare of the Filipinos, it had failed in its avowed objectives of reforming society; if it had removed one set of oligarchs, it was only to replace them by others.

Dictatorship was not the solution for the Philippine multifarious problems. It never had been; and our history as a people, marked by determined effort by a ceaseless struggle for freedom attested to that. All political leaders of the world envisioned to leave a legacy for their people to emulate their accomplishments. Marcos political slogan in his 1965 presidential campaign was that "The Nation Can Be Great Again." In his "New Society" Marcos declared that it came into being with the people to have a new sense of discipline, uprightness and love of country. To do this, martial law was declared and the 1973 Constitution was framed, "ratified" and put into operation. By and large, the Constitution had various amendments and established a mixed presidential – parliamentary form of government for the Philippines, instead of a parliamentary government (British model) as provided in the original 1973 Constitution.

The First Presidential Election under the New Constitution. On June 16, 1981, two months and nine days after the people "ratified" the amended 1973 Constitution, the first Presidential Election was held.

Generally, the Filipinos have a passion for politics. It seems that many perceived politics as an investment so they looked forward to an election period with enthusiasm and optimism; but in this presidential election, contenders for various political groups who did not belong to the KBL party were adamant to participate. They believed that this will not be a credible election and another "show" for democratic process. One of the criteria of a credible election especially on the presidential post is intellectual and moral integrity. The three main candidates for presidency were President Marcos of the Kilusang Bagong Lipunan (KBL), Alejo Santos of the Nationalista Party (NP), and Bartolome Cabangbang of the Federal Party (FP). Many unknown men and women joined the presidential election, but they were only nuisance candidates.

Undoubtedly, President Marcos and other candidates of the ruling party, the KBL handily won. The principles inherent in a democracy that "sovereignty resides in the people and all government authority emanates from them" is morally and legally derived from the citizens through suffrage. According to Justice Enrique Fernando, "the right to vote has reference to constitutional guarantee of utmost significance. It is a right without which the principle of sovereignty residing in the people became negatory. This right to vote is a political right enabling every citizen to participate in the process of government to assure him that it derives its power from the consent of the people.

To give meaningful expression to the rights of suffrage in the context of representative government, citizens must be able to participate freely in competitive elections that should be clean, honest, peaceful and credible so that elected officials of government can exercise political authority.

Having observed and participated in scores of election, one may have the impression that the just-concluded Presidential election was full of flaws. Political analysts and observers and majority of the Filipinos perceived that this political exercise where candidates of the KBL won was a sham.

On June 30, 1981, Marcos was inaugurated amidst colorful ceremonies and lavish fanfare at the Rizal Park as President.

The Downfall of Marcos. The assassination of former

Senator Benigno S. Aquino, Jr., the leading opposition leader and a staunch critic of the Marcos government returned from a three-year exile in the United States. Hardly had Aquino's plane landed in Manila International Airport when he was met by a group of soldiers and hustled out of the plane. Seconds later, shots rang out, and Aquino was shot in the head and killed as he was escorted off an airplane at Manila International Airport by soldiers of the Aviation Security Command on August 21, 1983. The government's claim that he was the victim of a lone communist gunman, Rolando Galman (who was conveniently killed by Aviation Security Command troops after the alleged act) was unconvincing. A commission appointed by Marcos and headed by jurist Corazon Agrava concluded in their findings announced in late October, 1984, that the assassination was the result of military conspiracy. Marcos' credibility, both domestically and overseas, was mortally wounded when the Sandiganbayan, a high court charged with prosecuting government officials for crimes, ignored the Agrava findings, upheld the government's story, and acquitted Ver and twenty-four other military officers and one civilian in December, 1985.

Although ultimate responsibility for the act still had not been clearly determined, on September 28, 1990, a special court convicted General Luther Custodio and fifteen other officers and enlisted members of the Aviation Security Command of murdering Aquino and Galman. Most observers believed, however, that Imelda Marcos and Fabian Ver wanted Aquino assassinated.

A question may be asked: Who was the mastermind behind that dastard act? Only God knows. The tragic crime that jolted the nation on August 31, 1983, continues to blow the pain and suffering to the innocent, not the guilty. The brutal murder brought greater anguish to the Filipino people.

Aquino's Funeral Procession. After a Requiem Mass at Sto. Domingo Church in Quezon City, the Aquino, funeral procession started from Sto. Domingo Church to Parañaque on August 31, 1983. It was the longest and the largest procession in Philippine history, attended by more than two million people from all walks of life. As the casket, where the remains of the late senator were placed and driven by a military vehicle, a big crowd of people screamed into the streets in an unprecedented outpouring of sorrow and shock.

In September, after he was laid to rest, church bells started to peal twenty times before and after a five-minute prayer at noon. According to Cardinal Jaime L. Sin, the church bells shall continue to ring until such time as truth, justice and reconciliation are finally achieved in our beloved land.

In the weeks and months that followed, street vendors, professionals, students, businessman, workers, urban poor and radicals all awoke from years of resignation to condemn that diabolic act and cried out their rage.

The assassination of Aquino became the focal point of a renewed and more heavily supported opposition to Marcos' repressive rule. By late 1985 Marcos, under mounting pressure, both inside and outside the Philippines, called a snap presidential election on February 1986. Corazon C. Aquino, Benigno's widow, became the candidate of a coalition of opposition parties. Marcos was declared the official winner, but strong public outcry over the election results was marred by massive cheating.

Ninoy's Brilliant Trait. "I have decided to challenge death. I do not believe I'm sinning against my Creator because, in the end, I am not really my own executioner. By my example, I can inspire others. Like the dominoes, one has to fall to create the chain reaction," says Ninoy.

Knowing his own death, he pursued on going back to his homeland to continue fighting for the truth. This is just a proof that Ninoy is really determined to continue what he had started.

Yes, Ninoy did possess the traits of becoming a hero. And everyone does. What makes Ninoy differ from others is that he did use the traits for the truth, for JUSTICE.

Ninoy's Heroic Deeds. Ninoy's legacy was his exemplary courage and love for country, that eventually became the culmination of the Filipinos' struggle to attain freedom.

"I have died, I told you. This is a second life I can give up. Besides, if they shoot me, they'll make me a hero," Ninoy said in one of the last interviews on board the plane.

Risking your life for the sake of your fellowmen is considered as the toughest way of proving your love to your country. Ninoy did it successfully for his death led to the restoration of our freedom.

Ninoy is the only figure that can rally the citizenry today. As a hero, he is contemporary. We have nobody like him since Jose Rizal, Andres Bonifacio and Apolinario Mabini perished 100 years ago.

Making Ninoy as a hero should help to remind us of what he fought for while he lived. It should help remind us of what we fought for in his name after he died. We need his ideals and this should be kept alive.

The good thing with all this is that even as we need heroes, we don't have to invent one. Ninoy was one. Ninoy is one.

It was Napoleon who said that a great man is the product of an encounter between a great mind and a great opportunity. Well, Ninoy was that man. He converted a small, damp, forlorn prison cell into a tabernacle. His mind soared to great heights. He leaped from politician to pilgrim. In that loneliness, he was able to touch the tip of heaven because these were the only things he could really touch in seven years and seven months of solitary imprisonment.

In this sense, we also recall Albert Einstein who said: "The true value of a human being is determined by the measure and the sense in which he has affirmed liberation from self." YES. Ninoy said the Filipino is worth dying for. Ninoy deserved to be a hero – because his heroism brought back the freedom to his fellowmen.

Study Guides

A. Terms/Concepts to Understand

Martial Law	authoritarian
invasion	despotic rule
insurrection	anarchy
Habeas Corpus	emancipation
arbitrary	deliberation

B. Questions to Answer

1. What are the grounds when the president can declare Martial Law?

2. What are the rights of the citizens that may be violated during Martial Law?

3. Enumerate the government reforms made by President Marcos under the Martial Law.

4. What do you consider the best reform made by the Marcos government under Martial Law? Explain your answer.

5. What do you think are the contributions of Martial Law that are worth remembering, if there are any?

6. What are the reforms conceived and instituted by the New Society of President Marcos?

7. Enumerate the educational reforms the government instituted during Martial Law.

8. What development programs were launched by the Department of Tourism during Martial Law that boost Philippine economy?

9. What important role did the barangay, as a basic political unit, play during the Martial Law period?

10. Do you favor the parliamentary form of government created under the Constitution of 1972? Explain your answer.

Chapter 17

Restoration of Democracy and Political Transformation

The state of the nation for eight years of Martial Law did not solve our political, social and economic and cultural problems. Political analysts and observers viewed that martial law had virtually destroyed the country's political, economic and social institutions and these even became worse. The Filipino people had reached the point of disillusionment with Ferdinand Marcos. His administration had been rocked by serious allegations of corruption, greed, cronyism, extravagance, deceit, vengeance, and abuse of power. In a time of grave crises plaguing the country, the Filipinos lost their trust in Marcos and looked for a leader who can bring their freedom and bring honesty to public service, which they can be proud of.

After suffering for 300 years from Spanish repressive rule, a half century by the American exploitation, more than three years of undergoing the dangerous and rigorous life under the Japanese occupation, and enduring the abuse and tyranny of Martial rule, the Filipinos were able to withstand tremendous trials with courage, fortitude, wisdom and optimism.

The transition from authoritarian rule to democracy is not easy and is very crucial to the life and future of a nation. The circumstances of Cory Aquino's ascent to presidency required selflessness, dedication, perseverance, and a passion for righteousness not demanded of political leaders in normal times and the unwavering support of every Filipino.

259

CORAZON C. AQUINO (1986-1992) The Seventh and First Woman President of the Republic of the Philippines. Corazon C. Aquino became actively involved in politics, as her husband Benigno, was a popular critic of the Marcos dictatorship in the Philippines. Marcos imprisoned Benigno and had agreed to free him if he left the Philippines. Benigno only agreed when he needed critical heart surgery, which would be done in Boston.

However, Benigno decided to return to Manila to run for the presidential election of 1984, but he was shot in the head when he got out of the plane in Manila in 1983. Corazon Aquino had hoped that the party would find someone else to run against Marcos; so that she would not have to be considered. She agreed to run if she had a million signatures on petitions requesting her to run, and so she did.

Marcos, thinking that he still had the Filipino people behind him, called for a snap election in 1986. It was then that Cory became the unified opposition's candidate for presidency. She lost the election to Marcos, but people believed that Marcos rigged the elections, and due to his mass corruption, he lost the support of the U.S. and the people. On February 25, 1986, both Aquino and Marcos were inaugurated as President by their respective supporters. Soon the implausible turned into the improbable. Defense Minister Juan Ponce Enrile, the architect of Marcos' martial law, and Lieut. General Fidel Ramos, the deputy chief of the armed forces, broke away from the government, claiming that Aquino was the true winner. As the rebels barricaded themselves inside two military camps, first hundreds, then thousands, then tens of thousands of common citizens poured into the streets to offer food, support and protection, if need be with their bodies, to the maverick soldiers and Aquino backers. As civilians, bearing only flags and flowers, took up positions to defend the military men, the world knew that it was watching more than just an electoral upheaval.

Finally, the improbable became the impossible. Marcos' tanks rolled toward the crowds, only to be stopped by nuns kneeling in their path, reciting the rosary. Old women went up to gun-toting marines and disarmed them with motherly hugs. Little girls offered their flowers to hardened combat veterans. In the face of such quiet heroism, thousands of Marcos loyalists defected, many simply broke down in tears.

Less than 24 hours after Marcos had himself inaugurated, he was being helped off a plane in Hawaii, sickly, exiled and bewildered. His former home, Malacanang Palace, was now a melancholy tableau of abandoned power, overrun by thousands of revelers. The new leader of the Philippines was the reserved housewife who had worn plain yellow dresses every day of her campaign.

Cory's People Power. With Marcos gone, President Aquino is now struggling to make a born-again democracy work.

"Cory! Cory! Cory!" The chant roared across the Philippines, welling up into an overwhelming display of People Power. The currents swept away Ferdinand Marcos, bringing justice and office to Corazon Aquino. While Marcos, tagging after "Baby Doc" Duvalier, prepared to escape aboard an American jet, Aquino was sworn in as president of the Philippines. In triumph, she became an emotional embodiment of democracy itself. Facing down a strongman's army, her followers brought 20 years of despotic rule to a nearly bloodless end. "The world saw and recorded a people who knelt in the path of oncoming tanks and subdued with embraces of friendship the battle-hardened troops sent out to disperse them," she said. "All the world wondered as they witnessed ... a people lift themselves from humiliation to the greatest pride."

For Marcos, it was an ignominious end. He had cringed in his palace for three disastrous days, watching incredulously as a desperate mutiny by a handful of soldiers blossomed into full scale revolt. His once loyal military turned against him in an avalanche of revulsion: hostile crowds threatened to storm the palace gates. It was finally left to his old ally Ronald Reagan to inform the fading dictator that he was through. Four U.S. Air Forces helicopters arrived at Malacanang Palace to take a tearful Marcos and his remaining entourage on the first leg of a journey into exile and disgrace.

"Today," declared Reagan, "the Filipino people celebrate the triumph of democracy, and the world celebrates with them." The happy ending for Mrs. Aquino vindicated the professional strategies within the Reagan administration who had orchestrated two years of escalating pressure on Marcos. Their goal had been to encourage a moderate alternative to the communist insurgents. With the people passionately behind her, Aquino was well positioned to attack the political, military and economic problems crippling the Philippines. A U.S. Congress poised to stop payment on aid to Marcos and suddenly outdid itself in promising to help her.

She was sure to need all the help she could get. She inherited a looted and inefficient economy, a military helpless against a communist insurgency and a political system grown flaccid and corrupt under Marcos' autocratic rule. She has no stable political organization and no experience as an administrator; one of her first tasks must be to harmonize a coalition that managed to unite only in its opposition to Marcos. She is surrounded by talented advisers, though and backed by the Roman Catholic Church. And as Marcos learned too late, she is a woman with a way around power.

Aquino Sworn into Office. After her oath-taking at Club Filipino, Corazon Aquino appointed the first members of her cabinet. She appointed Vice-President Salvador Laurel as Prime Minister and concurrently Minister of Foreign Affairs. She appointed Juan Ponce Enrile as the Minister of National Defense. Fidel V. Ramos was named Chief-of-Staff of the New Armed Forces of the Philippines (NAFP) and was promoted to the rank of full General.

The other members of the cabinet were Executuve secretary Joker Arroyo, Minister of Justice Neptali Gonzales, Agrarian Reform Minister Heherson Alvarez, Minister of Local Government Aquilino Pimentel Jr., Minister of Natural Resources Ernesto Maceda, Minister of Agriculture and Food Ramon Mitra and Minister of Education, Culture and Sports Lourdes Quisumbing.

Since Corazon Aquino did come into power by virtue of the 1973 Constitution, she established a revolutionary government upon her assumption into office on February 25, 1986. This early government was provisional and transition government. It was a temporary government that existed only while a new constitution was being prepared. With the ratification of the 1987 Constitution on February 2, 1987, the temporary government was dissolved and the new one was enforced.

Reorganization of the Government. President Aquino saw the need of reorganizing the government upon her assumption in office. A Commission was created and prepared a comprehensive government reorganization plan which became the basis of the changes that President Aquino made in the government.

Aquino changed the members of the Supreme Court created by Marcos. She chose people who were known for their competence in legal matters, integrity and independence. Senior Associate Justice Claudio Teehankee was named Chief Justice of the Aquino Supreme Court.

Aquino also abolished the Batasang Pambansa controlled by Marcos and assumed legislative powers. She issued executive orders. She authorized the removal of all KBL, local elective officials – governors, vice-governors, mayors, vice-mayors, barangay captains – and replaced them with officer-in-charge (OICs).

True to her promise to restore freedom in the country, President Aquino lifted the suspension of the privilege of the writ of habeas corpus in the two regions of Mindanao on March 1, 1986. She freed the political prisoners under the Marcos dictatorship; among them, Jose Ma. Sison, the alleged founder of the Communists Party of the Philippines (CPP), Commander Dante (Bernabe Buscayno), founder of the New Peoples Army of the Philippines and Victor Corpus, a former PC lieutenant who defected to the NPA.

President Aquino also recognized the need to investigate the human rights violation during the Marcos Regime. For this purpose, she created the Presidential Commission on Human Rights to investigate human rights violations, especially those committed by the abusive elements of the armed forces of Marcos. Former Senator Jose W. Diokno was appointed head of the Commission.

Corollary to the foregoing, President Aquino abolished the dread laws that empowered Marcos to order the arrest and indefinite detention of people suspected of being subversives.

The Freedom Constitution of President Corazon Aquino. After the overthrow of Marcos, President Aquino issued Proclamation No. 3, adopting a temporary constitution for the Philippines. This was called Freedom Constitution, which took effect on March 25, 1986, one month after the people power revolution. Proclamation No. 3 also declared the national policy "to implement reforms mandated by the people." It provided for the smooth transition of a government under the new constitution.

The Freedom Constitution had the following features:

1. It abolished certain constitutional positions. The Freedom Constitution dissolved the Batasang Pambansa and the position of prime minister.

2. It granted almost absolute powers to the President. The temporary constitution granted the President both executive and legislative powers. It also empowered the President to remove all appointees and elective officials and to appoint their replacements.

3. It was a temporary constitution. The Freedom constitution was not intended to be permanent. In fact, it provided for the creation of a Constitutional Commission that would draft a new constitution.

The Framing of the 1987 RP Constitution. In April , 1986, President Aquino issued Proclamation No. 9, creating a Constitutional Commission to draft a new constitution as provided for in the Freedom Constitution.

The members of the Constitutional Commission (CONCOM) were appointed by President Aquino on May 26 from a list of persons nominated by various groups and individuals. They represented all sectors of Philippine Society – education, labor, agriculture, business and industry, youth, military, mass media, cause-oriented groups, cultural minorities and the religious sector.

The members of the Constitutional Commission were: former Speaker Jose B. laurel, Jr., former Senator Francisco "Soc" Rodrigo, Decoroso Rosales, Ambrosio Padilla, Domocao Alonto and Lorenzo Sumulong; former Supreme Court Chief Justice Roberto Concepcion, former 1971 Constitutional Convention delegate Napoleon Rama, U.P. Student Council President Chito Gascon, Ateneo University President Father Joaquin Bernas, S.J., Bishop Teodoro Bacani, Sister Christine Tan, Rev. Pastor Cirilo Rios, and economist Bernardo Villegas. President Aquino also included former KBL members namely, former labor Minister Blas Ople and former MP Teodulo Natividad.

The Commission formally opened its session at the former Batasang Pambansa building in Quezon City on June 2, 1986, President Aquino addressed the opening session. Former Associate Justice of the Supreme Court Cecilia Munoz Palma was elected president of the Constitutional Commission.

Heated arguments took place regarding the controversial RP-US Military Bases Agreement (MBA), land reform and foreign investments. A walk-out was staged by several commissioners in protest against the approval of some economic provisions to which they strongly objected. One commissioner who walked out was Lino Brocka, a well-known film director.

After 11 days of debates and revisions of provisions, committee hearings and provincial consultation, the Constitutional Commission finally finished its work. On October 12, 1986, the commissioners approved by a vote of 45-2 the draft of the new constitution and signed it on October 15. The said constitution was submitted to President Aquino on the same day. Commissioner Jaime Tadeo and Jose Suarez voted against the new constitution.

Ratification of the 1987 Constitution

The draft of the 1987 Constitution was submitted to the people in the February 2, 1987 plebiscite for ratification. About 86% of the 25 million registered voters voted in favor of the New Constitution. It was reported as the biggest election turn out in the political history of the nation. The official count of the Commission on Election showed that there were 17,059,495 "Yes" votes while the "No" votes had only 5,058,714. The big turnout of the "Yes" votes confirmed the massive popular support for President Aquino.

On February 11, 1987, President Aquino issued Proclamation No. 58 declaring that the New Constitution has been approved by the Filipino people and is therefore, in "Full force and effect." On the same day, President Aquino and other government officials pledged allegiance to the New Constitution.

The ratification of the 1987 Constitution ended the revolutionary government of Aquino, which was established on February 25, 1986. It heralded the restoration of the Philippines to a full democratic form of government for the first time after the Marcos dictatorship.

Significant Features of the 1987 Constitution

The 1987 Constitution contains 18 articles, 306 sections and more than 20,000 words. It includes an ordinance apportioning the 200 seats of the House of Representatives to the different legislative districts.

The 1987 Constitution had several significant features. It includes safeguards that will prevent a new dictatorship. For example, certain checks on the power of the President to declare Martial Law have been included. Article VII, Sec. 18 of the New Constitution, provides that Martial Law will last for not more than 60 days unless Congress decides to extend the period. Congress was also given the power to revoke the martial law proclamation of the President. Also, private citizen may question before the Supreme Court whether or not there were sufficient reasons for the President to declare martial law.

The new constitution seeks to prevent the violation of human rights that was rampant during the Marcos regime. Article III, the Bill of Rights, prohibits the use of torture on any person under investigation, as well as the use of secret detention places. It also provided that "no person shall be detained solely by reason of his political beliefs and aspirations." In this connection, a new independent constitutional body called the Commission on Human Rights, to be composed by a chairman and four members was created. The body has the duty to investigate all forms of human rights violations and to help the victims of such violations.

The New Constitution recognized people power. The power to make laws is shared, by the Congress with the people. Under Article VI, the people can directly propose and enact laws, or approve or reject any act or law or a part of that law passed by the Congress or a local legislative body. This may be done in the form of a petition signed by at least 10% of the total number of registered voters all over the country. Also in Section 2 Article XVII, the people may directly propose amendments to the constitution through a process called "initiative upon a petition of at least 12% of the total number of voters nationwide.

The Launching of the
Kabisig People's Movement

Inspired by the People Power Revolution at EDSA in 1986, the Kabisig People's Movement (KPM) or simply KABISIG was formally launched by President Corazon Aquino on June 12, 1990. There were four basic reasons why KABISIG was organized by Aquino:

1. To institutionalize participatory democracy;

2. To use the collective strength borne out of the peoples' active achievement in participatory democracy for the poverty alleviation efforts;

3. To present any attempt in the future in returning the country to a dictatorship;

4. To give life to provisions of the 1987 Constitution that enshrine the ideals of people empowerment (Sections 15 and 17, Article XIII).

The KABISIG was a non-partisan, multisectoral, and voluntary movement of concerned citizens who seek only the best interests of the country and the people. The KABISIG slogan "Magtulungan Tayo" indicates that more can be achieved if the energies of our people can be harnessed and translated into a collective strength to deliver services for the people and discover for themselves their capabilities for self-development.

To institutionalize the movement, Proclamation No. 650 was issued which provides among others, the establishment of the KABISIG People's Movement National Operations Center (KPMNOC) to serve as the implementing arm of the Movement.

Corazon C. Aquino – Housewife and Crusader of Justice

President Aquino was portrayed in the media as just an ordinary housewife who was challenging a 20-year dictator for presidency, but this was never true. As she had been tutored in politics from an early age, was college educated, was part of a wealthy political family, and had a husband with political instinct and ambition. She came to power as a "clean-up mom," trying to move her country out of social and financial turmoil, and she also wanted to keep her husband's political vision alive. She appeared shy and a silent student and wife, but she is also seen as eventually growing into the role of a leader.

Although many saw her weakness and delay, Aquino did not waiver from her decision that the most important legacy of her presidency would be her presidential leadership style, as she was always more concerned with process over policy. In March 1986, she proclaimed a provisional Constitution; and soon after appointed a commission to write a new Constitution. This document was ratified by a landslide popular vote in February 1987. She served for one term that lasted six years as defined by the new Constitution, as she decided not to seek re-election.

Aquino epitomizes the virtues of grace and humility, honesty and sincerity, endowed with personal courage, moral integrity and unflinching commitment to non-violence as a means of achieving justice for the common good and general welfare for all men.

There was however, no change in the social and economic circumstances under Aquino's government. It is important to realize that her government was pressured by huge popular expectations, as the people prior to her had been living under martial law for 14 years. She saw herself, as a transition president, from going to dictatorship to democracy, as she believed the Philippines would take at least 10 years to recover after Marcos Regime. It is also important to understand, that what could have impacted her ability to create change was the fact that she had to survive six coup attempts that kept her government seem unfocused for most of her term. The government survived; but the recurrent threats of a coup disrupted out political life.

As far as her impact on the lives of women both generally and politically, in the Philippines, Aquino accomplished a lot for women in terms of being the first woman president of the Philippines; but she did not deal specifically with women's issues. Many of her proclaimed policy priorities, addressing poverty, would have had a positive impact on women, as the majority of those impoverished are women. Also, two women ran after her for president. Although these women did not win, the fact that they even ran, illustrates that, in some regards, Corazon Aquino is partially responsible for "breaking the glass ceiling" in the Philippines.

Cory Aquino received her education at the Assumption Convent in the Philippines, Ravenhill Academy in Philadelphia, Notre Dame Convent School in New York, College of Mount Saint Vincent in New York and Far Eastern University in the Philippines.

Her honorary degrees include Doctor of Humane Letters, College of Mount Saint Vincent (NY), Ateneo de Manila University and Xavier University (Philippines), Doctor of Laws from the University of the Philippines, and *Honoris Causa*, Boston University, Fordham University, Waseda University (Tokyo), Far Eastern University and University of Sto. Tomas (Manila), as well as Doctor of Humanities, Stonehill College in Massachusetts.

President Aquino's awards and distinctions are numerous. Some include: Woman of the Year, Time Magazine, the Eleanor Roosevelt Human Rights Award, the United Nations Silver Medal, and the Canadian International Prize for Freedom. It is with great pride that Women's International Center honors the perseverance and dedication of Corazon Aquino with the International Leadership Living Legacy Award.

The End of Aquino's Administration

Whatever else happens in her rule, Aquino had already given her country a bright, and inviolate, memory. More important, she had also resuscitated its sense of identity and pride. In the Philippines, those luxuries are especially precious. Almost alone among the countries of Asia, it has never been steadied by an ancient culture; its sense of itself, and its potential, was further worn away by nearly four centuries of Spanish and American colonialism. The absence of a spirit of national unity has also made democracy elusive. Even Jose Rizal, a political reformer, shot by the Spanish and a national hero, called the Filipinos "a people without a soul." Yet in

February, for a few extraordinary moments, the people of the Philippines proved their bravery to the world, and to themselves. For her determination and courage in leading a democratic revolution that captured the world's imagination, Corazon C. Aquino is TIME's Woman of the Year for 1986.

President Aquino did not run for a second term. Claiming that hers was only a "transition government" she refused to run for re-election. She endorsed and supported the candidacy of former Defense Secretary Fidel V. Ramos from Asingan, Pangasinan on the May 11, 1992 presidential election.

As President of the Republic of the Philippines, Corazon Aquino led her country's difficult transition from dictatorship to democracy. After re-establishing the democratic institutions, her administration made them work, bringing about substantive economic and social reforms. Through great personal courage and unwavering commitment to non-violence, she successfully served her term in office. Ultimately, Corazon C. Aquino should be remembered for her unwavering commitment to democracy.

Fidel Valdez Ramos (1992-1998)

The Eighth President of the Republic of the Philippines.

Fidel Valdez Ramos, military hero of the 1986 Philippine People Power Revolution in February 1986 and victor in the first multi-party presidential elections of the country, became the 8th President of the Republic of the Philippines on June 30, 1992.

The President took over the reins of a newly-restored democracy, which he helped recover from a 20-year dictatorship and successfully defended against a series of adventurous military take-over attempts. Today, this non-traditional President has made big strides in bringing about a new social and political order by actively reaching out to even political opponents and insurgents to unite the nation behind a common vision.

In 1946, Ramos, through competitive examinations won a government scholarship to the U.S. Military Academy in West point, New York. Seeing the need to help raise his country from the ruins of war, he pursued further studies in engineering following his graduation from West Point in 1950, obtaining a Master Degree in Civil Engineering in the University of Illinois in 1951, still a government scholar.

In his military career, Fidel "Eddie" Ramos, rose from 2nd Lieutenant infantry platoon leader in the Philippine Expeditionary Force in 1952 during the Korean War to Chief of Staff of the Philippine Civil Action Group to Vietnam in 1966 -1968. He is also known as the "father" of Philippine Army Special Forces, an elite paratroop unit skilled in community development, as well as fighting communist insurgents. Later, he was appointed Deputy Chief of Staff for Home Defense of the Armed Forces, Chief of the Philippine Constabulary, reaching the zenith of his military career in February 1986 when he was named Chief of Staff of the Armed Forces of the Philippines, as a four-star general.

In January 1988 Fidel V. Ramos took over the stewardship of the nation's Department of National Defense in the cabinet of President Corazon C. Aquino. In this role, he introduced systematic response mechanisms as concurrent head of the National Disaster Coordinating Council. He provided effective impetus to national stability programs as Vice-Chairman of the National Peace and Order Council and spurred President Ramos' ascent to the highest office of the land through peaceful, democratic elections was a masterpiece of political daring and calculation. He founded the Partido Lakas Tao (People Power Party), espousing his long-held political doctrine of people empowerment, seeking to bring to the people "greater control over their livelihood, culture, politics and all aspects of their lives." He formed the winning coalition of similar parties such as the National Union of Christian Democrats/United Muslim Democrats of the Philippines and consolidated the strength of non-government organizations and marginalized sectors composed the majority of the electorate. President Ramos is married to the former Amelita

"Ming" Martinez and they have 5 daughters. Mrs. Ramos is herself a low-profile but hard-working First Lady, whose long experience in education, sports development and plant propagation has enabled her to spearhead projects in environmental protection, culture and arts development, and livelihood generation.

Aquino nominated Ramos as her choice for President in the 1992 elections. Ramos won a narrow victory to become the 12th president of the Philippine Republic. His immediate priorities were to deal with the energy crisis and the economy; he tackled economic problems through policies of fiscal transparency and deregulation, as well as less popular methods such as extending value added tax. Ramos also sought to end insurgencies by Communist and Muslim rebels, and formed a National Unification Commission in August 1992 to oversee this. In the same month, he gave permission for the return of Ferdinand Marcos's remains to the Philippines. Legislative elections held in June 1995 that were presented by Ramos in a referendum on his administration led to an overwhelming victory for his supporters; by this time, his policies had reformed the Philippine economy and lifted its growth rate closer to that of other Pacific Rim "tiger economies." In October, he took personal charge of the government's campaign against organized crime. The withdrawal of the Lakas ng Edsa party from the ruling coalition weakened Ramos's support; but he was still able to put through an important economic liberalization package in March 1996. In September, the government concluded a landmark agreement with the Muslim secessionist Moro National Liberation Front in Mindanao, ending the long-term insurgency there.

Program of Government

The Ramos framework of governance is founded on a Five-Point Program: peace and stability; economic growth and sustainable development; energy and power generation; environmental protection; and a streamlined bureaucracy.

The Ramos administration has anchored its governance on the philosophy of "People Empowerment" as the engine to operationalize economic growth, social equity, and national solidarity. It is focusing on a five-point program: peace and stability; economic growth and sustainable development; energy and power generation; environmental protection; and a streamlined bureaucracy.

The Ramos Administration was characterized by landmark reforms including the deregulation of key industries, the privatization of public entities, and dismantling of monopolies. These paved the way to significant economic transformation. Thus, the FVR Research Chair in Policy Studies was launched to institutionalize the "Ramos Trademark" and gave due recognition to his performance that put the Philippines back on the international investment map.

The Ramos administration has been continuing the structural reforms initiated by the Aquino administration. The main objectives are trade and investment liberalization, privatization of public corporations, deregulation and tax reform.

Accomplishments:

Environment and Natural Resources Pursued Economic Growth Within the Framework of Sustainable Development

Recognizing the long-term implications of this situation on our economy and national life as a whole, he set out to ensure that our economic agenda are not pursued at the expense of our environment and natural resources. To this end, the Philippines participated and committed to the principles of the 1992 Rio Earth Summit, which in essence, required the adoption of sustainable development as the country's development policy framework. This is to ensure that environment considerations are placed in the mainstream of national development efforts. In pursuit of this, it formulated the Philippine Agenda 21, which consists of strategies that would integrate sustainable development in its development efforts. To provide a mechanism that will ensure the integration of these strategies in national policies, plans and programs, it created the Philippine Council for Sustainable Development (Executive Order 15, September 1, 1992) headed by NEDA.

Using Agenda 21 as its guidepost, the government vigorously pursued the implementation of the environmental protection programs and projects and adopted innovative approaches and mechanism to deepen public awareness on the causes and costs of environmental degradation. It also streamlined the environmental protection mechanism and systems towards making them more responsive to present and future requirements.

It focused its efforts on protecting and conserving our national resources and on rehabilitating our degraded ecosystems and pursued with greater vigor, the implementation of programs and aimed at preserving the genetic diversity of our wildlife. To ensure the preservation of their natural habitats and rationalize the exploration and development of our natural resources, it identified and segregated critical areas and put in place institutional mechanism to coordinate their development and protection.

It also adopted and implemented policies and programs to conserve and protect our forest, mineral and land resources. To augment government resources, it enlisted the support and participation of our communities, local government units, the private sector and other countries and international donor institutions in pursuit of our goals for the sector.

It extended its commitment to the protection and preservation of our natural resources and environment in the international arena by taking an active advocacy role in the first Asia Pacific Economic Council (APEC) Meeting on Sustainable Development, and successfully advocated for APEC's commitment to sustainable development and generated an Action Program towards ensuring the operationalization of the concepts in APEC member-countries.

All these contributed significantly to the attainment of our economic goals within the framework of sustainable development; and thus, ensured the continued sustainability of national efforts towards economic growth. Our success in these endeavors have earned for us the recognition as the World Bank's First Green Tiger and Asia's Emerging Green Tiger by Newsweek Magazine, sterling tributes to our commitment to, and pursuit of, sustainable development.

Environmental Protection

The government promoted an ecologically sound environment and reduced land, sea and air pollution through the implementation of various programs, adoption of innovative schemes and the streamlining of environmental protection systems and focused resources on the implementation of programs and projects that directly address the causes of pollution, in collaboration with the local government units and the private sectors.

Implemented Waste Disposal Projects. It launched the Ecological Waste Management Program under which Local Government Units (LGUs), communities and the private sector are provided technical assistance to promote and speed up the transfer of information and technology on the proper management and disposal of solid wastes, as well as guidance on the preparation of the requirements of the Environmental Impact Assessment System. To date, it entered into a Memorandum of Agreement with 134 LGUs; identified 736 potential landfill sites and implemented 32 pilot waste disposal projects on composting and recycling nationwide.

Furthermore, as part of its technical assistance to LGUs and other concerned groups, it formulated and published the following waste management manuals, plans and other relevant documents to serve as guide to users:

a. Handbook on Solid Waste Management for Local Government

b. Guidelines for the Preparation of Solid Waste Management Master Plan

c. Criteria for the Selection of a Potential Sanitary Landfill Site

d. Manual on Sanitary Landfill

e. Sanitary Landfill Design and Construction Manual

f. Leachate Stabilization Ponds Design and Construction

g. Internal Criteria for the Initial Evaluation of Solid Waste Management Projects Proposed Under the Built-Operate-Transfer (BOT) Scheme.

h. Scooping Guidelines for the Conduct of Environment Impact Assessment (EIA) for Thermal Conversion/ Waster-to-Energy (Incineration) Facility.

To complement the effort of the LGUs, the government set up waste disposal projects nationwide to ensure that appropriate technologies and procedures in the collection, storage, processing, transport and disposal of solid waste are widely disseminated and properly observed. It operationalized the San Mateo and Carmona Landfills and the Las Pinas Transfer station to address the waste disposal problem in Metro Manila.

Intensified Clean Air Campaign. It pursued our drive against smoke belchers and tapped the LGUs to implement the Comprehensive Anti-Smoke Belching Program. In support of the Program, it completed the revision of the IRRs on the Anti-smoke Belching Law (PD 1081) for the law's more effective implementation.

It complemented the Anti-Smoke Belching Program with the promotion of the use of lead-free gasoline, which significantly contributed to the reduction of noxious gases in the air. A total of 953 gasoline stations nationwide are now selling unleaded gasoline.

It also continuously monitored air quality and upgraded our monitoring stations to get a more accurate and up-to-date information. It acquired two (2) units of mobile air laboratory van to augment the existing stations.

Rehabilitated and Protected Major Bodies of Water. It intensified the protection and rehabilitation of heavily polluted major bodies of water.

a. *Pasig River.* It created the Presidential Task Force on Pasig River Rehabilitation under Administrative Order No. 74 dated 29 July 1993 to speed up the rehabilitation of the Pasig River and to upgrade its water quality by the year 2005. Toward this, it enlisted the support of our local communities, NGOs and private sector in the implementation of the Waste Minimization Program and resettled 3,583 families living on stilts along the Pasig River. The Biological Oxygen Demand (BOD) load was reduced from 330 metric tons per day (MTPD) in 1990 to 283 MTPD in 1996. These resulted in significant improvement in the ability of the river to sustain marine life.

b. *Laguna Lake and Tributaries.* It also pursued the implementation of the Sagip Ilog/River Rehabilitation Program, a multi-sectoral approach to clean and rehabilitate the biologically dead and polluted rivers in the nine (9) priority river systems in the Laguna Lake Basin.

c. *Boac River.* It rehabilitated the Boac River, which was damaged by Marcopper's mine tailings, in partnership with the private sector as well as the concerned LGUs and communities. Expenses for the rehabilitation activities was drawn from the Environmental Guarantee Fund established by Marcopper Company.

d. *Pasak River.* It removed and blasted illegal fishpond dikes and structures causing the siltation of the Pasak River and the flooding of San Fernando, Pampanga area and surrounding barangays. As a result, it reduced flooding in said areas.

e. *Pansipit River.* It dismantled about 2,951 (out of

3,440) illegal fishcages, fishpens, fishtraps and other aquaculture in Pansipit River to prevent the lake from further pollution due to excessive feeding of cultured fishes, and to save its endemic species such as Maliputo and Tawilis.

Implemented Clean and Green Program. It implemented the Clean and Green Program to instill in the minds of our local communities and LGUs the need for a clean and green environment. As part of the program, it distributed a total of 75.5 million seedlings and saplings to the LGUs for planting in their localities. It also established 457 mini parks nationwide and conducted the annual search (starting 1993) for the cleanest and greenest LGUs and bodies of water and reorganized and elevated to the Hall of Fame, the Cities of Baguio and Puerto Princesa, for winning the cleanest and greenest local government unit award for three (3) consecutive years.

Strengthened Environmental Impact Statement System. It revised the implementing rules and regulations on the Environmental Impact Statement System to make it a more responsive instrument in addressing the increasing pressures on the environment and simplified its requirements and mandated the conduct of the EIA simultaneous to that of the pre-feasibility study for environmentally-critical projects. This resulted in the reduction of processing time in the issuance of Environmental Compliance Certificates (ICC) to only 90 days. As insurance against possible harm to the environment and communities arising from the implementation of high-risk projects, it required firms to put up an Environment Guarantee Fund prior to the start of the project, and an Environment Monitoring fund to ensure that projects are monitored, in terms of their impact on the environment, from start to completion. In the same vein, it required social acceptability as one of the major criterion for the release of the ECC.

Closed Down Establishment Violating Pollution Control Laws. The government waged an all-out war against industrial polluters identified to be sources of pollution through the issuance of 286 Cease and Desist Orders (CDO) to industrial establishments operating without the required waste treatment facilities and discharging toxic chemicals and waste into the air, water, as well as those operating open dumpsites.

Developed the Smokey Mountain.   It closed the 20-hectare Smokey Mountain open dumpsite and disposed about 5 million cubic meters of garbage to develop it into a port-related, commercial and industrial area with housing units for its resident and constructed at least 33 temporary housing building in the Smokey Mountain which is now occupied by 2,700 Smokey Mountain households and drew up a development plan for the area, a component of which is the development of a 79 hectare reclaimed for the purpose. This is to include economic growth and provide employment opportunities to the residents of Smokey Mountain. It also provided basic services and alternative Mountain and also provided basic services and alternative livelihood to the scavenger families displaced by the closure of the dumpsite.

Adopted New Concepts and Measures to Protect the Environment.   It adopted innovative programs and market-based instruments aimed at influencing industrial firms and local government units to take deliberate efforts to protect the environment and to pursue more environmental friendly ways in their operations.

Imposed Emission and Effluent Charges.   It started charging pollution fees to industrial firms releasing pollution substances into the environment, based on the "Polluters Pay Principle" to put pressure on them to put in place waste minimization or waste treatment facilities. The concept is currently being piloted in the Laguna Lake region.

Adopted Color-Coding for Industrial Firms. Under the project, industrial firms are color-coded based on their environmental responsiveness, for disclosure to the public. "Gold" denotes excellent performance; "blue", sufficient compliance; "red", insufficient compliance and "black", non-compliance. The system is slated to be piloted in NCR and Laguna Lake region and will initially focus on the biochemical oxygen demand (BOD) concentration of a firm's effluent.

Comprehensive Ecological Labeling Project. Under the Project, LGUs were rated and ranked according to their performance in enforcing development and environmental functions such as compliance to environmental standards like water supply, sewerage treatment facilities, and solid waste management.

Banned the Entry of Toxic Waste. A signatory to the Basel Convention, it banned the importation, storage or transport of toxic or nuclear waste into or through our country. To further regulate the movement of hazardous waste, it also prohibited the importation of recyclable materials containing hazardous substance (DENR Administrative Order No. 28, S. 1998).

The Ramos administration's over all objectives were higher economic growth with equity and poverty alleviation through people empowerment. It offered a vision of a Philippines where people under God, can live together in freedom, dignity and prosperity, in one nation and one with the world.

According to President Ramos, "This is the challenge to our leadership today: that we cast away the old politics that divides us and work together for the common good and national welfare."

The six-year term of President Ramos is looked upon with much optimism, not only for his clear vision of the future but also his hand-on style of leadership in addressing the challenges facing the Filipino nation. As Centennial President, a name conferred on him because his term coincides with 100th year anniversary in 1998 of the declaration of Philippine Independence from Spain, the nation looks forward to attaining full political stability, sustained economic development and social justice by the turn of the 21st century.

Joseph Ejercito Estrada (1998-2001)

Ninth President of the Republic of the Philippines

JOSEPH EJERCITO ESTRADA, a college dropout who made it big in movies and then became a bigger star in politics assumed the highest elective public official of the Philippines.

Estrada called the proclamation of the Congress of the Philippines a "triumph of Philippine democracy," and thanked his supporters, "especially the masa" or masses.

Estrada gained a devoted following, particularly among the country's many poor, during several decades as an actor in B-movies playing the roles of tough guys who stood up against justice.

He parlayed his popularity into a successful political career, first winning election as mayor of San Juan Rizal, then as a Senator and as Vice-President.

Estrada, whose inauguration is June 30, said that he would continue most of Ramos' policies but will focus on helping the poor and building up agriculture. He also has pledged to crack down on official corruption and solve the country's severe crime problem within six months. In Congress' tabulation, Estrada led the presidential race with 10.7 million votes. De Venecia, the administration candidate, was a distant second with 4.3 million.

Right after Estrada took his oath of office as the country's 9th president before Chief Justice Andres Narvasa at 12 noon, at Barasoain Church, Malolos, Bulacan, the Armed Forces of the Philippines gave a 21-gun salute as church bells pealed and the University of the Philippines Singing Ambassadors sang Handel's "Hallelujah Chorus."

After the inauguration, former President Corazon C. Aquino, who was personally invited by President Estrada to attend the affair, said she was wishing the Estrada administration "nothing but the best."

"We should all rally behind our new President so that he will succeed in enhancing our democracy and improving the lives of the majority of our people." Mrs. Aquino said.

She also welcomed President Estrada's assurance that the annual celebration of the 1986 People Power Revolution would be continued during his six-year tenure in Malacanang.

Former President Ramos reiterated his support to the administration of the President Estrada for the speedy recovery of the Philippines from the regional currency turmoil.

President Estrada's 10-Point Agenda

Fighting poverty through people empowerment was the noble and lofty plan of the Estrada administration, which it hoped to leave as a legacy to the Filipino people. He directed government resources toward addressing the immediate concerns affecting the economy and promoting the welfare of the Filipinos, particularly the poor.

President Estrada's 10-point Action Plan Agenda are:

1. *Governance.* Government must be transparent. All decision-making processes are publicly disclosed. Immediate objective is to restore public confidence through the restoration of peace and order establishing a responsive government.

   Immediately arrest the most notorious criminals and drug pushers and prosecute tax evaders and corrupt officials and law enforcers.

   Reorganize the Office of the President in order to bring it closer to the citizenry. This may involve extending the presence of the Office of the President to each of the three major regions (Luzon, Visayas, and Mindanao).

2. *Fiscal Policy.* Build framework for economic growth and deliver necessary social services. It must be majoritarian. Government will work closely with civil

society, and favor broader over narrower constituencies on any given issue.

Consider the granting of tax amnesties in order to accelerate collection of past dues and encourage compliance in the future by non-salary-based taxpayers. Following the grant of amnesty, all tax evaders shall be prosecuted to the fullest extent of the law.

Abolish the Presidential Commission on Good Government (PCGG), which has outlived its usefulness, and resolve all legal impediments to the immediate disposition of sequestered assets.

3. *Monetary Policy and Financial Reforms.* Facilitate reduction in market interest rates in order to stimulate new investment from domestic and international sources. As investor confidence returns and the regional currency crisis eases, improvement in liquidity must be directed towards rebuilding our foreign exchange reserves rather than allowing the peso to appreciate unduly.

Long term objectives are to keep the average inflation rate at/or below 5%, maintain the peso at an internationally competitive level, maintain our foreign exchange reserves against future economic shocks, and continue the liberalization of the financial sector, led by the commercial banking system, as the engine for increasing domestic savings and channeling it to the most efficient uses.

Promote and maintain an internationally competitive peso through appropriate monetary and exchange rate policies.

4. *Exports and Investments.* Restore market confidence in our commitment to the various bilateral and multilateral agreements that comprise the framework for a global free market and an open world economy.

Open up to foreign capital and technology to

augment low domestic savings rate and acquire advance technologies abroad. Our long-term objective is for the private manufacture sector to increase its growth rates from 2% currently to at least 10% annually.

Increase official support for the Export Development Council in order to mount a fully coordinated and monitored export offensive.

Review the liberalization of foreign investment ownership rules, with a view towards opening of additional areas of the economy. These restricted areas may include retail trade, mass media, and even land ownership.

5. *Infrastructure.* Deregulation and privatization will continue to be a commitment to transparency and full disclosure especially for large flagship projects.

Expand the build-operate-transfer (BOT) approach to private-public sector partnership on large-scale infrastructure programs, as well as variants like build-operate-own (BOO) in relation to privatization.

Accelerate deregulation of inter-island shipping and the abolition of monopolistic privileges in that industry. Our domestic shipping costs run as high as 200% of the equivalent costs for international shipping or comparable distances.

In telecommunications, continue deregulation initiatives, improve interconnection performance, and strengthen the supervisory capabilities of the National Telecommunications Commission (NTC).

6. *Agriculture.* Central issue in agriculture and agrarian reform is the productivity of land use, not simply land ownership. Agricultural growth rates have been less than 2% annually a situation aggravated by improper policies on food price support and consumer subsidies.

286 PHILIPPINE HISTORY AND GOVERNMENT THROUGH THE YEARS

Direct the Department of Agrarian Reform to complete the full implementation of agrarian reform within the next four years, as measured principally by completion of the land transfer process.

Direct the Department of Justice to resolve immediately all problems related to ownership of the coconut levy fund.

Abolish the National Food Authority (NFA) monopoly on rice imports and allow private traders to import rice at any time, subject only to the tariffs and usual standards of government oversight.

Replace quantitative restrictions and bureaucratic decisions on rice imports with a system of tariffs. Tariff revenues then become available to finance livelihood and safety net programs for the rural poor.

Privatize and separate the marketing and trading functions of the NFA and limit its role to the administration of necessary regulations and management of our strategic stockpile and other food grains.

7. *Safety Nets and Social Services.* Commitment to the establishment of social safety nets that will cushion the poorest of our poor and prevent them from being marginalized. Such programs must proceed from a well-defined social policy and include provisions for social assistance, social insurance and employment generation.

Operationalize the inter-agency National Anti-Poverty Commission under the leadership of the President and develop its capacity for policy formulation, monitoring poverty, and the integration and coordination of service delivery.

The Department of Health and Department of Interior and Local Government (DILG) will be responsible for devolving health care to local governments, particularly through barangay health stations and rural staffed by trained midwives and nurses. Special emphasis will be given to municipalities without a municipal health officer as well as prioritize poverty alleviation target areas.

8. *Education.* Strengthen primary education, which is both a great social equalizer and the building block for future educational achievement.

Direct the DECS to review and upgrade salary and benefit levels of teachers for consideration in our budgetary allocation process, if feasible, through full or partial exemption from the Salary Standardization Law.

Direct the DECS, TESDA and CHED to adopt programs to improve the quality of teacher performance.

Create a muti-sectoral Presidential Commission Education Reform comprising of representatives of government line agencies, public and private schools at all levels. Teachers, private industry, NGOs and other concerned sectors.

9. *Science and Technology.* The low level of so-called "non-factor productivity improvement" characterizes the technology handicaps in our current economy. This must be addressed if we are to progress along so-called "technology learning curve," learn and adapt modern technologies, and become a nation of high value-added producers.

Promote linkages across the value chain between large corporations and small and medium enterprises by which technology will be transferred and integrated into the entire production and distribution process.

Encourage businesses to provide specialized training and continuing employee education, perhaps along the lines of German-type-apprenticeship programs.

10. *Environmental Protection.* Natural resources management must become the responsibility of local communities who are both familiar with, and attached to, these resources.

Intensify enforcement of environmental control laws and administer required sanctions on polluting firms and other violators. DENR will be directed to submit a Report of Compliance within one hundred days.

Launch a nationwide civic effort to re-green the country. Community programs must focus on rehabilitating community forests and other green spaces, and cleaning up polluted rivers and water systems.

The Rise and Fall of Estrada

Former President Joseph Ejercito Estrada was a grand spectacle never before seen in the Philippines political landscape. So great, yet so controversial, was his impact on the lives of our people. For Estrada – also known as Asiong Salonga, during his less than a three-year stint in the highest elective position in the land – earned for himself a niche in Philippine history, not for any significant achievement he had done but for his colossal failure of governance that plunged the nation into crisis. His impeachment by the lower house of Congress and the subsequent trial at the Senate which convened as a court with the presiding officer, Chief Justice Hilario Davide, Jr., of the Supreme Court, moved the entire nation to militancy and led serious loss of credibility for his eleven allies in the Senate, who acted like his lawyers, instead of as his judges.

Ironically, the disgraced president assumed the mantle of leadership of the nation in an atmosphere of hope among the poor and deprived masses of our people that he would lift them from their impoverished existence and bring the whole country to prosperity. Elected with more than 10 million votes, the biggest majority for any president in the nation's political history, he had campaigned with the slogan, "Erap para sa mahirap" and during his inaugural oath-taking, he swore on his family's Bible before the then Chief Justice Andres Narvasa that he would upholdthe Constitution and do justice to every man. At his inaugural address, he told a wildly cheering crowd that he would govern without fear or favor.

What Erap did instead is now history. In October 2000, on the floor of the senate and before the Senate Blue Ribbon Committee, Erap was accused by then Senate minority leader, Teofisto Guingona, of receiving bribe money from gambling lords engaged in *jueteng* (illegal numbers game) and pocketing more than P400 million of this money. It was a bombshell exposé which reverberated throughout the nation and led to his impeachment and subsequent trial by the Senate. Because the trial turned out to be highly partisan in favor of Erap, the Filipino people who were scandalized and humiliated by the un-Filipino behavior of their President, went to the streets to demand for Erap's resignation. This explosion of rage led to EDSA People Power 2 – and the ascension into office of then vice-president Gloria Macapagal-Arroyo, in a constitutional takeover of government and the humiliating ouster of Erap!

The Impeachment Trial of Estrada. Joseph Ejercito Estrada was the first head of state in the Philippines to be impeached. The impeachment trial has opened the eyes of many Filipinos to the many shortcomings of the leader to whom they had entrusted the steering of the ship of the state.

The Articles of Impeachment denounced President Estrada for bribery, graft and corruption, betrayal of public trust and culpable violation of Constitution. The House Panel of prosecutors accuses him of stealing hundreds of millions of pesos in jueteng payola and the tobacco excise taxes, maintaining secret billion peso bank accounts from which he has acquired mansions for his several mistresses, falsifying his sworn statement of assets and liabilities, appointing his subordinates to multiple positions despite the constitutional prohibitions and other impeachment offenses.

The incredible revelations at the impeachment trial, which was televised nationwide have betrayed another facet of Mr. Estrada's public character and political role as a head of government. It is unfortunate that a president elected by an overwhelming majority must be ousted from office after thirty-one months of office.

In deed, the impeachment trial is a rare opportunity and a learning experience for the Filipino people to test their capacity to engage in discourse, to make valid claims, to lay bare the bases of these claims, to vindicate them, and make their own judgment.

Joseph Estrada – The Actor and Politician. Joseph E. Estrada was born on April 19, 1937 in Tondo, Manila and once the home to the toughies and poorest of the poor, to Engr. Emilio Ejercito (deceased) and Maria Marcelo. His father worked for the government, Joseph's mother, Maria Marcelo, a simple housewife, studied music at the Colegio de Santa Rosa.

After high school, Joseph decided to study engineering to follow the footsteps of his father; but in his third year at Mapua, he decided to try the movies. Displeased with his decision to drop out of college, his parents forbade him to use his family name, which forced him to adopt "Estrada" (Spanish for street) as a screen name, and "Erap" ("Pare" or friend spelled backwards) as a nickname. During his movie career, he played the lead role in several movies and produced more than 70 films. He was the first FAMAS Hall of Fame awardee for Best Actor (1981) and also became a Hall of Fame awardee as a Producer (1983).

Estrada entered politics when he ran for Mayor of San Juan in 1968. He was proclaimed mayor only in 1969, after he won an electoral protest against Dr. Braulio Sto. Domingo. As mayor (1969-1986), Estrada was named one of the Ten Outstanding Mayor and Foremost Nationalist (1972) and Most Outstanding Metro Manila Mayor (1972). The EDSA Revolution in 1986 brought about the end of his 16-year stint as mayor and was replaced by an officer-in-charge as part of the organization of local governments. Of all the Metro Manila Mayors who were replaced, he was the only one who left behind savings in the Municipal Treasurer – almost P24 Million.

Estrada's political career was not meant to end just yet. The following year, he ran for Senator, and again, contrary to the expectations of many, he won despite running in the opposition party. He was proclaimed in 1987, and held office there for five years. As a legislator, he followed a nationalistic and pro-poor agenda. He chaired the Senate Committee on Rural Development, authoring and sponsoring the law to promote rural development by providing an accelerated program for the construction of irrigation projects within a 10-year period.

He sponsored several bills and resolution for the protection and promotion of the interest of indigenous cultural communities. He also co-authorized the law requiring court stenographers to give free transcripts of notes to indigent/ low-income litigants. He also authored an act creating the Philippine Carabao Center for the propagation of the carabao to enable farmers, particularly the small landowners and agrarian reform beneficiaries to avail of good quality stock at reasonable prices.

He was one of the most vocal opponents of the RP-US Military Bases Agreement. In 1991, when the agreement was up for renewal, Estrada was the first Senator to deliver a privilege speech against the extension of the agreement, and he voted for the agreement's termination. He explained that it was not because he had anything against Americans but that because he wanted the Philippines to reclaim its full sovereignty. On January 14, 1989, he was named Outstanding Senator by the Philippines Free Press.

From his being a senator, he ran for Vice-President in the 1992 elections under the Nationalist People's Coalition-Partido ng Masang Pilipino, which he easily won by a big margin. As the elected Vice-President, there were those who thought he would soon fade into oblivion, having no definite role to play in the government and belonging to a different political party from the President. He was, however, given by President Fidel V. Ramos the task of heading the newly-created Presidential Anti-Crime Commission (PACC), a superbody mandated to go after organized crime and their perpetrators. He made headlines bagging kidnappers and other criminals.

In his private capacity, Vice-President Estrada continues to be active in several organizations involved in matters close to his heart. He is the Founder and President of the Movie Workers Welfare Foundation (MOWELFUND), a Governor of the Film Academy of the Philippines and adviser of the Philippine Motion Picture Producers Association. He is also the Founder and President of ERAP para sa Mahihirap Foundation, the Police and Fire Trust Fund, and the Philippine Drug Abuse Resistance Education, Inc. (PHILDARE).

JOSEPH EJERCITO ESTRADA –
"A President of Ironies"

The Estrada administration is like a movie against a backdrop of ironies. After establishing a big unprecedented lead over his political rivals in the 1998 Philippine presidential elections he declared, "I will not play politics, I will not rule with vengeance, and I will give the last and greatest performance of my life in the service of the nation, and the upliftment of the lives of our people."

This was the very essence of his inaugural address when he told emphatically a big wildly-cheering crowd that he would govern his country and his people without fear and favor anchored on honesty, justice, and equality. His political campaign with the slogan, "Erap para sa Mahirap" were empty rhetoric and paradoxical. The masa or the "bakya crowd" swooned to their idol in the movies whenever they saw him. They are totally misled and refused to see reality. While they lived in extreme poverty and want with limited opportunities to improve their living conditions. Estrada is living in luxury. Erap refused to tame his legendary appetites – for food, drink and women. Erap and his friends and close political associates in Malacañang Palace had drinking sprees almost every night with the red wine (preferably the $1,000 – per bottle Chateau Petrus). He also maintains several mistresses and fathered a number of children who live in mansions in exclusive areas in Metro Manila.

The president's days in power established shots that defined the personality of the lead actor as well as the setting he portrayed his role. His remaining days in power were scenes through which a keen viewer can tell what lies ahead be they ecstatic or tragic. His role in the Philippine political landscape was phenomenal; so great, yet controversial.

Like a movie, the political drama as it unfolded ended Erap's reign of political power on January 20, 2001 when he hurriedly left Maloacanang Palace via the backdoor on a barge at the Pasig River with his family, friends and political supporters.

After leaving the Palace, Erap still insisted that he was still the *de jure* President, having been elected by more than ten million votes, while denying vehemently that he had committed wrong against the Filipino people – despite a unanimous Supreme Court 13-0 judgment that he had resigned from his post and therefore, liable for criminal and civil charges that would be filed against him.

While the viewers believed that Erap betrayed the Filipino people, and his struggle to hold desperately on to power, the movie ended like a tragedy – typically of a person who had noble intentions whose character is flawed by a single weakness as greed and pride and immorality, which caused him to break a divine law or moral precept and leads inevitably to his downfall.

Philippine politics sometimes seems like the stage of a dramatic morality play, because leaders like Joseph Estrada whose political slogans is "Erap para sa Mahihirap" and Ferdinand Marcos, "This nation can be Great Again" respectively, inspired a moral crusade because of their monumental sins. It seemed like the stage for a Greek tragedy, because of the genuine affection with which these presidents

were catapulted to power with their excessive arrogance and
self-confidence that marred their rule, the Filipino people's
popular outrage drove them out of Malacanang.

Gloria Macapagal Arroyo (2001-   )

Tenth President of the
Republic of the Philippines

When she was still Vice-President of the Philippines,
Gloria Macapagal-Arroyo had not displayed much of her
natural-born leadership. This is because the Office of the Vice-
President is simply not the Office of the President that directs
major national and international affairs affecting the nation's
entire operations. It just supports the undertakings of the
premier office of the land. Media seldom focused eyes on the
Vice-President because the President was hugging the
limelight. However, during her stint as Vice-President and
concurrently as Secretary of the Department of Social Welfare
and Development, GMA had done much to improve the plight
of the marginal sectors of society.

Now that she is President of the Republic, President Gloria
Macapagal-Arroyo is proving her worth as leader of a nation
embroiled in domestic problems. The characteristics of
statesmen are gradually emerging in her person: firm yet
compassionate, with a brilliant mind that may lead this nation
to economic prosperity. There had been many who said that
we need an economist for a President to release us from
economic bondage. Well, now they have the answer, President
Arroyo is an economist.

President Gloria Macapagal-Arroyo has such an
impressive record, aside from being a daughter of the late
Philippine President Diosdado P. Macapagal who was known
for his integrity and dignified lifestyle. During the Presidency
of Diosdado P. Macapagal, the Philippines was second only
to Japan in economic progress in Asia.

Elected as senator during her first try in politics in 1992,

President Arroyo was re-elected senator in 1995 with nearly 16 million votes. She was elected Vice-President of the Philippines in 1998 with almost 10 million votes, the largest mandate in the history of vice-presidential elections.

President Gloria Macapagal-Arroyo, born on April 5, 1947, was valedictorian of her high school class at Assumption Convent. She was consistently on the Dean's List in Georgetown University in Washington, DC, and graduated *magna cum laude* at the Assumption College. She obtained a Master's degree in Economics from the Ateneo de Manila University and a Doctorate in Economics from the University of the Philippines.

President Gloria Macapagal-Arroyo began her professional career as a teacher at the Assumption College. She later became Assistant Professor at the Ateneo de Manila University, and Senior Lecturer at the UP School of Economics.

She joined the Philippine government in 1986 during the administration of President Corazon Cojuangco-Aquino, who appointed her Trade and Industry Undersecreatry. During her tenure in the Senate, she authored 55 laws on economic and social reforms and was named outstanding Senator several times. When she was elected Vice-President, President Joseph Ejercito Estrada appointed her as concurrent Social Welfare and Development Secretary, a post she held until her resignation from the Cabinet on October 12, 2000.

Gloria Macapagal-Arroyo's Ascension to Presidency

For the second time in 15 years, Filipinos unleashed people power to force the resignation of their President in a bloodless and legal transfer of power from Joseph Ejercito Estrada to Vice-President Gloria Macapagal-Arroyo.

Gloria Macapagal-Arroyo was sworn into office before more than a million people, who had gone to the streets to demand Estrada's resignation, at historic EDSA where in February 1986, millions of Filipinos braved tanks to topple the 14 year dictatorship of Ferdinand Marcos. The Filipinos did it again after five days of people-power demonstrations in protest; this was triggered by the Senate's vote not to disclose evidence in Estrada's impeachment trial.

What was remarkable with People Power 2, which former President Fidel Ramos described as a reprise of the 1986 EDSA Revolution "done better," was that the Filipinos demonstrated that they can change disgraced leaders with pressure from the streets within constitutional and legal methods, and without shedding blood.

Fears that People Power 2 would turn violent, given President Estrada's belligerent statements that he would never resign, did not materialize, repeating the non-violent transfer of power in 1986 after Marcos resigned. The power handed over virtually ending the country's political crisis, demonstrated the strength and resilience of the country's democratic institutions and traditions.

With the transfer of power, Estrada went down in the archives as the shortest-serving president (31 months) in the post-war history of the Republic, as well as the first Filipino president to be impeached.

It is historically significant that Gloria Macapagal-Arroyo, took her oath as a constitutional successor before Chief Justice Hilario Davide Jr., with the blessings of Jaime Cardinal Sin, in the presence of the Armed Forces Chief of Staff Gen. Angelo Reyes, leaders of Congress and the leaders of civil society forces which were the dynamo of the second People Power upheaval. The presence of two key players in EDSA 1 – former president Corazon Aquino and former President Fidel Ramos – forged the historical link between the two people-driven uprising in the streets to replace leaders who had lost their mandate. At the new President's swearing in, the leaders of the key Philippine political and social institutions, including the Senate and the Church, closed ranks to give the new government constitutional and moral legitimacy.

The constitutional and non-violent succession of President Macapagal-Arroyo was facilitated by the decisive withdrawal by the Armed Forces of the Philippines and the Philippine National Police of their support for Estrada and their swift transfer of loyalty to his constitutional successor. This breakaway repeated the military defection from Marcos in 1986, and, in this crisis, it knocked down the main pillar of support for Estrada; ignited the resignations of most of the members of his Cabinet; and precipitated the collapse of his government.

It is reflection of the strength of the Filipino democratic culture that the military did not take advantage of the crisis to seize power, preferring to mediate the resignation of Estrada and the transition to the next government. In EDSA 2, the military took a lower profile than in EDSA 1, when it sent tanks to the streets. While giving credit to the role of military defection in making Estrada realize that his time was up, it was people power itself massed in the streets that was the most decisive factor in the resignation of Estrada.

It was a revolution, Filipino-style. For four days and nights protesters sang and danced in the streets, nuns and priests held prayer vigils and behind the scenes the opposition worked feverishly to persuade the military to abandon President Joseph Estrada.

In the end, a weary president with no soldiers left to command walked out of the Malacanang presidential palace and, without a shot being fired in anger, his vice-president, Gloria Macapagal Arroyo, was sworn in.

They're calling it People Power 2, the sequel to the 1986 ouster of Ferdinand Marcos. That first revolt became a model for civilian uprisings against dictator around the world. But the second revolution is already being criticized as a "soft coup" that ejected an elected president in order to return the old, wealthy political and business elite to power. Many ordinary Filipinos are eager to believe that's not the case and are relying on Arroyo's new administration to stamp out corruption.

Arroyo's Task. Arroyo certainly faces a daunting task. She must end the pork-barrel politics that have dominated the

Philippines through dictatorship and democracy. She must improve the lot of the millions of impoverished Filipinos who elected the populist Estrada with a huge majority in 1998. She must strengthen the nation's faith in its democratic institutions.

Whether she will be helped or hurt in that quest by the dizzyingly broad coalition of interests that brought her to power remains to be seen. Middle-class civil-society groups, left-wing trade unions and the Catholic Church got people out in the streets; political backing came from the traditional political elite of former presidents Corazon Aquino and Fidel Ramos; and big businesses showed their support for president Arroyo.

More ominously for a new civilian leader, the fatal blow to Estrada was delivered by the military, when it announced it would no longer recognize him as commander-in-chief.

Some of these elements will now be clamoring for change; in particular, the middle classes and some businesses. Others, especially politicians who prospered under the old system, would want to preserve the *status quo.*

"There is a genuine constituency for reform," says Sheila Colonel, executive director of the not-for-profit Philippine Center for Investigative Journalism. But with politicians already prominent in Arroyo's camp from the Ramos and Aquino administrations, which were both accused of failing to stamp out corruption, "I very much doubt if it will be a reformist government," says Coronel. "I was at her headquarters and I could see the old faces coming out, people who have been accused of corruption in the past."

Clearly, the battle for reform will be difficult. Arroyo will be hoping that it won't be made harder still by the role the military played in the political transition. With the armed forces largely depoliticized since Marcos' day, outright interference in government isn't expected. Nevertheless, the fact that the new president needed to secure the support of the military underscores just how frail democracy still is in the Philippines.

Retired generals, including Ramos, had been openly calling on active officers to betray their president for weeks. Reports are now emerging that the chief of staff of the Armed Forces, Gen. Angelo Reyes, fearing his own troops could start to divide along pro and anti-Estrada lines, abandoned Estrada to forestall cracks in the ranks.

How close the country came to armed conflict isn't clear; but as recently as December 30, more than 20m people died in a series of blasts in Manila, for which no group has claimed responsibility. In the days leading up to Estrada's ouster, there was the worrying sight of tense stand-offs between anti-Estrada demonstrators and small groups of hard-core Estrada supporters.

Few have forgotten that Aquino's administration was marred by seven coup attempts in the years following the Marcos dictatorship. Some observers are concerned that the reappearance of the military in Philippine politics casts a shadow over the president's ability and desire to strengthen civilian institutions.

The story of Estrada's fall from grace is a case in point. When the president, who had been plagued by corruption scandals since he took office, was impeached in November, it was hailed as a great advance in maturity for the country's democracy; but as the trial wore on, Filipinos became increasingly convinced that the legal and democratic process would be thwarted by the president's power to call in personal favours and persuade the senators sitting in judgment to block his conviction.

The final straw came on January 16, when more than half of the senators voted to block the opening of bank documents, which prosecutors said contained evidence that Estrada had accepted millions of dollars in kickbacks. The decision immediately sent hundreds of Filipinos out into the streets, triggering rallies that swelled into a massive four-day demonstration.

But while anger was apparent among the middle classes, Estrada, a master of the common touch, still retained largely passive support among the poorest Filipinos. Citing that mandate and exploiting the letter of the constitution, which stipulates that a written resignation must be presented, he refused to step down, even after all of the armed forces, the police and most of his cabinet members withdrew their support for him.

Instead, Estrada holed up with his family and remaining allies in Malacanang palace and stalled for time, reportedly arguing for concessions such as immunity from prosecution and keeping some of his alleged ill-gotten assets.

When an entire night passed without Estrada's resignation, tens of thousands of frustrated protesters marched to Malacanang to demand that the president leave office. An air force fighter jet and four military helicopters buzzed the palace to remind the president that he had lost the reins of power.

It finally took a controversial Supreme Court declaration that the presidency was effectively vacant to persuade Estrada to pack up and move out to his family home in Manila-still refusing to sign a letter of resignation and insisting that he was the legal president.

Gloria Macapagal-Arroyo's Program of Government. The Arroyo government is focused on poverty alleviation, political stability, peace and order and food security. Her pro-people program are anchored on new politics based on platform on order to create fertile grounds for genuine political reforms. The politics of personality and patronage must give way to a new politics of new programs and process of dialogue with the people through consultation, good governance supported by high moral and ethical standards, and leadership by example.

The Arroyo administration is confronted by the chaos that had ensued from the open political wounds caused by the ouster of her predecessor, Joseph Ejercito Estrada. Other serious problems confronting her administration is the uphill drive against graft and corruption in government, the unresolved communist and Muslim insurgencies, and the damage to the national image caused by the Abu Sayyaf bandit group in Mindanao, poverty, unemployment, kidnapping and drug trafficking.

The President is determined to address these various problems and these can be facilitated with the cooperative effort of all sectors of society, including politicians siding or not with the President.

President Gloria Macapagal-Arroyo envisions to established a robust economy that can sustain all sectors in the country.

Epifanio Delos Santos Avenue (EDSA)

EDSA – symbol of courage, fortitude, unity, justice, truth and tenacity of spirit exemplified the Filipino character at its highest and loftiest measure to dramatize their legitimate grievances.

EDSA 1 was hailed as a legitimate uprising of the Filipino people against the excesses of Ferdinand E. Marcos during more than thirteen intolerable years of despotic rule. It was received with universal commendation of deposing a president who would not want to relinquish power. The significant fact that this political upheaval was effected without bloodshed made it doubly extraordinary and praiseworthy before the eyes of the world. There was a minimum of violence in this historic event in the life of a nation that virtually emphasized the level-headedness of the Filipinos in resisting tyrannical and dictatorial rule. Despite the unbearable oppression for many years of the hated regime, we still avoided the threat or force of arms and mayhem. We relied instead on our freedom of expression and assembly to articulate our thoughts and sentiments to a repressive regime as our most formidable weapon of peaceful protest coupled with prayers. The exuberance did not cry for vengeance as Marcos, Imelda, his family and cronies fled, but only exhibited the nationwide euphoria over the end of the despised dictatorship. People went to the streets and danced while church bells continuously rang.

The peaceful uprising in EDSA will always be remembered as the Filipino people's shining moment in history because they stood up to answer the call for love of country. Their only weapons against a formidable force were their collective expression of opposition against authoritarian rule were songs, prayers, religions, icons and yellow daisies to oust a dictator through a dramatic end. This EDSA event, which the whole world watched with awe as it unfolded gave the Filipino people the opportunity to regain their freedom.

EDSA 2. This People Power was an event skeptics thought could never happen but it galvanized the normally passive middle-class members of the societal strata to the streets and pressed for Joseph Estrada's resignation. EDSA 2 was spontaneous and hailed by majority of the Filipino people especially the middle class – the intellectuals, professionals, businessmen, political figures, priests, nuns, civil societies, students, and officers and members of organizations against crimes and corruption and adherents of good government. It received national protest when eleven administration senators blocked the opening of the second envelop of the damaging evidence against Estrada, where Clarissa Ocampo, the prosecutions surprise witness Senior Vice-President for trust of Equitable PCI Bank testified that she was just a foot away when Joseph Estrada assumed Jose Velarde's identity by signing documents pertinent to a P500 million trust account. The cowardice of that servile vote virtually transferred the impeachment trials yielding chamber dominated by the senators who were loyal to Estrada to the court of the people at EDSA.

Joseph Estrada was perceived by his detractors as a loyal follower and emulator of Marcos who may have exceeded his model and idol in debasing the high office of the President of the Republic of the Philippines.

It is also interesting to note that this significant historical event of stripping the powers entrusted to him was also affected without bloodshed. This explicitly implied that the Filipino people can force a head of state to give up his powers because of the people's mounting rage. The outraged Filipinos, including the thinking and disenchanted masses, who idolized and lionized him before, finally joined in the widespread demand for their disgraced idol to step down. EDSA 2 was a triumph of civil society. It was crises and an upheaval which the Filipinos resolved themselves for the first time without foreign intervention. It helped us regain our national pride and dignity.

EDSA 2 may be viewed of a culmination of a movement to restore accountability and idealism in government. The moving spirit constituted the young, the students, the middle class and the educated who refused to be led any further by an incompetent, corrupt and immoral president. By and large, the Filipino people did the right decision. They got rid of a president by a non-institutional route and, at the same time, saved the constitutional order.

The political, economic and social conditions were less than ideal. The failure of the new government under President Arroyo to relieve the suffering of the poor in any meaningful way had made it hard for her to win over the masses who idolized Estrada. Some political analysts and observers inferred that she seems to worry over her tenuous grip on the presidency and, in effect, this inclines her even more to prioritize political consolidation over the much-needed reform.

Despite all this, let us not blame the government for all these problems. If we want the spirit and the flame of EDSA 2 to live, let us begin to demand of ourselves the same selflessness and sacrifice for a common good.

Comparison of EDSA 1 and EDSA 2

In EDSA 1, the people protested the massive election fraud during the Snap Presidential Elections held during the first week of February 1986. Many supporters of Corazon Aquino were not able to vote because their names were allegedly deleted from the registered voter's list. Members of the Commission on Election walked out from their work because, according to them, the then President Ferdinand Marcos was forcing them to declare him the winner.

In EDSA 2, the people protested the pro-Estrada senators' barring of a set of evidence that will convict the president in the on-going impeachment trial. This is what the people claimed as "suppression of truth." People of EDSA 2 have lost faith in the integrity of the impeachment court and were predicting an acquittal verdict by a majority of the senators. The people then gathered in EDSA to continue the battle in the streets rather than in court.

EDSA 1 lasted for 5 days (February 21-25, 1986), while EDSA 2 lasted for 4 days only (January 17-29, 2001).

Ferdinand Marcos left Malacañang and went to Hawaii. Estrada left the palace but stayed in the country.

In both EDSA 1 and EDSA 2, Jaime Cardinal Sin called on the people to gather at EDSA through Radio Veritas.

There was no EDSA flyovers and EDSA Shrine yet during EDSA 1. These structures, including the EDSA Monument," was called "Pamana ng 1986 EDSA People Power."

There were no presence of tanks and heavily armed soldiers during EDSA 2 unlike EDSA 1. Both ended peacefully.

People wore something yellow during EDSA 1, while something black during EDSA 2. Yellow symbolizes democracy which was being cried for in 1986 while Black was worn in 2001 because of the "death" of justice in the Impeachment trial.

EDSA 1 was more of a solemn crusade, while EDSA 2 was more like a party. Both were supported by the religious sectors.

"EDSA 1 involved the exercise of the people power of revolution which overthrew the whole government. EDSA 2 is an exercise of people power for redress of grievances which only affected the office of the President. EDSA 1 is extra-constitutional and the legitimacy of the new government that resulted from it cannot be the subject of judicial review, but EDSA 2 is intra-constitutional and the resignation of the incumbent President and the succession of the Vice-President as President are subject to judicial review. EDSA 1 presented a political question; EDSA 2 involved legal questions." (G.R. 146738, Estrada vs. Arroyo, p. 32).

Then the question of whether or not Erap resigned was debated in all sectors. Finally, the Supreme Court handed down its verdict. Citing the diary of the then Executive Secretary Edgardo Angara, published in full by the Philippine Daily Inquirer, the details of Erap's final hours in Malacanang were revealed. Although many of the quotations of Angara may, in a strict legal sense, be classified as hearsay, Erap's words were put together to analyze his then state of mind. Such words as quoted, "Pagod na pagod na ako. Ayoko na, masyado nang masakit. Xxx" (I am very tired. I don't want anymore of this; it's very painful.) – These words signify resignation, coupled with his overt acts, such as showing himself on national television, proposing a snap election in May, without his participation.

The series of negotiation between the Erap camp and GMA faction, discussing a peaceful and orderly transfer of power, at which point Erap was supposed to have a five-day grace period to stay in Malacanang, and the subsequent message that he signed where he acknowleged the oath-taking of GMA and announced that he was leaving the palace to start a healing process, all told, speaks of resignation. He did not say that he was leaving the Palace due to any kind of inability and that he was going to re-assume the presidency as soon as the disability disappears. As the Supreme Court puts it, Erap's presidency is now in the past tense.

The issue of immunity has also been resolved but its finality is yet to be counted 15 days after the decision was handed, and if any motion is filed, the resolution of said motion may take another few weeks. It's just a matter of time. When it happens, an ex-President will stand criminal trial. Ironically but true in every sense, it is a case of the People of the Philippines against Joseph Estrada, a case of plunder involving hundred of millions of pesos.

People Power 2 was undoubtedly achieved! No wonder. The Spirit of EDSA Lives On! ... so it was not the straw that broke the camel's back, it was the ENVELOPE. If only those 11 senators chose to open the mysterious envelope, the people would have not protested in EDSA, and People Power 2 would have not taken place. However, the people in EDSA are a little bit glad with those eleven senators' decision not to open the envelope, because it all ended up to an infamous president's removal from office and once again Filipinos have shown to the entire world, through EDSA People Power 2, the Filipinos' sense of unity, peaceful non-violent attitude and that democracy works in our country! God bless the Philippines!

Weeks after EDSA 2, Estrada insisted that he never really resigned, and therefore he is still the president. He added that Gloria Arroyo is merely an acting president. The president insisted on these in order to gain immunity from the plunder and other charges filed against him since the president and other high-ranking public officials have immunity from charges until their term expires. However, the Justices of the Supreme Court, using the actions of the former president during his last days in office as basis, unanimously agreed that he undoubtedly resigned from office and because of this, he no longer enjoys immunity from the charges. Estrada appealed to the Supreme Court for a decision, but the appeal was unanimously denied. During the last week of April 2001, Estrada was arrested for plunder charges. The supporters of Estrada protested the arrest by staging what they called "EDSA 3." It lasted for nearly four days. It was said that most of the people in the crowd were "paid" to support EDSA 3 by public officials who are allies with the former president. They demanded Estrada's return to power even though there is no LEGAL or lawful way he can return to office. Estrada's allies in politics persuaded the protestors to march towards Malacanang. At early morning of May 1, they marched to Malacanang and attempted to enter the residential palace. Unfortunately for them, military men have already barricaded it and, using maximum tolerance, made the pro-Estrada crowd retreat. The supporters of Estrada created a riot by throwing rocks, burning cars, destroying police stations, hurting policemen and even news reporters. They failed in their endeavor to let the current president resign and bring Estrada back! They, along with the Estrada allies who persuaded them to march to Malacanang were accused of "Rebellion." This gathering cannot be truly called EDSA 3 because rallies in EDSA are always characterized by peaceful protests. By the unquestionably rude and cruel attitudes and actions of the Estrada supporters, this rally is NOT worth being called EDSA 3.

EDSA 3 was participated in, also by some opposition political leaders and loyal followers of Estrada. At the start, it was deliberate and was clearly a devious and crafty conspiracy, led by the disgruntled politicians in the newly installed government by plotting to destabilize for their personal sinister purposes. The ultimate objectives of this group of plotters against the government were to restore the Estrada regime that had been deposed in an eruption of fury and hatred against its abuses and incompetence. It was motivated by an alleged loyalty to Erap as the champion of masses. Incited by senators and other politicians identified with Estrada's Pwersa ng Masa Party, they attacked Malacanang on May 1, 2001. This crowd was characterized by unruly, riotous and lawless group of people reflecting lowest intellectual level, fueled by giving money and food, drugs and other psychoactive-minded-altering substances intended to lose their rationality to make them run berserk. This motley mob, stimulating one another to excitement and losing ordinary rational control over their activity resulting in disorderly behavior attempted to seize the country's seat of power but were repulsed by the combined police and military forces.

EDSA 3 was devoid of rationality of purpose. It was simply a mob action whose leaders pricked their followers with promises of worldly goodies and a little cash, only to desert them later when they sensed that their objective was an exercise of futility. The mob left to their resources and misleading directions, resorted to indiscriminate burning of property, overturning and burning of vehicles, assaulting and injuring lawmen, smashing store windows and virtually running berserk, enraged out of depravity and vandalism.

What is deplorable about this despicable and shameful event that no prominent figure who conspired with the mob had been arrested and prosecuted. The perpetrators of this destructive political event had been forgiven by the administration, perhaps hesitant to offend the unruly crowd whose electoral support it will need in the election of 2004.

What is apparent is that we have defiled the meaning of EDSA 1 and EDSA 2. Perhaps the only tangible proof and the good results were that, the people were able to oust Marcos and Estrada. Little has changed in our various institutions especially in the political system.

Study Guides

A. Terms/Concepts to Understand

plague	impeachment
transformation	payola
empowerment	vindicate
marginalize	plunder
sustainable development	*de facto* president

B. Questions to Answer

1. What is democracy? Enumerate the rights and privileges a citizen enjoys in a democratic form of government.

2. What is the freedom constitution of President Corazon C. Aquino? Enumerate its important features.

3. In your opinion, what is the most significant achievement of the Aquino Administration?

4. Enumerate the most important achievement of the Ramos Administration.

5. What do you think should be the most important qualifications of a candidate for the president in any country? Explain your answer.

6. What were the objectives of the Estrada Administration? Can you site some?

7. What were the accusations against President Estrada? Why was he impeached?

8. What do you think were the causes of the EDSA 2? Explain your answer.

9. What are the important programs of the Arroyo Administration? Can you identify them and explain one of them?

10. What is the difference between EDSA 1 and EDSA 2? Explain your answer.

Chapter 18

Graft and Corruption: Its Nature and Origin

Graft and corruption are moral perversion, which are very complex and exist in any society throughout the world. Perhaps the only difference lies in the range and degree and the time related to their stage of growth.

Most social scientists observed that corruption is evidently rampant in colonized and transitional societies and newly independent states. It is marked and usually prevalent during the period of rapid social transformation and economic growth. This prevailing condition may be attributed to the discrepancy between the cultural norms and the legal norms of a particular society.

Corruption is moral perversion of integrity. It is behavior and attitude, which are not in accord with accepted rules of standard approved of a civilized society. It is the impairment of moral principle characterized by dishonest practices and applied to a person, especially in public office, who acts on mercenary motives without regard to honor, right or justice. Examples of corrupt practices include acquisition of explained wealth, "juicy" position even if these are not qualified, big profit by dishonest and questionable means, taking advantage of public office or position of trust or employment to obtain fees, profits or anomalous contracts or pay for work not done or service not rendered.

On the other hand, graft is acquisition of gain or advantage by dishonest, unfair or sordid means, especially through the abuses of one's position or influence in politics and business. An example of this is the embezzlement or illegal appropriation of public funds by officials especially in the government.

Graft and corruption is prevalent in large organizations and in administrative agencies of the government, which are often referred to as bureaucracy. Bureaucracy is looked upon as an administrative and social instrument in a political environment.

Corruption in Public Service.   The accountability of public officials is enshrined in the Constitution of 1987, as it has been in the Malolos Constitution of 1898, the Commonwealth Constitution of 1935 and the Constitution of 1973, the Martial Law period.

Article XI of the Constitution of 1987, entitled "Accountability of Public Officers," states the fundamental principle of public office as a public trust. It requires full accountability and integrity among public officers and employees.

The Philippine government is directed to maintain honesty and integrity in public service, and to take action against graft and corruption (Section 27, Article II). It is also directed to give full public disclosure of all transactions involving public interest (Section 28, Article II). This provision is complemented by the Bill of Rights within the Constitution, which gives people the right to information on matter of public concern, to include official records, documents and papers pertaining to officials acts, transactions or decisions, and to government research data used as basis for policy development (Section 7, Article III).

Graft and corruption were further specified in Republic Act No. 3019 (Anti-Graft and Corrupt Practices Act), which prohibits the following acts:

1. Accepting or having any member of the family accept

employment in a private enterprise which has pending official business with his office.

2. Causing undue injury to any party or giving any private party unwarranted benefits or advantage in the discharge of official, administrative or judicial functions.

3. Neglect/refusal, after due demand or request, any matter pending before him for the purpose of gaining pecuniary material benefit or giving undue advantage or discrimination against any party.

4. Entering into any transaction or contract on behalf of the government which will result in the disadvantage of the latter.

5. Directly or indirectly having financial pecuniary interest in any business, contract or transaction in which he takes part in his official capacity.

6. Directly or indirectly becoming interested in personal gain or having material gain in any transaction or activity requiring the approval of the board or panel of which he is a member.

7. Knowingly approving or granting licenses, permits, privileges or benefits to persons not qualified or not legally entitled to such.

8. Divulging valuable information of confidential nature.

Penalties of the violation of the above-mentioned provisions range from imprisonment for not less than six years but nor more than fifteen years, perpetual disqualification from public office and confiscation or forfeiture in favor of the government of any interest or unexplained wealth (Section 9).

Following the overthrow of Marcos, a form of corruption, called plunder, entered the law books. "Plunder" is the acquisition of ill-gotten wealth, either directly or in accordance with members of his family, relatives, business associates or any other person that amounts to a total value of at least seventy-five million pesos (P75,000,000). Ill-gotten-wealth may be any asset, property, business enterprise or material possession acquired by means of:

- misappropriation, conversion or malversation of public funds;

- receiving shares, gifts, commission or any other form of pecuniary benefit in connection with government contracts or transactions;

- fraudulent conveyance of government assets;

- receiving or accepting directly or indirectly any form of interest or participation in any enterprise or undertaking;

- establishing agricultural, industrial or commercial monopolies and implementation of decrees and decrees in favor or benefit particular persons or interests, and

- taking undue advantage of official position, authority, connection or influence to enrich himself at the expense and damage of the country and the Filipino people.

The public-interest-centered definition sets a higher standard than law in defining corrupt acts. It sets up public interest as the norm, and may be used in situations where corruption itself allows the legislation or judicial enforcement of laws that contravene justice, human rights and other standards of the public good.

Violations of public duty for personal gain are usually referred to as "graft and corruption." Although often used interchangeably, they differ in the inclusion or exclusion of clients in the corrupt act. "Graft" is an act of an individual or group of individuals in government for personal gain without any external party, as for instance, when disbursing officers pad receipts and charge higher expenses to government. Meanwhile, "corruption" is not unilateral, and as the term implies, has at least two parties, which influence each other (i.e., "corrupt") to benefit themselves and violate the law.

Causes of Graft and Corruption in the Philippines

Political scientists maintain that graft and corruption is common and prevalent in developing societies, particularly, the inability of the modernizing states to cope with the complex and multiple demands and problems in moving towards modernization. These problems confronting developing society, from a colonial status to self-government, the inequality in the distribution of land due to rapid population growth, and the concomitant problems brought about by industrial development and urbanization, and multitude pressure for public welfare.

Other related causes of graft and corruption include:

1. Unrealistic salaries of government employees and officials that they become susceptible to accept money or in kind,

2. The excessive discretionary powers extended to high government officials.

3. The cumbersome red tape in the bureaucracy that usually resulted in corruption due to tempting juicy inducements that may be offered under the circumstance,

4. The bad example set by leadership in the bureaucracy. If the head of the office of an agency is corrupt, the subordinates are likely to be the same,

5. The complex and dragging system of administration of justice which normally hinders and causes delay in the prosecution of public servants accused of corrupt practices.

Graft and Corruption in the Philippines

Moral alienation which causes many Filipino to withdraw behind a skewed system of values, of which the epigrammatic examples are the attitude of *bahala na* (this term actually means "Let the evil take the hindmost," contrary to its literal interpretation of "Leave it to God"), *utang na loob* (an accepted favor is a blood debt, the repayment of which takes precedence over the moral and legal considerations), and *hiya* (loss of face or public humiliation is unacceptable because it is the ultimate defeat, and must, therefore, be prevented by any means, no matter how questionable). When it may enhance the culture of corruption, this state of moral alienation does not strictly conclude the corruption. These values were already ingrained in the Philippine society in prewar period, when concededly, the culture did not flourish. For in fact, these native values, if properly programmed, could serve to limit the culture.

To gain insight and a better understanding of the origin of corruption in our country, we should study its historical roots. According to Dr. Onofre Corpuz, this evil malpractice can be traced from the character of the relationship between government and the Filipino people.

When the Spanish government was established in the Philippines, the whole archipelago was considered private property of the King of Spain. The term property included in its definition the colonial offices, privileges and various gainful positions in the colonies. A Spanish officer can buy an office at a "bargain" and employ someone else to discharge the function of the position for him at a very much lower price in terms of salary. The position can be renounced and resold anytime.

This situation in the bureaucracy left a profound impact in the minds of every Filipino. The institutions of government were agents of abuses and oppression.

Whenever a Filipino has transactions with any government office, at first he tries to avail himself of family connections. Nepotism is rampant in almost all administrations up to the present. Promotions are influenced by personalistic considerations. Family influence works far beyond employment. Family influence or "pull" is restored to as a matter of course in application for business licenses, franchises and government contracts.

Family values and interest largely depend and support the dynastic structure and political systems, especially in the rural areas. The network of family ties offers a ready-made political machine in support of electoral candidates. Voting depends more on how close the members of the family are and how much the family can depend on a particular candidate, and ask for help irrespective of his intellectual and moral qualifications. The compadre syndrome contributes immensely to illegal practices that are based on the exchange of favors.

It is unfortunate that, as the moral values of the people deteriorated, more corruption continued even starting from top to bottom of the bureaucracy. Influence peddling, kickbacks, overpricing, rigged bidding, padded project expenses, expense accounts and payrolls, use public funds for vote-buying and personal expenses, nepotism, cronyism, tampering of public documents and election returns, paid prosecutory and judicial decisions, smuggling, test leakages for government and board examinations, bribery and even insertion of questional clauses and provisions in congressional bills.

Corruption is massive and had gone beyond the realm of family and personalistic considerations. Even professionals misdeclare their incomes for tax evasion and those who travel as "tourists" bring and smuggle goods as "personal effects" to avoid paying correct taxes.

Commentary on Graft and Corruption in the Philippines

Some political analysts view that the real problem of the Philippines as a developing state is not poverty but graft and corruption. The Philippines is not inherently a poor country because it abounds in vast natural resources; e.g., the marine life of its archipelago waters, the fertile volcanic soil of the islands, the forest of the mountainsides, geothermal sources of energy, and a cornucopia of natural resources including oil, gold, silver, copper, chromite, manganese, and zinc. Some of these resources have been depleted by ecological abuse and human greed, but certain downtrends can still be averted. Furthermore, the country boasts of human resources, consisting of work force that has one of the highest literacy rates in Asia and is uniformly fluent in English, and adapts easily to Western technologies. Thus, in terms of both natural and human resources, the country cannot be classified as poor.

Corruption in any government agency seems to be a way of life that it muffles any sense of faith and hope. It is so comprehensive that it has almost developed into an entire culture of corruption.

The political system, which is supposed to be the main force in society with capability to change the environment, has itself turned into the culture medium. Politics in the hands of the powerful elite has been sterilized of any authentic opposition to the culture, and it has been suitably prepared for the controlled growth of corrupt politicians prepared to defend themselves by immoral means against any form of attack. The power brokers of the corrupt system wield tremendous connections with powerful politicians.

To end one culture and begin another is a cataclysmic endeavor, and those who would advocate a cataclysmal theory of politics must prepare themselves to be challenged by forces they unleash. The web of corruption in our government seems difficult to stop.

While it might be very difficult for an individual to challenge the culture of corruption, society itself has no choice; it must reform in order to survive. History teaches us that this can be done by a supreme act of the will. If there is any single individual in whom this executive will repossess, it is the President of the Philippines. The President, clothed with the constitutional authority, in a political sense, is one of the most powerful executives in the world. Therefore, the Filipinos who seek to reform the culture of corruption will have to access the formidable resources and executive will of the office of the president.

Many Filipinos during presidential elections, for many reasons have sought the presidency. Almost every presidential candidate aspiring to be the top executive of the land will promise to stop graft and corruption. After he is elected into office, the promise to institute reforms will just vanish into thin air.

Of the Philippine presidents, the most vocal about reforms was Ferdinand Marcos. He became president for two terms, and was disqualified from seeking a third term under the Constitution. In a stunning maneuver, toward the end of his term, he imposed martial law, and was able to secure ratification of his new constitution, which allowed him to extend his tenure of office. He justified imposition of martial law with the repeated slogan: "To save the Republic and reform society." He even bragged about the new society. As a skilled orator, he frequently expounded on the need to reform society to get rid of graft and corruption, but at the end, he virtually failed as an administrator, and after his death, political scientists could only point to a redesigned agrarian reform program as a political and economic reform of note that could be credited to him. In fact, by the time of his overthrow in 1986, after that historic event of EDSA 1, he had turned into the paradigm of a society that desperately needed to reform. After his twenty years of rule, the Philippines was still languishing in an abject poverty because of overwhelming graft and corruption in every branch of the government.

The government during Marcos years, felt piling up of a gargantuan foreign debt that, together with the mounting domestic debt, and consequently, plunged deeper into the ravine of poverty under the sheer weight of its own graft and corruption.

It may be interesting to note that, according to some political scientists the only Philippine president who achieved any lasting attitudinal reform in the culture of corruption was Ramon Magsaysay. Magsaysay was not only an honest president; he was also perceived to be honest by Filipinos. So rare is honesty as an official virtue in the Philippines that Magsaysay remains the best-loved and most popular figure in this country, especially the masses on the strength alone of his honesty in public service and in private actuations. Ramon Magsaysay became the embodiment of clean and honest government.

With Magsaysay's premature death in a plane crash, everything in the presidency went downhill fast. Succeeding presidents simply lost control, as the bureaucracy slided on the side of bribery, extortion, and plain malversation of the public funds. Some political scientist perceive that corruption has become a way of life. Many Filipinos either accept it, or ignore it. Those who accept it defend the system and destroy their detractors. On the other hand, those who ignore it dispute their critics. In this culture of corruption, the practitioners and adherents are bound by a conspiracy of silence. Corruption, as a societal phenomenon, is a moral perversion, and is discussed only in certain acceptable ways by parties or persons who endorse this immoral practices, especially in politics.

Corruption imposes its own language. Under this lexicon, the term "graft and corruption" applies only to the wrongdoing of the underprivileged, but not of the rapacious privileged, whose normal rhetoric is reported only by means of acceptable euphemisms; e.g., "under process," "congressional investigation," "media exposé," and "preliminary investigation for probable cause," all of which are common methodologies of extortion and intimidation. Because the culture has succeeded in creating its own language, the society that accepts this language has become accustomed to any kind of denunciation by those who are victimized and injured.

It is common knowledge and vicious practice in Philippine society that it seems that it is acceptable to denounce graft and corruption, as long as the targets are people who have no capability for self-defense, and much less, for retaliation.

Apparently, no high officials in government has ever been jailed for graft and corruption. A number of cases are brought in court every year, but they are only investigated; no tangible results, especially if the accused is rich and a powerful politician. If the respondent has established any kind of connection with the party in power, the case filed against him most likely will be dismissed. On the other hand, if elections catch up with the proceedings and effect a reversal of the political configuration, then the case will either languish in judicial limbo or simply be forgotten.

Ironically, the voluminous 1987 Constitution devotes an entire article in graft and corruption. This Article 11 entitled "Accountability of Public Officers," with all of eighteen sections, beginning with Section 1, which makes the following declaration: "Public office is a public trust. Public officers and employees must at all times, be accountable to the people, serve them with utmost responsibility, integrity, loyalty and efficiency, act with patriotism and justice, and lead modest lives."

Under Section 2, certain high officials may be removed from office on impeachment for, and conviction of graft and corruption, and other high crimes or betrayal of public trust. These officials are the President, Vice President, members of the Supreme Court, members of the Constitutional Commissions, and the Ombudsman. A similar section was contained in the 1935 and 1972 Constitution. Former President, Joseph Ejercito Estrada was the only president in the Philippines ever impeached.

The big wheels are naturally found at the very top, the high and the mighty among the rich, and the famous, who occasionally inflict themselves on society with a speech or a talk-show interview, where they advocate change to reform society, the very same society that makes them rich and famous at the expense of middle class professionals and upper class business executives who faithfully pay the taxes to support government programs.

Effects of Graft and Corruption

1. Graft and corruption lessen allegiance and loyalty to the government and counteracts the development of

nationalism among the citizens. It hampers the spirit of unity in government leadership and endangers political stability.

2. Corruption impairs national economic planning and management; and introduces an element of irrationality in plan development.

3. Corruption gives emphasis to existing inequalities by providing more power and opportunities to those who are already powerful.

4. Corruption causes wasteful depletion of government resources by increasing the cost of programs and projects for development because, in most cases, appropriated funds for intended purposes are channeled outside the government to questionable pockets.

5. The cost of corruption is eventually passed on the taxpayers who carry the brunt in the form of taxation. Whatever amount is legally spent, the people shoulder the cost because public funds are the taxpayers' money.

The establishment and strengthening of morality and the inculcation of the concepts of public service as a public trust and the supremacy of public good and welfare over the Filipino personalistic considerations are indeed a gigantic responsibility of the national leadership – political, economic, social and cultural. It should be the primary goal and deliberate total efforts of the whole community and its citizenry.

Study Guides

A. Terms/Concepts to Understand

corruption	malpractice
transitional	languish
perversion	configuration
embezzlement	depletion
bureaucracy	irrationality

B. Questions to Answer

1. Identify the nature and origin of graft and corruption.
2. What could be the reasons why corruption is evidently rampant in colonized and transitional societies?
3. Give examples of corrupt practices committed by public officials in government.
4. Why is graft and corruption prevalent in large organizations and administrative agencies in government? Explain your answer.
5. Why does the "compadre syndrome" in the Philippines contributed immensely to illegal practices?
6. As a student, what would you suggest to minimize graft and corruption in the government?
7. According to some political analysts, the only President who, to a certain extent, achieved a lasting attitudinal reform in the culture of corruption was Ramon Magsaysay. What do you think were the reasons?
8. Why did graft and corruption become a vicious practice in Philippine society?
9. Apparently, it seems that no high officials in government has even been jailed for graft and corruption. What do you think about this perception?
10. Identify the officials in government who may be charged with graft and corruption through impeachment.

Bibliography

A. Books

Agoncillo, Teodoro A. and Milagros C. Guerrero, *History of the Filipino People*. Quezon City: R.P. Garcia Publishing Company, 1975.

Agoncillo, Teodoro A. *Malolos: The Crises of the Republic,* Quezon City, 1960.

Agoncillo, Teodoro A. *The Revolt of the Masses: The Story of Bonifacio and the Katipunan*. Quezon City, 1956

Bazaco, Evergisto. *The Church in the Philippines*. Manila, 1939.

Beyer, H. Otley and Jaime C. de Veyra. *Philippine Saga*. Manila, 1947.

Cameron, Forbes W. *The Philippine Islands*. Boston and New York, 1928, 2 vols.

Corpuz, Onofre D. *The Philippine Englewood Cliffs*. New Jersey, 1956.

Kahayon, Alicia H. and Celia A. Zulueta. *Philippine Literature Through the Years*. Mandaluyong City: National Book Store, Inc., 2000.

Kalaw, Maximo M. *The Philippines Under the Jones Law*. 1927.

Kalaw, Teodoro M. *The Philippine Revolution*. Reprint. Manila, 1969.

Mabini, Apolinario. *La Revolucion Filipina*. English translation by Leon Ma. Guerrero II, 1969.

Majul, Cesar A. *Muslims in the Philippines*. Quezon City: University of the Philippines Press, 1973.

Malay, Armando. *Occupied Philippines: The Role of Jorge B.*

Vargas During the Japanese Occupation. Manila: Filipiniana Book Guild, 1967.

Morton, Lonis. *The Fall of the Philippines.* Washington D.C., 1953.

Nowell, Charles E. (ed.) *Magellan's Voyage Around the World. Three Contemporary Accounts.* Evanston, 1962.

Ocampo, Esteban A. de: *The Life and Achievements of Bonifacio.* Manila, 1966.

Osmeña, Sergio: *Our Struggle for Independence.* Manila, 1956.

Recto, Claro M. *Three Years of Enemy Occupation.* Manila: People's Publishers, 1946.

Robinson, Albert G. *The Philippines, the War and the People.* New York, 1901.

Worcester, Dean C. *The Philippines: Past and Present.* New York, 1900.

Zaide, Gregorio F. and Sonia Z. Pritchard. *History of the Republic of the Philippines* (College edition) National Book Store, Inc., Manila, 1983.

Zulueta, Francisco M. *General Sociology.* Academic Publishing Corporation, Mandaluyong City, 1998.

B.   Other Materials

Archipelago – The International Magazine of the Philippines, April 1979.

Filipino Heritage: The Making of a Nation, Vols. 1 to 10.

Philippine History. Metro Manila: Social Studies Publications, Inc., 1982.

Readings in Philippine Prehistory by Filipino Book Guild, Inc., Cultural Center of the Philippines Encyclopedia.

Philippine History Through Selected Sources. Quezon City: Alemars -- Phoenix Publishing House, 1967.

Vital Documents on Proclamation 1081 Declaring a State of Martial Law in the Philippines.

President Marcos. Notes on the New Society of the Philippines. Manila, 1973.

Marcos, "The Democratic Revolution on the Philippines."

The State of the Nation after Three Years of Martial Law. September 21, 1975, Civil Liberties Union of the Philippines, Makati.

"Accused." Newsweek, November 5, 1984.

"The Philippines Another Iran? Washington Backs Away from Marcos." Newsweek, November 4, 1985.

"The Moment of Truth." Newsweek, February 2, 1986.

"Battling on. Has Reagan Made the Crises Worse?" February 24, 1986.

Kilosbayan, Shalom Conference Center. Manila: November 13, 1998.

The Philippine Daily Inquirer. Sunday, February 4, 2001.

Important Events, Persons, Concepts, Places and Things to Remember in Philippine History and Government

1250. Chieftains Led by Datu Puti built a Malay Settlement in Panay: Datu Sumakwel wrote the oldest known code of written laws called the Maragtas Code.

1380. Islam reaches the Philippines with the arrival of Arab teacher, Karim-ul Makhdum in Sulu.

1450-1475. The sultanate was founded by Abu Bakar in Sulu and in Maguindanao, by Serif Kabungsuwan. Muslims conquered Mindanao.

1433. Code of Kalantiyaw, written by Datu Kalantiyaw, which contained the 18 orders on various crimes committed and the corresponding penalties.

1521 March 31. The First Christian Mass was celebrated in Limasawa.

1521 April 14. Rajah Humabon and 800 other Cebuanos became the first Filipino Christian converts.

1521 April 1. The blood compact between Magellan and Rajah Humabon to establish friendly relations and converted about 800 natives.

1521 April 27. The Battle of Mactan Chieftain Lapu-Lapu defeated the leader of the Spanish expedition, Ferdinand Magellan.

1565. The First missionaries, the Augustinians, under Father Andres de Urdaneta, reached the Philippines with Miguel Lopez de Legazpi. The Franciscans in 1577; the Jesuits in 1581; the Dominicans in 1587; the Recollects in 1696; and the Benedictines in 1865.

1571 January 1. Legaspi established the first permanent Spanish settlement in Cebu, the La Villa de Santisimo Nombre de Jesus.

1571   June 1. Legaspi declared Manila, then the Islamic Kingdom of Rajah Sulayman, a Spanish city.

1578.   A Franciscan lay brother named Juan Clemente founded the first hospital in Manila which is now Hospital de San Juan de Dios.

1585 May 15. The Royal Audiencia was established by virtue of the Royal Decree of the Spanish Crown.

1593.   The first book, *Doctrina Cristina*, was printed in the Philippines.

1593.   The Galleon Trade between Manila and Acapulco began to eclipse all other economic activities.

1625.   The University of Sto. Tomas got a university rank to become the only royal Pontifical University in Asia. It is 25 years older than Harvard University, the American oldest University.

1565-1898. The Muslim of Mindanao and Sulu put up their fiercest resistance against the Spaniards. In 1656, Sultan Kudarat declared the first *jihad* (holy war) against the Spaniards.

1670.   Tomas Pinpin of Mabatang, Abucay, Bataan, was known as the first Filipino printer. He published the first Tagalog book, "Librong Pag-aaralan ng mga Tagalog nang Wikang Castila (Book the Tagalogs Should Study to Learn Spanish).

1729.   The Walls of Intramuros, seat of Sapanish state and church rule, were completed.

1744.   Francisco Dagohoy led 3,000 Boholanos to fight the longest revolt against the Spaniards, 85 years.

1762-1763. Diego Silang led an uprising over excessive tribute and forced labor in Ilocos province. His wife, Gabriela, took command of his forces after he was killed.

1774   November 9. A royal decree was promulgated by

Archbishop Basilio Santa Justa, ordering the secularization of parishes (or the turn over of parishes administered by friar curates to the seculars).

1814   February 1. The eruption of Mount Mayon where an avalanche of its flaming rocks, molten lava and billowing smoke utterly destroyed the town of Cagsawa and buried hundreds of people.

1818.   The Las Piñas bamboo organ, the only organ of its kind in the world, was built by Father Diego Cerra, a Recollect priest-musician.

1849   November 11. Filipinos adopted Spanish surnames per order of Governor-General Claveria.

1851   August 11. The Banco Español de Isabel II, the first regular bank, was established. It is now the Bank of the Philippine Islands.

1861   June 19. Birth date of Dr. Jose Rizal, a Nationalist Martyr.

1863   June 3. The most tragic and frightful earthquake to rock Manila and its suburbs where the Manila Cathedral, many churches, bridges and buildings were destroyed. It was estimated that more than 400 people died and many were injured.

1872   January 20. The Cavite Mutiny led by a group of Filipino artillerymen, marines and workers in the Cavite arsenal as an off shoot of the disgruntled Filipino workers at the arsenal and the navy yard revolted in strong protest against the unjust treatment of governor Izquierdo's despotic administration.

1865.   The Observatory of Manila, known for its accurate forecast of typhoons and its scientific recordings of earthquakes, was founded by the Jesuits. The observatory is the oldest in the far East.

1872   February 12. Filipino priest Mariano Gomez, Jose Burgos and Jacinto Zamora (GOMBURZA), who actively campaigned for the secularization of the parishes, were garroted in Bagumbayan (now Rizal Park) for complicity in the Cavite Mutiny. Their deaths sparked the National Movement of the Revolution of 1898.

1892 July 3. The La Liga Filipina was to unite the whole archipelago into one compact, vigorous and homogeneous body; and ultimately, promoted the general welfare of every Filipino.

1872-1892. Jose Rizal, Marcelo H. del Pilar, Graciano Lopez-Jaena, Antonio and Juan Luna, Mariano Ponce, and other young Filipino patriots led the Propaganda Movement, the crusade for reforms.

1887. Dr. Jose Rizal published *Noli Me Tangere* in Berlin, Germany; *El Filibusterismo* was published in 1891.

1896 January 20. Death of Graciano Lopez-Jaena in Barcelona, Spain, leaving a legacy of unwavering commitment for reforms.

1896 August 19. The discovery of the Katipunan, because a certain Patiño revealed its existence to Father Mariano Gil.

1896 August 23. The Cry of Balintawak where Bonifacio and his followers brought out their cedulas (their identity papers) and simultaneously tore them to pieces as a symbolic act of defiance against Spanish imperialism and, with determined efforts, to take up arms against Spanish authorities amidst the thunderous cry of "Long Live the Philippine Independence!"

1896 December 30. Death of Jose Rizal at Bagong Bayan, now Luneta Park, Manila.

1898. Treaty of Paris was signed. This treaty was a very significant act between Spain and the United States for it initiated and drew up the peace agreement, ending the Spanish-American war.

1898   June 11-12. The National Anthem, originally known as *Marcha Magdalo Filipina,* was played for the first time on the eve of the proclamation of Philippine Independence at Kawit, Cavite.

1898   June 12. Proclamation of the Philippine Independence at Kawit, Cavite.

1898   September 15. The Malolos Congress was inaugurated in the Barasoain Church in Malolos, Bulacan.

1898   September 29. The ratification of the Philippine Independence.

1898   October 19. The issuance of a decree by Emilio Aguinaldo, creating the Literary University of the Philippines.

1898   October 20. Gregorio Aglipay was appointed Military Vicar General – the religious leader of the revolutionary movement by General Aguinaldo.

1898   Novemebr 29. The approval of the Malolos Constitution by a majority vote of the members of Congress and by President Emilio Aguinaldo.

1898   December 10. The signing of the Treaty of Paris with these provisions: 1) Spain ceded the Philippines, Guam and Puerto Rico to the United States, 2) the United States paid Spain the sum of $20,000,000, 3) Spain withdrew her sovereignty from Cuba, and 4) the civil and political status of the inhabitants in the ceded territories were to be determined by U.S. Congress.

1899.   The *La Solidaridad* was founded by the Reformists with Graciano Lopez-Jaena as its first editor. This newspaper served as the mouthpiece of the reformists to articulate their legitimate grievances against the Spanish authorities.

1899   January 21. Emilio Aguinaldo promulgated the first Philippine Constitution that embodied the ideology, belief system and values of the Filipino people in

Barasoain Church in Malolos, Bulacan. The First Philippine Republic from January 23, 1899 to March 23, 1901 had Aguinaldo as President.

1899   January 28. The First Philippine Republic was established in Malolos, Bulacan.

1899   February 4. The first shot exchanged between Filipino and American soldiers on San Juan del Monte Bridge that started the Filipino-American war when Willie W. Grayon shot and killed a Filipino soldier.

1900   September 9. The Philippine Commission enacted the Civil Service Act No. 5 which places all classified employees of all divisions, and agencies of insular, provincial and municipal governments under the administrative control of the Bureau of Civil Service.

1901   July 4. The Civil Government was established; it replaced the Military Government in the Philippines during the American Rule.

1901-1907. Era of suppressed nationalism with the Americans' Anti-Sedition Law (1901) and the Flag Law (1907),which banned the public display of the Filipino flag.

1902   July 1. The United States Congress passed the Philippine Bill and established the Philippine Assembly.

1916.   The Jones Law was enacted as the first American formal and official commitment to grant independence to the Philippines.

1916   February. The Civil Retirement Act No. 2589. was enacted and further accelerated Filipinization.

1916   October 16. The inauguration of the Philippine Legislature under the Jones Law where Manuel L. Quezon was elected President of the Senate, while Sergio Osmena was elected Speaker of the House of the Representatives.

1918   November 7. The Philippine Legislature created the

Commission of Independence to study all matters relating to "the negotiation and organization of independence" of the Philippines.

1919   February 23. The First Philippine Independence Mission, headed by Senate President Quezon left Manila for Washington.

1920   December 20. President Wilson, in his farewell address to the United States Congress, recommended favorably the granting of Philippine Independence.

1933   January 17. The Hare-Hawes-Cutting Bill became a law.

1934   March 24. The Tydings-McDuffie Law was signed into law by President Roosevelt granting Philippine Independence with certain provisions one of which was a ten-year transition period under the Commonwealth of the Philippines preparatory to the grant of independence on July 4, 1946.

1935   March 23. President Roosevelt approved the Constitution of the Philippines, tailored after the American Constitution, which "embodies the ideals of liberty and democracy of the Filipino people."

1935   November 15. The Commonwealth was inaugurated with Manuel . Quezon and Sergio Osmena as its president and vice-president, respectively.

1937   April 30. Filipino women were given the right to vote in a plebiscite.

1940   June 7. President Quezon approved Commonwealth Act No. 570, declaring the National Language (Tagalog) one of the official languages of the Philippines.

1941   December 8. The Japanese naval bombers attacked Pearl Harbor in Hawaii, resulting in heavy American military losses.

1941   December 8. At 6:30 a.m., the Japanese bombed Davao, Tuguegarao, Baguio, Iba, and Tarlac. Manila was bombed the next day.

1941   December 24. Christmas Eve, President Quezon, his

family and members of his cabinet moved to the island fortress, Corregidor, on board S.S. Mayon, where the Commonwealth Government was transferred.

1941   December 25. Was a bleak Christmas for many Filipinos because they could not celebrate the coming of the Lord Jesus on Christmas day.

1941   December 29. General Douglas MacArthur declared Manila an open city to be spared from further destruction.

1942   January 2. The Japanese tanks entered the city of Manila.

1942   February 18. President Quezon, his family and members of his cabinet were picked up by a submarine *Swordfish*, successfully eluded the Japanese blockade and were fetched by a plane for Australia.

1942   April 9. The Fall of Bataan under General Edward P. King to prevent further injury to the helpless defender due to the unstoppable Japanese attack, while waiting for U.S. reinforcement that never came.

1942   April 10. The Infamous Death March started from Cabcabin, Mariveles, Bataan, marching on foot, the 112 kilometers stretch to San Fernando, Pampanga, under the scorching heat of the sun. Those who could not walk because of physical weakness due to hunger, fatigue and sickness were either shot down or bayoneted by the Japanese soldiers.

1942   April 15. Only about 58,000 prisoners reached Camp O'Donnel, Capas, Tarlac, alive, after enduring the harrowing ordeal. Many died along the way due to sickness and physical exhaustion and Japanese brutality. About 7,000 to 10,000 Filipino-American soldiers died in route to the concentration camp.

1942   May 6. The Fall of Corregidor under the General Jonathan Wainwright. The impregnable and defiant

ROCK-Corregidor, guarding the entrance to Manila Bay, finally fell because of continuous artillery pounding and successive bombings of the Japanese forces.

1943   September 25. The National Assembly elected Jose P. Laurel, President of the Republic.

1943   October 14. The Declaration of Independence was read and subsequently, inaugurated with the induction into office of President Laurel of the Japanese-sponsored Republic.

1944   July 26. The Potsdam Proclamation by the allies through President Truman and Prime Minister Churchill, calling upon Japan to surrender unconditionally or face "prompt and utter destruction."

1944   August. The Battle of the Philippine Sea between the American and Japanese forces began.

1944   April 19. President Quezon, his family and his party left for the United States on board the ship President *Collidge.*

1944   August 1. President Quezon died in Saranac, Lake Sanitarium, New York.

1944   October 20. General Douglas MacArthur fulfilled his promise: "I shall return," landing in Palo, Leyte. The liberation of the Philippines began.

1945   February 27. The turn-over of the Commonwealth Government to President Osmena by General MacArthur in a simple ceremony.

1945   June 14. Ended the battle of Besang Pass, which was characterized by courage and heroism as well as bloodshed, immortalized the bravery of the Filipino soldiers.

1945   July 26. The Three Allied Powers – Great Britain, China and the United States through President Truman and Prime Minister Churchill issued the Potsdam

Proclamation, urging Japan to surrender unconditionally or face "prompt and utter destruction."

1945   August 6. The United States Air Force dropped the deadly Atomic (Uranium) bomb on the Japanese City of Hiroshima. It destroyed over half of the city, killed about 60,000 persons outright and wounded 100,000 others.

1945   August 8. Another atomic bomb fell on Nagasaki that was actuated by the fission of plutonium, an artificial radio active element derived from bombardment of uranium by neutrons in atomic reactors built for that purpose in the United States. It flattened a square mile of Nagasaki and took a heavy toll in life.

1945   September 2. Japan signed the terms and conditions of surrender on board the battleship USS *Missouri* at Tokyo Bay-General MacArthur, newly-appointed Supreme Commander of the Allied Powers (SCAP) in Japan, presided over the historic ceremonies finally, ending the war.

1946   April 23. The last national election under the Commonwealth was held where Manuel A. Roxas and Elpidio Quirino were elected President and Vice-President, respectively.

1946   May 26. Manuel A. Roxas was inaugurated the last President of Commonwealth.

1946   July 4. The Republic of the Philippines was inaugurated in the City of Manila and Philippine Independence was proclaimed to the world by Harry S. Truman, President of the United States of America, Manuel A. Roxas as first President of the postwar Republic amidst the jubilant Filipino rejoicing for the regained freedom.

1946   July 27. The return of the mortal remains of the late President Manuel L. Quezon to Manila on board the United States aircraft carrier Princeton.

1947   March 14. The Military Bases Agreement allowed the United States to maintain bases in the Philippines.

1947   March 21. The Military Assistance Pact was concluded between the two countries under which the United States would furnish arms, equipment and supplies to the armed forces of the Philippines.

1948   April 15. President Manuel A. Roxas died of a heart attack at Clark Field, Pampanga, after delivering a speech to the United States Air Force.

1949   April 28. Mrs. Aurora Aragon Quezon, wife of the late President Quezon, her daughter, Baby and other members of the group were ambushed and shot to death mercilessly in Bongabon, Nueva Ecija.

1950   October 22. President Elpidio Quirino suspended the *writ of habeas corpus* to suppress the Hukbalahap rebellion escalating in some provinces, especially in Central Luzon.

1954   May 17. Luis Taruc surrendered to the government after four months of negotiations with then newsman Benigno "Ninoy" Aquino, Jr., Magsaysay's personal emissary.

1955   February 19. The Southeast Asia Treaty Organization (SEATO) formally came into being with the ratification of the treaty by all the member-states.

1956   May 9. Reparation Agreement with Japan was concluded in which Japan agreed to pay the Philippines the amount of $800 million.

1957   March 17. President Magsaysay and his party, aboard the presidential plane crashed on Mt. Manunggal, Cebu. Magsaysay and members of his party died, except Nestor Mata, a journalist.

1960   October 2. Senator Claro M. Recto, lawyer, nationalist and statesman died in Rome.

1963   July 31. The Manila Accord (Maphilindo) was approved and signed by Pres. Diosdado Macapagal, Pres. Sukarno of Indonesia and Prime Minister Tunku Abdul Rahman of the Federation of Malaya.

1967   August 8. The Association of Southeast Asian Nation
        (ASEAN) was founded in Bangkok, Thailand, for the
        promotion of the general welfare of the member-states.

1970   January 30. Radical students launched a wave of
        protest against the rule of President Marcos, known as
        the First Quarter Storm, after a violent and bloody
        dispersal by riot police.

1972   September 21. President Marcos, by virtue of
        Proclamation No. 1081, placed the entire Philippines
        under Martial Law.

1975   April 15. The Kabataang Barangay was created through
        Presidential Decree No. 684 to broaden the participation
        in the democratic process of the youth on national
        issues affecting them.

1976   August 17. The most destructive earthquake that
        occurred in the Philippines with a tremendous force of
        8.2 magnitude on the Ritcher scale with epicenter in
        Mindanao Gulf. It was accompanied by tidal waves,
        which caused the death of hundreds of people;
        rendered many families homeless; and destroyed
        property amounting to millions of pesos.

1977   November 25. Ninoy Aquino was sentenced to death
        by a military tribunal.

1981   January 17. The end of Martial Law in the Philippines-
        eight years and four months by virtue of the Marcos
        Proclamation No. 2045 with certain conditions.

1983   August 21. Benigno S. Aquino, the opposition leader,
        was assassinated at the Manila International Airport,
        becoming a martyr in the Philippines' struggle for
        freedom and democracy.

1983   August 31. The remains of the late Ninoy Aquino were
        laid to rest. This was preceded by a Requiem Mass at
        Sto. Domingo Church in Quezon City and a very long
        funeral procession attended by more than two million
        people from all walks of life.

338   PHILIPPINE HISTORY AND GOVERNMENT THROUGH THE YEARS

1986   **February 7.** The "Snap" presidential election were held before the fall of Marcos.

1986   **February 16.** Corazon Aquino led millions of Filipinos at the *Tagumpay ng Bayan* (Peoples' Victory Rally) at the Luneta, to launch a nationwide campaign for civil disobedience to force Marcos to step down.

1986   **February 22-25.** The People's Revolution at EDSA, where not a single shot was fired, led to the fall of Marcos. Marcos, his family and his cronies with General Fabian Ver fled into exile.

1986   **April.** President Aquino issued Proclamation No. 9, creating a Constitutional commission to draft a new constitution as provided for in the Freedom Constitution.

1986   **September 5.** President Aquino and MNLF Chairman Nur Misuari signed an agreement in Jolo, Sulu, to end hostilities between the government and the Muslim rebels.

1987   **February 2.** Filipinos ratified the 1986 Freedom Constitution in a crucial show of support for President Aquino. Congress opened, marking the country's return to constitutional democracy.

1987   **February 11.** President Aquino issued Proclamation No. 58, declaring that the New Constitution of the Republic of the Philippines has been approved by the Filipino people and is, therefore, in "Full force and effect."

1987   **February 25.** The ratification of the new Constitution ended the revolutionary government of Corazon Aquino, which was established and has heralded the restoration of democracy after the Marcos dictatorship.

1987   **August 28.** Army Lt. Col. Gregorio "Gringo" Honasan, Reform the Armed Forces Movement officers, staged a coup d'etat but failed.

1987   October 18. Lorenzo Ruiz became the first Filipino canonized saint.

1989   December 1-7. Dismissed Lt. Col. Honasan staged the bloodies coup d'etat against the Corazon Aquino government.

1991   June 9. Mt. Pinatubo, dormant for over 400 years, erupted at 2:55 p.m. causing massive destruction to human lives and property.

1991   September 16. The senate rejected the treaty, granting a 10-year extension of the U.S. Military Bases in the Philippines.

1991   November 26. The U.S. government turned over Clark Air Base to the Philippines after nearly a century of control.

1991   December. The Philippine government officially asked the United States to withdraw completely from Subic Naval Base.

2000   December 7. The Impeachment Trial of President Estrada started with 21 senators acting as jurors, while a panel of congressmen, assisted by volunteer lawyers, composed the prosecution.

2000   December 22. Clarissa Ocampo, senior vice-president of Equitable PCI Bank, said that she saw Estrada signed Jose Velarde.

2001   January 16. Senator-judges in the impeachment trial of Estrada voted 11-10 not to open the envelope where bank documents were kept secret. Senate President Aquilino Pimentel quits in protest.

2001   January 20. Gloria Macapagal-Arroyo was sworn in as the 14th President of the Republic of the Philippines by Chief Justice Hilario G. Davide, Jr., after the members of the Supreme Court unanimously declared the position of the President vacant, the second woman to be swept into the Presidency by a People Power revolution popularly called EDSA 2.

IMPORTANT PERSONS

Pigafetta. The chronicler of the Magellan expedition which arrived in the Philippines in 1521.

Dr. Joaquin Gonzales. The first president of the Literary University of the Philippines.

Dr. Pedro A. Paterno. Wrote the first Filipino novel, *Ninay.*

General Camilo Polavieja. The shrewd and aristocratic Spanish Chief executive. He was the governor-general who approved the death sentence of Dr. Jose Rizal on a farce trial by a military court on charges of "rebellion, sedition, and illicit association."

Major Lazaro Macapagal. The man ordered by General Mariano Noriel to bring out the Bonifacio brothers from jail on May 10, 1897, where he was handed a sealed letter with specific orders to read the contents only after reaching Mount Buntis about four kilometers from Maragondon.

Julian Felipe. Composer of the Philippine National Anthem which was the greatest musical legacy of the Revolution.

Melchora Aquino. She was known as Tandang Sora, "Mother of Balintawak," a principled Filipino woman who rendered patriotic services to Bonifacio and to the *Katipuneros.*

Felipe G. Calderon. Lawyer, writer, scholar and patriot who drafted the Constitution of the First Republic of the Philippines.

Januario Galut. This was the Igorot who led the Americans to the secret trail leading to Tirad Pass where General Gregorio del Pilar was shot during the brief encounter with the American soldiers.

General Macario Sakay. The last Filipino general to surrender to the American authorities.

Apolinario Mabini. The "Sublime Paralytic," lawyer, philosopher, patriot and writer called the "Brains of the Philippine Revolution." He composed the True Decalogue.

Andres Bonifacio. The Great Plebian, founder and organizer of the Katipunan who was born on November 30, 1863, grew up in a slum environment; and deprived of the benefits of a prosperous life. He was the legitimate Father of the Philippine Revolution during the Spanish era.

Gregoria de Jesus. Wife of Gat Andres Bonifacio who made the flag of the Katipunan as its first official flag. She was the *Lakambini* (Muse) of the Women's chapter of the Katipunan.

Emilio Jacinto. "The Brain of the Katipunan" who was trusted by Bonifacio and eventually became his adviser.

Daniel Tirona. A member of the Magdalo Faction who questioned the qualifications of Bonifacio as Secretary of the Interior who was elected during the Tejeros Convention as an insult and humiliation.

Cayetano Arellano. A native of Orion, Bataan, who was appointed the first justice of the Royal Audencia (The present Supreme Court).

Justice Jose Abad Santos. Died in the hands of the Japanese, because of his refusal to take an oath of allegiance to the Japanese authorities. It was an eloquent manifestation that the Filipinos were ready to die for love of their country.

Father Francisco Foradada. A Spanish and author of a book on the Philippines to work on the Filipino priest who exerted all his power of persuasion to win back Aglipay to the Catholic fold.

William H. Taft. First American civil governor of the Philippines.

Frank Murphy. The last American Governor-General in the Philippines who helped the Filipino people in their campaign for independence.

Commodore George Dewey. The U.S. Commander of the Asiatic Squadron who led the destruction of the Spanish fleet in the Battle of Manila Bay. Dewey's victory marked the end of Spain's dominant colonial rule as a world power and heralded the beginning of the United States ascension to the "World Empire."

Carlos P. Romulo. Diplomat, soldier, and orator who served as President of the United Nations General Assembly in 1949. He was the first Asian to preside over the sessions of this international body.

General Douglas MacArthur. Military Commander of the USAFFE and military adviser to the Commonwealth and Chief of the United States Military Mission to the Philippines. He was largely responsible for the Philippine Military defense system.

Masaharu Homma. The Commander-in-Chief of the Japanese Imperial Forces who led the Japanese invasion in the Philippines during World War II.

IMPORTANT CONCEPTS, PLACES AND THINGS

Pleistocene. Noting or pertaining to the epoch forming the earlier half of the Quarternary or one part of the Neocene period, originating about one million years ago, characterized by widespread glacial ice and by the appearance of man.

Narra. (Ptercarpus indicus). This is the national tree of the Philippines.

Sampaguita. The Philippines' national flower with white small petals and pleasing small usually made into leis and placed around the neck of visiting heads of state, dignitaries, and prominent personalities.

Tarsier. (genus tarsius). This aboreal, nocturnal primate, having a long tail and very big eyes is said to be the smallest monkey in the world.

Mouse-deer. (Tragulidae). The world's smallest deer found in Balbac Island.

"Pearl of Allah." This is considered the world's largest natural pearl found in Palawan by a Muslim diver.

Tamaraw. (Bubalus Mindorensis). The unique small buffalo, having thick brown hair and short massive horns; a symbol of people's dangerous grace.

Banawe Ifugao Rice Terraces. These are found in Northern Luzon, built more than 2,000 years ago by the Ifugaos on the slopes of the mountain and acclaimed as the "Eighth Wonder of the World."

Mayon Volcano. This is in Albay Province with "the perfect cone" and its majestic and serene beauty is indeed a scenic spot to behold, but it has a grim, horrible and tragic history.

Zebronkey. This is the half-zebra and half-donkey, which was bred at the Manila Zoo in 1962.

Babaylan. A native priest during the early decade of the Spanish rule perceived to have the craft of magic and idolatry.

Biag-ni Lam-ang. This was an epic of adventure among the Ilocanos.

Kartilla. This was a primer, which consisted of the teachings of the Katipunan to indoctrinate the members of the secret about its ideals.

Tobacco Monopoly. The government designated Nueva Ecija, Cagayan Valley, Marinduque, Abra, Isabela, La Union, Ilocos Norte, and Ilocos Sur as places confined to tobacco planting, causing compulsory labor and a tremendous decline of food production because the government compelled the natives to produce nothing but tobacco.

Polistas. These were native laborers who were hauled off from their homes to serve as archers or rowers for Spanish expeditions, to build ships in Cavite navy yard, or to work in roads, bridges, and church construction. They were not paid any allowance.

Encomienda. This was a favor from the King of Spain, whereby the encomiendero, the holder of an encomienda, was given the right to collect taxes from the people under his jurisdiction. It became a source of evil and corrupt practices, resulting in the exploitation of the Filipinos.

Falla. This was a form of fee, which allowed Spaniards to be exempted from forced labor.

Bandala. This was an arbitrary practice where the authorities compelled the natives to sell their produce to the government.

Obras Pias. This literally means "pious works." Foundations, which invest their money in trade and devoted their profit coming therefrom to charitable works." They were controlled by the friars who the *Obras Pias*. Unfortunately, the friars generally did not pay back the government and the *Obras Pias*, resulting in their bankruptcy.

Peninsulares. These were the Spanish born in Spain and felt that they were superior to the Filipinos.

Insulares. The Spaniards born in the Philippines.

Illustrados. These were the cultured and educated Filipinos who found the vanguard of the Propaganda Movement. They exposed the great spiritual crises that engulfed the Filipinos and attempted to convince the Spanish authorities of the imperative need for reforms to avert the outbreak of the revolution.

Dimasalang and Laonlaan, pen names of Dr. Jose Rizal; Plaridel, Marcelo del Pilar and Tikbalang, Mariano Ponce. In writing for the Sol, the Filipino reformists used pen names for obvious reasons.

El Heraldo de la Revolucion. (Herald of the Revolution). This was the first official organ of the Revolutionary Republic that served as a mouthpiece that conveyed the ideals and aspirations of the Filipino people.

Propaganda Movement. This was a peaceful campaign by Dr. Jose Rizal and other Filipino intellectuals for reforms, which began in 1872.

The Tejeros Convention. This convention was primarily held to resolve the internal problems of the *Magdalo and Magdiwang* factions on March 22, 1897.

Religious Schism. The separation of Gregorio Aglipay and the Filipino clergy from the Catholic Church as a religious revolt against the Vatican.

Aglipayan Church. The birth of the Aglipayan Church in the Philippines was considered a tangible result of the Revolution attributed to the Struggle of the Filipino priests to have control in the administration of the Catholic Church in the Philippines.

"Thomasites," American teachers who came to the Philippines on board the S.S. Thomas to teach Filipinos and prepare them for civic duties.

Hare-Hawes Cutting Act was the bill that provided for a ten-year transition period, at the end of which the United States would grant and recognize the independence of the Philippines.

Olympia. The flagship of Commodore George Dewey in the Battle of Manila Bay.

Bataan. A peninsula on Western Luzon surrounded by mountain ranges and irregular coastlines along Manila Bay where General Dougals MacArthur and his army troops retreated was a brillant maneuver as a military strategy for he outwitted General Homa, the Japanese Commander-in-Chief with his superior ingenuity who failed to encircle the USAFFE. A battleground that exemplified the Filipino-American troops' heroic stand against Japanese forces that was drenched with blood and tears that became a hallowed ground for their love of country to be immortalized by freedom-loving people of the world.

The Battle of Besang Pass. This battle may be considered one of the fiercest and dangerous battles between the American forces and the Japanese soldiers because the fury was day and night and continued over five months, resulting in heavy casualties, which General Yamashita had strongly fortified.

USAFFE. United States Army Forces in the Far East. This military organization constituted the Filipino-American courageous soldiers that stood for justice, freedom and peace until the fall of Bataan and Corregidor.

KALIBAPI. (Kapisanan sa Paglilingkod sa Bagong Pilipinas). This was a body organized during the Japanese occupation with Jose P. Laurel as President and Benigno S. Aquino and Ramon Avanceña as Vice-Presidents.

HUKBALAHAP. (Hukbo ng Bayan Laban sa Hapon). This Hukbalahap Movement has its deep roots in the Spanish *encomienda* system which began and developed into a system of exploitation. These were the Filipinos who fought against the Japanese during the war but not given reward and recognition by the government. The social uprising was due to the numerous injustices and abuses perpetuated by the landlords, especially in Central Luzon, upon the poor peasants.

MAKAPILI. The Filipino spies and notorious collaborators who were loyal to the Japanese who squealed the names of the guerrillas and their activities; as well as those who supported the resistance movement during the Japanese occupation.

Kempeitai. The dreaded Japanese Military Police during the Japanese occupation who had total disregard to human lives.

Kamikaze. (Divine Wind). The Japanese suicide pilots.

Corruption. This is a moral perversion of integrity. It is a behavior and attitude, which are not in accord with accepted rules of standard approved by a civilized society.

Plunder. Is the acquisition of ill-gotten wealth, either directly or in connivance with the members of his family, relatives, business associates, or any other person that amounts to a total value of at least seventy-five (P75,000,000). Ill-gotten wealth may be any asset, property, business enterprise or material possession acquired by means of fraudulent practices to enrich oneself at the expense and damage of the country and the Filipino people.